POINT OF DEPARTURE

BOOKS BY JAMES CAMERON

POINT OF DEPARTURE

by

JAMES CAMERON

ORIEL PRESS

STOCKSFIELD

LONDON HENLEY BOSTON

Published by Oriel Press Limited (Routledge & Kegan Paul Limited)
at Stocksfield, Northumberland, NE43 7NA
Printed in Great Britain by
St Edmundsbury Press, Bury St Edmunds, Suffolk.
Reprinted 1985

ISBN 0 85362 175 6

To Elizabeth, Elma, Desmond and Fergus
who I hope understand
and to Emma, Andrew, and Philip
who will understand one day.

Contents

Contents

Foreword to the Present Edition

That this book first appeared as long as ten years ago gives it, in journalistic terms, a ripe old bouquet. Not much of the product of this vineyard in which we labour gets, as it were, Laid Down. Indeed in the neurotic heyday of national newspapers one was occasionally lucky to have one's story last the night, with such wild gusto did subeditors cast the type into limbo between editions. To see the resurrection of a book, very personal to me, is a rare compliment, and one I value.

In the years since *Point of Departure* I must have written a dozen or so forewords for other people's books. I became a sort of professional door-opener, like the sombre functionary who treads the Mace so solemnly through the Parliamentary lobby to inform the world that the Speaker is on his way. He has, as far as one knows, no other function at all. Nor have foreword-writers.

I will say, however, that it is a great deal easier doing the job for someone else. An appearance of objectivity can be maintained. A friendly colleague one may gravely salute; on a competitor, on the other hand, one must lavish effusive praise. He will see through it, but he will love it.

But to introduce a new printing of one's own book is very different. I would like to be modest about it – and indeed, as was said in another context, there is plenty to be modest about. At the same time, even with this gap in years, I can see in *Point of Departure* nothing of which I am ashamed, or not more so than any writer confronted with the pretensions of his past. Some of it I would necessarily, and with hindsight, have perhaps done otherwise, but very little. The story of Korea might well have been different had I then foreseen the shadow of the jailhouse of Viet Nam. The tale of the trip from Bengal to Tibet might have had a different poignancy had I known what was awaiting India, so soon afterwards. But these later traumas had to await later books; I have no regrets.

More than anything I would ask that this not be taken as a journalist's book – still less, god forbid, a book about journalism. I belong to that trade, indeed I know no other. I see its importance as rather more than that of a lawyer, and far less than that of a hospital nurse. I have no illusions whatever about its influence.

As Fleet Street stumbles into its terminal decay the 'power of the Press' is a very sick joke. I am glad I knew it in better days.

Still, it was a way of life that led me up some very odd byways, in company with some very odd people. It provided me, in Alan Moorhead's phrase, 'a late education', and goodness knows I had little other. Some of it – much of it – was a torment at the time. Looking back, however, I cannot seriously say that I would have chosen otherwise. I hope *Point of Departure* makes this clear. Its final chapter was written at a low point of my fortunes, but at least, said I, the title is optimistic. I was right, for once.

Foreword to the First Edition, 1967

THERE are few more daunting or pretentious words than 'autobiography'; it argues a very odd nature in a man who feels obliged to produce such a thing. In politicians and serious soldiers it can perhaps be mitigated by by-products of historical usefulness, but among writers to trade it suggests a kind of literary masturbation: have they nothing better to describe than themselves? I am constantly surprised to hear that people buy such books, which in no way impedes my earnest hope that they shall not stop now.

This is an autobiography only in the sense that much of it concerns aspects of my life that no one has hitherto paid me to describe. I have also drawn liberally on random writings over many years as an itinerant journeyman of my trade, and I am grateful for the indulgence of the ever-increasing multitude of editors and publishers who have at various times employed me, fired me, helped me, and despaired of me. My relations with most of them have been amiable, if erratic: in consequence my ex-masters are now numerous indeed. It would probably be typographically convenient to acknowledge them altogether: This Was My Press. Those whom I have offended will perhaps forgive me; those who have offended me must take their chance.

This is by no means a book about Fleet Street, which I inhabited for many years, and which now fatigues and bores me to the point that I have not, other than accidentally, set foot in it since the death of the *News Chronicle*. Neither is it a traveller's tale, since that would be absurd; a life of journeying has conveyed me somehow or other to almost every inhabited part of the world. I claim no advantage and certainly no wisdom from this; rather the contrary. Of some places with an especial call on my memories – Africa and India, China and Siam and the Americas and Viet Nam – I have said all that I have to say in other books. I would very much like to say it again, to be sure, but this is not the place.

Hume wrote in his *Treatise of Human Nature:* 'I may venture to affirm of mankind that they are nothing but a collection of perceptions which succeed each other with inconceivable rapidity and are in perpetual flux and movement.'

It is thus, I confess, that I see myself exactly; not as a character matured and fashioned by developing experience and increasing understanding. In many ways I am more of a fool now than I ever was. The writing of this book may well be evidence of that. I merely suppose that in every uneasy journalistic heart there lurks the hope to salvage from the ragbag of memory something that may not, or at least not instantly, vanish into the pulping-machines.

This is therefore the arbitrary reflections on a life which has had much good fortune, and some less good. It may be that the opportunities for this sort of gipsy existence are narrowing; one will not forever be able or even wish to continue. In the meantime it might not be a bad thing to remember, where one can; by and by one will perhaps not care, as much as one should.

Acknowledgements

CERTAIN passages in this book have been culled from, or adapted from, or remembered from, writings that have appeared in a variety of journals. Nothing I fear has survived intact; the process of distillation and adaptation has so blurred the outlines of their original form that I cannot specify what thoughts or what phrases came from where. At least two of the periodicals have preceded me into limbo; I salute the phantoms that squeak and gibber in Shoe Lane and Bouverie Street. For the rest, I am grateful to the following publications for allowing me to milk material acquired on their behalf:

Daily Express, Picture Post, News Chronicle, Daily Mail, Listener, New Statesman, Atlantic Monthly.

If a few phrases copyright elsewhere have slipped in inadvertently I apologize in advance: the brick is big and the straws are scarce.

Chapter One

I cannot remember when these curious moments of suspense first began, when I would find myself unanchored and adrift in the dark, groping for clues as to where I was. Sometimes, indeed, even who I was. These moments came, and still come, at the exact transition between sleep and awakening, lying on the edge of uncertainty: what is this bed, where is this room, what lies beyond it – Egypt, England, Berlin, Jerusalem, Moscow, Minneapolis, Peking; there have been so many places, and any of them could be the background of this vacuum.

Then of course the realization: the outline of a window, the shroud of a mosquito-net, and everything commonplace comes flooding back. But for that moment times hangs poised like a pendulum, and there is always one small peak of doubt when one could believe in the floating darkness that one had in fact died, and that this was it – anticlimax in an anonymous hotel room, with the light just filtering in. In a moment it is all over; a taxi calls in the street outside, and the day has no more mystery than another. One day, surely, the answer will never come: what then?

But it always does, and then it is time to go to work again.

As far as anything ever has a beginning, mine came to pass in the last few years before the first of two world wars altered all dimensions and ensured that I, and my generation, should never know that condition again.

It appears to have been a year singularly undistinguished even by the anodyne standards of the last Georgians; even the most pedantic historians concede that 1911 provided neither glory nor drama, no especial rejoicing and no memorable regret; no lights went out nor were illumined; no crises overcome, no truths revealed; no journalist ever evoked it as a punctuation-mark of any human consideration. How fortunate and decorous, then, to be born into an age of such tranquil anonymity – and indeed of prosperity abounding, for never in generations had Europe presented a countenance so smug, so buoyant and secure. It was a felicitous year, but seemingly dull.

Yet the records show – and tenuous though they are be sure I studied them for auguries – this anaesthetic year must have provided at least moments of passing interest – the coronation of a King, the voting of Members of Parliament that they should at last be paid. Somebody stole the Mona Lisa from the Louvre and, briefly blurring the cloudless humour of the scene, Italy declared war on Turkey. It came to little. There was a bland and sanguine temper to the times, though my father was to tell me of his outrage and dismay as the Income Tax soared to one-and-tenpence in the pound.

In the midsummer of this forgotten year I was born, prematurely and inconveniently and, as it seems, with some protest and resistance, in a gloomy but unchallengeably respectable apartment house in Battersea, London.

This in itself constituted an error of judgment, since all the circumstances of my arrival had been planned otherwise. My parents were Scottish and, while by no means subscribing to the expatriate enthusiasms so prevalent at the time, had the sentimental purpose of delivering me where we had all been delivered, and were indeed hastening north in what they believed to be good season. My mother and father had in fact been passing a final week or two in Monte Carlo, before parenthood put a stop to such diversions, and they were dutifully on their way to Clydeside for my debut when it became necessary to make other and abrupt arrangements. For some time I was held to blame for this, and perhaps I was; I have suffered all my life from impatience, and an eagerness to dispose of the inevitable.

My father, with whom I was to develop a relationship of a character difficult to define, so close did it become and, for a while, so poignant and dependent that its echoes are still meaningful for me thirty years after his death, was – as somehow seems inevitable in chronicles of this kind – a son of the Manse. At the time of my father's birth my grandfather was minister of the Victoria Church at Eglinton Toll in Glasgow, which I recall vaguely – it vanished long ago in one of the random and erratic developments of

Glasgow's South Side – as an edifice of stark and chilling ugliness at the junction of what must have been even then the two most lowering thoroughfares of that sombre city. I have only fugitive memories of my grandfather, for he died when I was ten, and far from Scotland; I remember an aquiline countenance of prophetic tranquility, with a long shaven upper lip and a white beard of such gossamer fineness that it stirred in the lightest breeze, and, as he sat down, would momentarily drift upwards and settle back, like silk. I was told that my grandfather had never shaved his chin in all his life – not to be sure from any reason of principle but because he had a delicate respiratory system and apparently suffered even as a child from what was then called clergyman's sore throat. It was, presumably, some precursor of the asthma that at one time or another was to seize on all our family, except me, and which was to turn my father's life into a martyrdom.

My father was born in 1881; he grew up thin and breathless but merry; he was a tremendous reader by inclination and long passages of illness in his boyhood provided the opportunity to fill his head with information and reflections of recondite and absorbing uselessness. From Glasgow High School he went to Glasgow University, where he graduated in arts and law, and forthwith departed for London, and finally began to practise as a barrister and member of the Inner Temple. He was from all accounts, and particularly his own, a counsel of singular inadequacy, or perhaps misfortune. The profession attracted him in its sociological implications, and bored him with its drudgery, its archaic technique and especially its penury. He found it extremely difficult to make a living. I would imagine that, thoughtful and volatile and accomplished as my father was, he was never any irreplaceable gift to the legal profession. There was an element of the capricious and quizzical in him, occasionally skipping into the fantastic, that would never have been really fulfilled in the Courts or the Temple. I think he must have appreciated this from the beginning, since his acquaintanceship and company was always found on the slightly unorthodox perimeter of London life – the theatre and the music-hall, the sporty peers, the Savage Club, and, of course, Fleet Street.

Somehow or other in this context he discovered in himself a sudden talent for writing. He had a tremendous aptitude for observation, and a truly telling facility of phrase. To some degree he evolved for himself a journalistic style that was distinctive for those days – elegant and urbane but meaty withal, treating commonplaces with a perception and wit that at once removed them from the commonplace. He began to contribute a weekly Letter, or column as it would be called today, to the Glasgow *Evening Citizen*; it was called 'Once a Week', and for a time it achieved a quite serious renown.

To his and everyone else's surprise, however, he abruptly found his true metier as a novelist. That is to say he began to write stories of an intricate and *nouvementé* kind, which found their expression in the great medium of those days of fifty years ago, the serial story. An early acquaintanceship with Lord Northcliffe achieved him the entry into the magazine field, the curious populous voracious market, long since sunk into the graveyard of English letters, of *Answers* and *Tit-Bits* and the *Strand Magazine*. For these papers he wrote his novels in weekly chapters, busy tales of shadowed marriages and undiscovered crime and venal judges and star-crossed love. They were not literature, nor ever did my father pretend that they were; at the same time they were very far from trash, and at least two have serious quality. I have them all in book form on my shelves today, titles most evocative of their time – *Such and Such Things, The Devil's Due, A Maid and her Money, The Knight's Move, The Mystery of Beaton Craig, The Mill, The Girl on the Green* – some two dozen of them, long forgotten by everyone in the world except me.

This development had one great repercussion on my father's life: in those days a barrister's career was set about with many elaborate bans and conventions, and professional authorship was in no way compatible with practice at the Bar, just as an association with Grub Street was held unseemly for a member of the Temple. My father's dilemma was that while he was not making a fortune from his stories it was at least eight times what he was making at the Bar or ever looked like making. At the same time he had no means of knowing how long this minor bonanza with the magazines was likely to last, and he was sentimentally reluctant to cut adrift from the Temple altogether. He resolved the difficulty in what seemed to him an ingenious and comparatively ethical way: he changed his name. For the purposes of the Bar and his private life he remained William Ernest Cameron, MA, LLB, and for the purposes of his writing he became Mark Allerton. How he landed upon his nom de plume I never completely understood; I believe he was never quite sure himself, for he gave me many different and elaborate explanations – but in the end it mattered little, since very soon the character and personality of Mark Allerton invaded and indeed superceded that of William Ernest Cameron to the point where, about the time of my birth, large numbers of his friends knew him as nothing else. By this time, of course, the stratagem had lost all its original validity, since the Bar came to mean less and less to my father, and eventually faded right away. He became increasingly known as 'Mark', and when the time came for him to find a name for me, that was the name he chose.[1]

By that time my father had been married four years to Margaret Douglas Robertson, my mother, whom my father loved extremely dearly, and whom he would appreciatively describe as a happy cross between Queen Alexandra and Marie Lloyd. I remember her as a kind of H. G. Wells heroine, full of a reflected gaiety, and of an endless patience.

I am obliged to linger somewhat on the nature of my father because it had without question a tremendous influence on my own. Physically I resemble him hardly at all, yet now I have reached the age at which I knew him best, and at which he died, I am vividly conscious of the perpetuation in me not only of aspects of character, both the good and the bad, but of actual physical traits, tricks of attitude and gesture – a stoop, a fashion of crouching with the elbows on the knees, a dawdling walk. The other day I came upon the manuscript of a lecture my father had given at the Kelvin Hall in Glasgow – I puzzled over it for some time, baffled as to when I could have composed this essay; so closely did the writing resemble my own that I was myself deceived.

My father was never rich – indeed on the contrary; my earliest memories are of periods of hard-upness that must have occasionally verged on the desperate, but which impressed themselves on my childhood as times of a rather mad improvisation, with my father and mother uproariously dressing for a dinner of boiled eggs.

[1] When I was born my father's close friend was the late J. J. Bell, the Scots novelist who had just had a success with a book called *Jim Crow*. The name, I regret to say, adhered to me in infancy, and for years to come. Indeed until I was in my twenties I had thought my registered names to be James Mark Cameron; only when some passport trouble obliged me for the first time to see my birth certificate did I realize that my name is Mark James. By this time it was rather late in the day to change.

Of the flat in Battersea I recall nothing whatever; I later heard
that its only claim to distinction was that the adjoining apartment
was the home of a talented youth involved in some way with the
stage, whose name was Noël Coward. There was a legend in the
family to the effect that the gifted youth had at one time upset my
pram, including myself, down the landing stairs; I have never
followed up this tenuous acquaintanceship.

Those were the days when the Balloon Races started from the
Park outside. I like to think I remember them – the great gay gas-
bags swelling and bobbing on the greenery, the earnest experts in
Norfolk jackets shouting orders from their little wickerwork
gondolas, the flurry of sand ballast as the pleasant fat things
drifted indolently over Wandsworth. I do not of course remember
them, though there was a curious sensation of the *déjà-vu* thirty
years later whenever I watched the barrage-balloons loafing over
London in the Second War – but dull military-coloured things,
sullen and tethered, not a patch on the elegant brown and blue
absurdities dangling their baskets full of moustaches. I imagine
life lost a lot with the passing of the balloon.

I was three when the first Great War began, and seven when it
ended; it could not be said therefore to have made much direct
impact on my life. I have a somewhat confused attitude to that
War, since while I can personally remember very little about it I
nevertheless had the impertinence a generation later to write two
books about it, called *1914* and *1916* – which required so much
research into the moods and manners of the time, so much absorb-
tion in the newspaper files of the period and discovery of contemporary detail, that for a while I felt I knew that epoch better
than my own. In consequence it is sometimes difficult for me to
distinguish between the true vestigeal memories of childhood and
the later impressions derived from diligent reading. Do I really
remember –as I seem to do – being taken to see General Sir
William Robertson reviewing a contingent of the BEF in Hyde
Park: the puttees and the flat caps and *Tipperary,* or have I described the scene so often on paper that I only imagine that I do?
Sometimes I could almost swear that I was myself aware of the
numbness of those years, of the paradoxes and tensions, even of
the Zeppelins . . . It is manifestly impossible.

My father, whose erratic health failed him at every medical
board, was directed to some vague job in the War Office, which

he later told me could have been done in half the time by a retarded child of eight. It succeeded, however, in unsettling him so much that as soon as the War was over we left the country.

It was during this second interlude that I began to grow up.

Back again plying his trade in what he called the Fiction Factory my father came to a big decision: since the Bar no longer either interested or supported him he might as well live anywhere. Those were the days when the pound sterling was a currency of real usefulness, and well regarded by other nations, and the modest amounts my father made would, he reckoned, go sensibly further in another country. So we packed up and left for Brittany.

Paramé in those days was a small and undistinguished resort a mile or so down the Channel coast from St Malo; later in life it gained a certain popularity for some reason with English schoolteachers of slender means, who in the early '20s were about the only low-income British group given to Continental vacations. They went to Brittany, I suppose, for the same reasons that had brought us there: it was accessible and it was cheap. It was also attractive, in its rather subfusc way – the flat sands stretched for miles, there were elaborate rock-formations and queer imponderable prehistoric remnants, splendid fishing-ports like Cancale and Roscoff, a cosy and restful river in the Rance, the walled town of St Malo itself. There was even one or two shabby and rickety casinos. Above all, a little money went a long way. Certainly my father felt that he had, for once, made a wise and prudent decision, and bustled around the neighbourhood seeking a base. He eventually found it in the Villa Le Chesnot, a small seaside house of a tasteless ugliness that approached the sublime, so sedulously had its creator invoked every single one of the more hideous manifestations of *art nouveau,* with such tormented ingenuity had its gimcrack bones been encased in gables and false timbers and crenellations. It looked like Balmoral seen through the wrong end of a telescope. My father was delighted by what he called the essential purity of its vulgarity. He was full of enthusiasm for the region. By and by it was to disenchant him, as everything sooner or later had to disenchant him, and he would grow fretful and restive; but to begin with he called a truce with his asthma and was in excellent form with the local café proprietors and small businessmen of the village.

The Bretons are probably among the most conservative people in Europe; most Frenchmen consider them frankly pagan. Certainly fairies and witches were said to abound, especially among the thudding echoing caves and the archaic monuments and standing-stones that no one ever tried to explain. My father greatly approved of this for some time, until he suddenly decided that superstition was not charming after all, but bogus and boring.

I was then sent to school.

To those who think of a Continental education in terms of an urbane and civilized course at Grenoble or the Sorbonne or the Ecole Normal or even any of the tidier lycées, the *externat* of St Servan, in the Department of Ile-et-Vilaine, would have presented some bleak surprises. It was the most utilitarian-looking of buildings – by which I mean paradoxically that it was as wholly unfunctional, crabbed and depressing as almost every village school built in Europe at the turn of the century. It was dark, and sombre, and awkward; it was howlingly noisy, and it contrived somehow to be both airless and draughty. It had another special disadvantage from my point of view: it was a good four kilometres from our villa, which meant that to arrive when school began, at half past seven in the morning, my day had to begin uncomfortably betimes. I would take a canvas satchel containing my *tartine* for lunch, a quarter of bread with a slice of paté embedded in the middle, and plod across the fields to where St Servan lay, separated from St Malo by an arm of the harbour, across which ran the Pont Roulant, an extraordinary affair that was half bridge and half train, rumbling over submarine rails with a lurching, clanking gait.

My first days of the school were a torture of inadequacy and embarrassment. We were crammed into a dozen or so rows of what even then seemed to me to be microscopic desks, all of us dressed alike in the practical but hideous black alpaca smocks that were – and still are, in the French countryside – standard uniform for elementary schoolboys. There would be a tremendous clattering of wooden-soled boots on the board floor while we shuffled and contended for some sort of comfort on the benches, until suddenly Monsieur Lhote, the master, would manifest himself before us in a dusty gown, carrying a cane, if you please, and initiating the day with the unchanging opening command: 'Prenez vos ardoises!' And we did; we must have been about the last schoolboys in

Europe to use slates. *Crash,* went the slates on the desks; from then on the leitmotif of education scratched and screeched its way into my memory forever: the dreadful abrasive whine of the slate-pencils on those scored and dismal slabs of stone.

For me those early days were as difficult, I believe, as any I remember since. My French at that time was I suppose adequate for ordinary purposes; it was a different matter trying to cope with the techniques of wholly unfamiliar subjects in the thick vowels and rough edges of Breton French, seasoned as it was sometimes by wholly incomprehensible Celtic variants. I would sometimes sit there in a cloud of incomprehension, recalled every so often to helpless attention by the phrase that brought everyone to heel like a dog: 'Deux avertissements, jeune homme!' – this meant I had been warned before; the next was a swift ragging cut on the bare knee from the tip of the cane.

Luckily for me the basis of instruction at our *externat* was of a form child-proof in any society: Monsieur wrote words on the blackboard, we copied them on our slates. Whatever phrases he wrote – and I recall some of them still: snatches of la Rochefoucauld, the five times table, the conquests of Charlemagne, eccentric dicta from the Radical Party – it was our duty to follow them literally, stroke by stroke, letter by letter, neither lagging nor anticipating, for if anyone was caught inscribing the final 'e' in 'patrie' while Monsieur was reaching only the penultimate 'i' there was great trouble, and from time to time the master would leap unexpectedly among us in mid-word, as it were, precisely to detect this deviation. I found this endlessly trying, as even an illiterate dolt like myself could move a pace or two ahead of Monsieur's copperplate inscription of 'Le travail, c'est le devoir du citoyen'. As I remember, our teaching took the form of the interminable repetition of unexceptional moralities and apothegms: 'Love of country is the passport to honour', 'Obedience is the key to the freedom of the soul', and so on. I grew up under the impression that all life hinged on the accurate reproduction of mottoes; I was persuaded that Monsieur Lhote had a special line to God, or whatever the post-war anticlericals used in his place.

Thus I sat there, scratching on my slate, wondering – I suppose I must have wondered – what on earth I was doing there at all, listening to the drone of Monsieur intoning the Napoleonic dates or the mysteries of dividing eight by two or the agricultural products of the regions of France, hearing in the background the sibilant provocations of my neighbours ('C'est vraiment toi qui as tué Jeanne d'Arc'), and praying to God or the President whom we were daily obliged to invoke to bring a thunderbolt down upon this hapless place so that dramatic death could relieve us all of the charade. I suppose this lasted a week or two, during which time I contrived to retreat deeper and deeper into the background of the schoolroom, waiting only for the 'Deux-avertissements, jeune-homme!' to restore me to a leaping pretence of vivid interest – until one day I discovered, without actually defining the moment, that I was in fact as alive to the happenings around me as anyone; that at last I had come to terms with the tongue, that I not only knew what was supposed to be going on but was, in some respects at least, ahead of it.

One hears so much of the tense and supercharged excellence of French education, of its universality and efficiency – of how, it was said, it was systematized to a point where the Ministry of Education had only to glance at the clock to know with certainty that exactly so many children of exactly twelve years old were simultaneously and at that precise moment reading the works of Racine, or studying vulgar fractions, or dissecting frogs, or whatever it might be. The anxieties and neurotic overwork of so many French adolescents harried by the cares of the *bachaud* seem to sustain this notion. All I can say is that if this was the case in the 1920s then my *externat* in the Ile-et-Vilaine had somehow eluded the exacting rigours of the system, since from the day of my arrival at school until my departure I recall learning virtually nothing whatever, except an accidental grasp of the common tongue, the verses of certain songs either official and patriotic – 'Le brave Charles, Roi de France, avait passé monts et torrents' – or unofficial and earthy: 'Quand j'ai vu Marie, tombée de sa bicyclette'; and an erratic mastery of the multiplication table up to and including seven times. It is an inexplicable thing to me that I never progressed any further than this arbitrary number. For the rest of my life that particular sense of helplessness has endured; confronted with the smallest and most infantile mathematical calculation I have been lost – not just inadequate, but abandoned. By good grace my life has never led me into paths where arithmetic has been imperative, and in later life where calculations have ever been required of me I have persuaded professionals to do them.

There existed a curious system at our school, the exact method and meaning of which I never wholly grasped, whereby at the end of every month some pupil or other was actually awarded a medal. It was of course always the same medal, and I can recall even now its shape and size, in cruciform enamel resembling, now I come to think of it, the medal of the Croix de Guerre – and indeed it occurs to me that this is possibly what it was. Anyhow, the boy who had succeeded somehow in winning the favour of Monsieur Lhote, or perhaps in incurring his displeasure less frequently than others, was formally entitled to pin this decoration on his alpaca overall, and by virtue of this was granted the right to a grace and favour position on the middle gangway of the front row of our bent and battered desks. It was a privilege fraught with disadvantages, since this was a very exposed position, and most of the *elèves distingués* were only too relieved to hand over to their successor when the time came.

I have to put on record that on at least one occasion I won this odd award, which is a sufficient indictment of the general scholastic level of our class. (We seem to have been indeed an outstandingly moronic intake; one or two of my coevals I suspected even at the time to be clinically subnormal; they were deposited in the back of the room and did, as far as was perceptible to the human eye, absolutely nothing at all, ever.)

It was while I was temporarily occupying this perilous seat of honour, for reasons that remain mysterious, that there befell me the most memorable and extraordinary incident of all my brief schooldays, that even now can bring a kind of *frisson* of alarm to me. Monsieur had been giving us some sort of history lesson, of a period that has left no impression on me since; in his usual habit, Monsieur had abandoned the thread of his discourse and had digressed into some reverie of his own. Imperceptibly he had drifted from whatever was on the curriculum to modern times – to the War, in fact, the War that was only in the immediate past, after all, and which was to Monsieur even now an ever-present thing. Monsieur was obsessed by the war, in which he had naturally fought, and I believe with honour. (Now I come to think of it, it was surely *his* Croix de Guerre that was the mark of his pupils' distinction, and that I was diffidently wearing at that very moment.) There were few contexts in which Monsieur could not involve the War, its horrors and enormities, its glories and scandals and shames and injustices, and in especial measure the guilt and villainy of the Germans. There were few people in France in those days who were prepared to think other than bitterly about the Germans, but Monsieur was anti-German almost beyond reason; his enduring hatred must have verged on the pathological. As he moved further from his original subject and deeper into his private memories his personality quite visibly changed, his voice grew hoarser, his eyes narrowed. He began to say 'Les salles Boches . . . qui m'ont fait . . .' and then he did the thing that has stayed in my memory most vividly ever since: he seized his left arm in his right fist and pulled it out by the roots.

For a moment he stood brandishing it like a club, held by its wrist; then he brought it down on my desk with a crash.

I think I very nearly fainted. The shock threw me back against the desk behind with such violence that I bruised my spine. The thing was unprecedented; I could not conceive of what trauma of passion could make it possible for a man to dismember himself in this terrible way, nor for what end the enormity of this gesture. I must have expected either the master or all of ourselves to complete the explosion by dropping dead on the spot. Never before had I witnessed an argument brought to such a ferocious and even magical climax.

This was the first knowledge I had ever had that the man had an artificial arm. It must have been for those days a very efficient and convincing one, since I had been quite unaware of its existence. I learned later that Monsieur was a *mutilé de guerre* and as such accepted in the special hierarchy of patriots, but the demonstration of this in such circumstances quite unnerved me. It clearly produced some sort of catharsis on Monsieur too, for at the conclusion he abruptly left the classroom, presumably to attach himself back into his arm; five minutes later he returned and resumed the lesson as though nothing had happened. I was never to look at him again without a sense of fearful apprehension.

As it turned out it did not matter greatly, since shortly afterwards my father ordained that we should move elsewhere, and for a while we travelled spasmodically from place to place, seeking sometimes the sun and sometimes the sea; for a while the mountains attracted my father and we investigated the Pyrenees. But already the adventure had lost its savour, and after a few years we returned, like weary and unfulfilled Crusaders, to England.

We then moved into a house called Bacombe Lodge in the Buckinghamshire village, as it then was, of Wendover; here, said my father, we should at last settle down. Here my brother Ken was born. Here we were able to pause and cohere for a time, and here as a family we finally disintegrated.

Our house was large and ungraceful and pleasant; it was a change from the Villa Le Chesnot in that it had been designed as a kind of huge square box without, as I recall, ornamentation of any kind; its exterior was spartan indeed, but it had great numbers of half-furnished rooms and grounds large enough for goats and garden-parties, and an enormous and fruitful mulberry tree on which my brother and I could rear silkworms. My father found it convenient for the Shoulder of Mutton inn by the railway station, and decided to make his life anew by abandoning his fancy Continental researches and taking up the game of bowls. He was always a man of profound concentration on the preoccupation of the moment, and for some time the Bowls Club of Wendover held his attention as assiduously as had the Breton gnomes of Rotheneuf not long before.

Here my mother grew mortally ill. She taxed herself hard in her ministrations to her demanding family; a condition of acute anaemia was treated by the administration of drugs to which she became, innocently and gratefully, addicted. The last year of her life was spent in bed, requesting with occasional flashes of her old Marie Lloyd charm, more of the stuff that was to kill her. My father and she consoled one another helplessly, discovering for the first time in their insecure and happy life together that love was not enough, and that while both of them had that in abundance, they had nothing else.

My mother's last years were spent in a painful effort to escape life; I have few recollections of her other than lying in bed, increasingly wasting, yet conveying still, after all those years, an impression of a sort of fey exasperation, a humorous acceptance of her illness punctuated by desperate interludes of hysteria; for it is the case that my mother had accompanied my father, gentle and well-intentioned souls that they were, into this retreat of drinking, a surrender that nobody would admit, any more than, years later, I was to admit my own. To her illness my mother added a nervous condition that some hasty medication compounded into a dependence on narcotics, so that the closing weeks of her life are locked in my mind as a continual plea for the sort of relief I barely understood at the time, and understand too well today.

Early one morning she had a cardiac spasm that lasted only a few moments; I recall not hers but my father's cry from the next room, of a kind I had never heard before but accepted at once as the signal of despair. There ensued a sequence of events that I can hardly rationalize to this day, but am persuaded in the truth: after the telephone-call to the doctor I shortly heard the slam of the doctor's door in the High Street; it was a mile away and it could nohow have been audible and yet I heard it, and the chunter of his little car all the way through the sleeping village to our house; I was able to follow the progress of this little old man every yard of the way to his knock on our front door. On later consideration I know it must have been impossible, yet I know it happened.

By the time the old doctor arrived my mother was dead. She was then forty-two years old; for months until that day she had looked at least sixty, but that morning she looked suddenly like a bride; death had left her with a smile of private contentment on her face, and I realized for the first time – not then, but later – that she had been very pretty. I was to see a lot of death in the years to come, mostly sudden and cruel and ugly, but this was the first time I had seen it, and to this day death has that face for me – all the others have been false and exceptional; all the other screaming distorted broken and bloody deaths have been aberrations, all the wounded and crumpled and frightened deaths of the kind my generation has seen too often were unreal; my mother died obviously pretending that the jest had gone on long enough, that it could be surrendered without especial rancour; and even as I cried and protested I knew I had lost only what I had barely known, and that when the time came anyone would settle for it in this fashion.

For my father it was the kind of catastrophe that I was to understand only years later, when it befell me even more bleakly. I suppose it was at that moment that my father conceded – perhaps gratefully – his inability to control the complications of life other than in an empty and desultory way. This had some meaning for me since from that moment my father and I became welded in an odd relationship, tender and perverse, and for his remaining years it was I who became the father to my father, so that in the end it was I who was for a time, to be rendered childless.

Chapter Two

THE next few years were of a kind of uneasy drabness that could be effectively described only in a psychological memoir of great insight and complexity, and by someone greatly more aware than I was of the processes of human development. I had grown up in circumstances of such flux and bewilderment that the next stage seemed no odder than the first. It was if anything rather more insecure, but there was nothing very new in that. Nor is there anything new in it to this day. I had long ago forgotten, if I had ever known, what it might have been to grow up gradually and with decorum; I was reconciled to a continual sequence of the unpredictable. I found myself hired by the Thomson Publications, who were then, and I believe still are, a phenomenon of the editorial industry, built on a principle of idiosyncratic paternalism. That was, even in my day, a survival from the past. The ramifications of their interests seemed unlimited; they produced everything from girls' twopenny weeklies, of a kind apparently unknown today, to schoolboy magazines and children's comics, to reputable newspapers and moralistic reviews, exactly as multiple bakers produce varieties of cakes and buns. I was attached to the Manchester office of the *Weekly News*, and thus did I most diffidently enter the back door of journalism, with the daily function of filling the paste-pots and impaling the other daily newspapers on the files. For this I was to be paid fifteen shillings a week. My father added to this another ten; on this I lived for some time.

My father, momentarily burying his concerns for his own future in the needs of mine, saw me into lodgings in Manchester, which were a very small room in a mournful rectilinear street at the back of Brooks's Bar. We shared a very tense parting dinner at the Midland Hotel, at which at his insistence we drank a bottle of champagne which we could not afford and which I could not enjoy. I saw him off from the station; as the train jolted away I felt the first grip of a loneliness that has, indeed, endured a long time. I was then nearly seventeen.

So I lived for a year or so between my lodging in Brooks's Bar and the Dickensian newspaper office in Chapel Street, Salford; I cannot imagine that I learned or forgot anything in either place. When I returned to Manchester not long ago, after thirty years, I walked back along that desolate stretch beside the River Irwell; it was like walking through walls of uneasiness and regret, but I remembered nothing.

Then my employers – perhaps out of consideration for my father more than for me – had me transferred to the headquarters in Dundee. For the first time in my life it occurred to me that there was a possibility of growing roots.

It was a curious context for such a consideration, since the city of Dundee in the early thirties was a place of singular desolation. The whole of industrial Britain in those days was gripped in depression, even despair, and Dundee could have stood as a symbol of a society that had gone sour. It had, for a start, the air of a place that from the beginning of time had reconciled itself to an intrinsic ugliness. This struck me even in my youth as being odd, even anomalous, since of all cities in the kingdom Dundee had been placed with the greatest potential for grace and charm: it was set on a firth of breadth and grandeur; it was built around the slopes of a small mountain, the Law Hill; it backed on to a hinterland of fields and glens – at one time or another Dundee had the makings of a kind of Naples, which, forgetting the punitive nature of its climate, it geographically resembled. Even in those days I had known Naples; I would often look at that bleak Angus shore half-expecting singing fishermen, and hoping for a drift of Vesuvius smoke from the summit of the Law.

Dundee, however, had for generations dedicated itself to a kind of commercial single-mindedness that had come to fruition, in my day, in black and terrible industrial depression. Even then I felt the impact of its brutal melancholy, the façade of unparalleled charmlessness, an absence of grace so total that it was almost a thing of wonder.

It maintained a gruesome derelict cemetery in the very heart of the business section. Its street scenes might have been created by a disillusioned designer of sets for the more embittered works of

Chekhov. It accepted all this sardonically, even proudly. The popular picture-postcard of the time was a wide-angle photographic view of the city, a dense and dreadful panorama of reeking factory chimneys: it was called 'Bonnie Dundee'.

But soon that irony became too much even for the Dundonians – because the chimneys smoked no more, the jute mills were empty; it was a community with an insured population of seventy thousand people, with more than forty thousand of them on the dole. The only plentiful thing was paradox: the opulence of the jute-wallahs in Broughty Ferry, the hopeless hovels of Hilltown and Blackscroft. That, and the phenomenon of Dundee, notoriously one of the most alcoholic towns of the nation, year after year returning to Westminster the only Prohibitionist Member of Parliament – the indestructible evangelist Mr Scrymgeour, endlessly voted for by the distracted wives in a hapless effort to keep the dole-money from the pubs.

That was Dundee in the late 1920s. All I could grasp, or more accurately assume, was that this sort of structure was unnatural, and therefore to be rejected – not at the time necessarily opposed; I knew no way of opposing it. I developed slowly into political thought, and with much inconsistency. I can recall no time when I was not a socialist; that is to say I can remember no conversion from anything else; from the moment when politics were anything more than a word I accepted socialism without any particular reasoning or argument. This was commonplace and inadequate, and all my life I have been exasperated at an insufficient grounding in the scientific basis of what I profess to believe. I imagine it is true that most people feel no compulsion to define what they intuitively comprehend, but they are better off if they can.

In the industrial graveyard of Dundee I could only equate class with poverty – not individual poverty, nor the knock-kneed hunchbacked poverty of one old jute-mill reject in the Overgate, but the poverty of what seemed an endless background of morally exhausted people: the poor who were always with us. Class existed, and was expressible in material terms, which were hateful. What made my own indignation especially feckless was my inability to establish myself in the pattern at all. I was extremely poor, frequently to the point of desperation – but I still lived in the part of town frequented by the less poor; I had few friends, but those I had were not millworkers or foundrymen. If the material conditions of life counted for anything I was working class, since I worked very hard for little pay, so much so that it left me thenceforth forever with a nagging compulsion to work, an uneasiness with leisure, a dread of being hard up, a self-defeating inability to relax. But it did not give me entrance to the confidence of true workers – at least not then – because, for one thing, I spoke wrongly.

The epithet 'education' was ironical indeed, since there was, and is, scarcely any civilized company anywhere in which I was not technically the least educated of all. The schooling I had was, as I have told, sketchy and erratic to the point of absurdity; in formal terms I had obviously learned less in five years than my own children learned in five months. In the years to come I required an ingenious and not altogether unpraiseworthy accomplishment of concealing or blurring this condition with fluent stratagems. It was perhaps inevitable that someone of my abject and total non-scholarship should wash up in the trade of journalism, at the same time both undemanding and exacting.

I settled down gladly enough. My father was now established as a more or less permanent resident of the Royal Hotel in Union Street. I drifted from lodgings to lodgings, until the greatest good fortune led me to a room in Reform Street, in the flat of Mrs Murray, a widow, the sister of Fiddes Watt, an RSA who had been a portraitist of some celebrity. She had three daughters, with the youngest of whom I fell in love. Her name was Elma, she was then sixteen and a student at Gray's School of Art in Aberdeen. It was the first time I had ever been in love.

My days were spent in the service of the Thomson Publications, then as now a patriarchal firm of significance in its own peculiar sphere, pre-eminent of its kind in the mass-production of an especially marketable type of sub-literature, of a strangely durable but ever-changing variety. Most of this quite considerable empire was divided into two fields, on the one hand Women's and on the other Boys'. The Women's section was presided over by Mr David Donald, the Boys' by Mr Robert Low. Both of them were to become generous and helpful friends, and introduced me to the pastime of Scottish mountaineering that became, and remained for many years, an obsessive occupation. In the office they were both very important men, while any position of less importance than mine had yet to be devised. Mr Low had under his wing the great organs of contemporary derring-do, the *Wizard*, the *Rover*, the *Hotspur*, and the like, all differing in fashions immediately perceptible to the initiate but to nobody else. Mr Donald was overlord of the *Weekly Welcome*, the *Red Letter* and the *Red Star Weekly*, each of which specialized – again in nuances not readily to be understood – in serial fiction of a nature which even after all these years I remember as either unbearably sweet and wholesome, or diabolically bloodthirsty. I was attached to the *Red Star Weekly*, which catered for a public of working girls whose tastes must have verged on the sadistic, so heavily were our pages soaked in gore. We had some sort of a lien on that hardy classic of Victorian violence, *Maria Marten, or the Murders in the Red Barn*. It seems to me that we were recounting that piece of durable *angst* for years, and when it stopped the intervals were filled with sequels, or developments, or associated crimes of passion; I am not sure that we did not have a *Son of Maria Marten*. These works were contributed by sundry authors over the country, my father among them, who were paid thirty shillings a thousand words for their not inconsiderable pains.

The memorable quality of these stories was, paradoxically, their purity. The most frightful things were encouraged to happen: stranglings, knifings, shootings, disembowellings, burials alive, hauntings, drownings, suffocations, torments of a rich and varied nature abounded, and each instalment was obliged to end with a suspenseful promise of worse to come, but in no circumstances and at no point was permitted even the hint of sexual impropriety. This was the ark of the covenant and the cornerstone of our editorial principles. No matter what ferocious indignities, disasters and deaths befell our heroines, it might never be even suggested, however obliquely, that there was ever any purpose behind these excesses other than good clean violence. This made much of the carryings-on somewhat inexplicable, but that was incidental and held to be no difficulty.

This curious attitude can be symbolized in the case of the Cover Picture. One of the functions that fell to my lot was the weekly selection of some particularly gripping or galvanic incident in our principal story that could be illustrated in a compelling way and used as the magazine's cover, as an earnest of the savours within. On one occasion we were beginning a serial based on an actual series of especially brutal murders that had much exercized the newspapers of the time, and which had been catalogued in the press as 'The Man With the Glaring Eyes'. No subject was more tailor-made for us, and with eager professional zeal and pride we had commissioned a fictionalized version of this rewarding series of crimes. In the real-life version the trouble had manifestly been caused by some unusually over-stimulated sexual psychopath; no such innuendo, however, was to be found in our version, in which a recurrent number of nubile virgins were vigorously done to death by some antisocial unknown apparently in pursuit of a wholly mysterious hobby.

On this occasion, then, I ordered from the artist what I felt to be an appropriate drawing that would do justice to our promising theme. When the rough appeared I was well satisfied: it portrayed a deeply sinister back-alley by night, lit only by the baleful gleam of an eerie street lamp, whose sickly beam threw into prominence a foreground of damp and lowering paving-stones, on which lay the true purpose of the composition: the body of a young woman, her throat most palpably cut from ear to ear. It was a highly successful realization; the draughtsman had clearly put his heart into his work, and he had delineated the character of the lady's injury with an almost clinical fidelity; hardly was a torn tendon or a severed blood-vessel out of place, and the blood that streamed into the rainswept gutter had been limned by an enthusiast. It did complete justice, I felt, to 'The Man With the Glaring Eyes'.

I took this along for Mr Donald's approval with a quiet and calm confidence. When he saw it he blenched. He tore it from my hand and studied it aghast, and in speechless outrage. Finally he said: 'You must be mad!'

Accepting that I might possibly on this occasion have overdone it, I murmured: 'It is a bit strong, maybe.'

'Strong, strong,' cried Mr Donald. 'It's no' a question o' strong; it's no' a bad scene. But for God's sake, boy – look at the lassie's skirt; it's awa' above her knees!'

Abashed, I realized what rule I had broken. I took the drawing back and had the hemline lowered a modest inch or two, and in the cover went, slit windpipe and all.

Thus I passed the hours of my trade; my leisure I spent exploring Scotland and climbing mountains; during my Dundee period I got to know the Highlands extremely well, and I believe it is true to say that there is not a Munro top (that is to say a peak of 3,000 feet or more) on which I have not sat at one time or another. In retrospect this seems to me to have been an uncommonly fatiguing and wasteful fashion of passing the time, since experience has taught me that mountains, as spectacles, have value only when seen from below, and preferably in comfort; however, I climbed up and down scores of them. For the rest, I spent my time with my father in the curious nest, half hermitage and half convivial, that he had created for himself in the hotel. I began to feel a sense of identity with him that was partly born of his manifest gratitude for companionship, and partly because he was, indeed, a rewarding companion, and we were oddly at ease with each other. Only with him and with Elma, to whom I had now become in a diffident sort of fashion engaged, did I ever feel complete. This is an odd thing to say of one who even then had pretensions to becoming a journalist, but it was the case.

My father, however, was not the easiest of men. The asthma that had persecuted him all his life never released him; there were times when it would abandon him capriciously for days or even weeks on end, and when that came to pass my father would seize on the situation and query and analyse every circumstance of the occasion to attempt to identify what factor or combination of factors had brought the miracle about. Was it the precise season of the year, was the wind in the west, had he been eating brown bread or white, was he at the beginning of a story or the middle or the end, was the moon at the full? Having over the years been experimented on with everything rational or scientific, he was prepared to investigate anything, even the most arcane and irrelevant possibilities. He once took a journey across the Atlantic to New York; during the whole week of the trip he suffered, he told me, not a whisper of the wheeze. It occurred to him then that perhaps the answer to his endless problem might be that he should spend his entire life travelling back and forth between Britain and the United States – but then he reflected that it might be not the voyage itself that had been so wonderfully beneficial but the exact conditions of the voyage; that is he would be obliged always to travel by Anchor Line, and always on the *Caledonia*. It was an interesting academic exercise, for there was naturally no chance whatever of his ever in his life being able to afford the experiment.

So more and more did my father come to terms with his difficulties – his illness, his loneliness – through the easement that was not only available but temporarily successful; as time went on his drinking became not intermittent but regular; his recourse to the glass increased with a sort of angry despair at the peaks of his illness, and established a norm that rose quite steadily. I never saw my father drunk – indeed it still seems to me an extraordinary thing that in all the years I knew him and in all the emergencies and vicissitudes that beset him until the last one, I can recall no occasion nor incident when he was incoherent or mean or banal, or indeed otherwise than agreeable. . . . Even at his worst times, when he would throw open the window of his claustrophobic room to the dank grey air of the town and lean gasping on the sill, his thin shoulders heaving in the effort of breathing, even then he could dredge from his situation a kind of very exhausted humour – largely, I think, to take the edge off the miserably helpless despair with which I watched him. 'Like – a – grampus,' he would say. 'The Tay, after all, was once the home of the grampus. The whale that lives in the sea can only breathe in the air, and that at infrequent intervals. How well I understand its dilemma. The difference is – that I – have – a deadline.'

It was a very long time indeed before I realized that my father had become an alcoholic. His physical deterioration was evident enough; he had begun to walk, in his fifties, like an old man, with the kind of deliberation and nervous concentration on crossing streets that became familiar enough to me in later years but which puzzled me then. I was sufficiently persuaded of the enduring qualities and propriety of my father that I attributed everything to the pitiable debilitation of his illness, without appreciating how he was compounding his troubles by his own anodynes. Sometimes when I would visit him at the hotel on my way to the newspaper office I would find him at the head of the stairs, on the lobby by the reception-desk, grasping the balustrade and waiting for me, his eyes clouded by what I took to be another asthmatic struggle, and which frequently was, and already at that hour sipping the whisky which was, he said, to give him enough breath to go upstairs and write another instalment of tosh about some Kailyard family that was even then required by this or that twopenny magazine. I did not know, then, that this process of escape was going on all day.

Even when I did come reluctantly to realize what everyone else in Dundee had apparently known for months, that my father was quietly and with discretion and infallible courtesy and consideration for others slipping into dipsomania, my response to this knowledge was of a kind of proprietorial concern and compassion; I saw the thing neither as a wrongdoing nor a weakness of will, but as a comprehensible effect of intolerable pressures. In view of my own experiences many years later this is understandable; I was already rationalizing what should have been opposed; I considered my father's drinking as something quite different from and even incompatible with his character; it was an aberration from which we would both be released one day, when we got the chance, when something splendid and unpredictable arrived from the blue and took us away from this bloody hotel, this bloody town, this bloody waiting for miracles.

About this time the publishing company decided to transfer me from Dundee to Glasgow. I was greatly torn about this, because while I was badly worried at the prospect of leaving the only two people who meant anything to me, Elma and my father, I felt by now so confined and exasperated by Dundee that I would have gone almost anywhere to escape it. In my case I had no particular choice, and so I moved southward again, and started work on the *Sunday Post* in Port Dundas Road, just below the Cowcaddens. There I remained for some five years, passing my days in the pursuit of a journalism the confused character of which must have been unusual even then, and would be totally and wildly impossible today.

In those days there was no tangible demarcation line between the functional processes in the editorial department of a provincial newspaper of this kind. Between the sub-editor branch and the reportorial staff no such schism or tribal difference existed as exists today, since everybody on the newspaper was both alternately, or even sometimes simultaneously. Much of my time was occupied in writing articles of a character almost excruciatingly homely and domestic, treating of the more trivial sort of family or social incident in a style, which I soon bitterly found came fairly easily to me, that somehow combined the facetious and the didactic, the worldly-wise and the innocent; an assemblage of recognizably nudging clichés that was defined in our literary terms as 'couthy'. Few essays before or since can have been as deadly, but the technique was not hard to master, and to this day I detect in myself sinister atavistic regressions into this appalling sly cosiness of style. This work was – in conformance with our editorial policy of refusing any employee the dignity of individuality – not signed, a fact which causes me great relief today; for the purposes of these compositions I would assume the character of A Feckless Housewife, A Henpecked Husband, Wee Wully, The Saftest o' the Family, Always a Wallflower, A Bairn Without a Name, and kindred archetypes of the ridiculous, eccentric, or pathetic. Everything had to be written in paragraphs one sentence long, and as far as possible in what was held to be the homely idiom of the Scottish working class, which is to say a costive coyness larded with apostrophes and Doricisms which bore as much likeness to the demotic speech of the Gorbals, say, as it did to Greek. Considerable value was placed on what were known as 'human stories', which by definition concerned animals. To this end I would be obliged to write under the title of Percy the Poodle, or An Unloved Alley-cat. In this character I authored some work so truly horrible that it met with heartfelt acclaim. From time to time I ghosted in serial form the life-stories of eminent boxers or released murderers or minor domestic functionaries of the Royal Household, all of whom, varied as their activities had presumably been, recounted their Exclusive Stories through me in a style uniformly homely, moving, gripping and couthy. It is true that in this way I came into contact with people and aspects of life that might otherwise have passed me by – for a time I became oddly involved in the activities of the professional boxing industry, in the wild macabre days of Benny Lynch, and a reluctant interest in that sad sport has never quite left me. I acted as journalistic amanuensis to an eerie creep who was contributing a series called 'Secrets of the Mayfair Vice Rings', who conscientiously established his bona-fides by attempting to seduce me on the top deck of a green tram. At intervals I would be despatched, at the conclusion of some especially repellent murder trial – and there seem to me to have been in those days about one a month – to call upon some distracted or avaricious mother up a close in Lanark or Motherwell and guide her hand through an article entitled 'Why My Boy Should Not Be Hanged'. Between these endeavours and my consistent *oeuvre* of canny suburban humour a kind of balance was maintained. I learned to do almost anything after a fashion, and nothing well. I was paid six pounds a week.

The great day was Saturday. This, being press day for our Sunday paper, was for me a regular climax of variety, a profess-ional routine that would be quite unimaginable today. It must be remembered that our organization was not only a non-union shop, but designedly and even militantly so. Only many years later did a fairly close association with my own Union reveal to me the outrages and heresies I had innocently committed long before against every sacred canon of organized labour. At the time it merely seemed to me that I was somewhat overworked. The principle was thus: early in the morning I would repair to the office to be informed what event or happening of the day would provide the most fruitful material for a 'nice wee middle'. It could be anything from a rugby international at Murrayfield to the opening of the General Assembly of the Church of Scotland; there were occasions when I did both at once. I would then attend this affair, return to the office and describe it in the kind of flippant and oblique style that was catalogued as 'light reading'. I would then sub-edit the copy – which, since it was my own story, en-tailed only the insertion of a few stylistic indications to the printer. While this prose was being set in type, I would then pro-duce pen and ink and a pad and make two drawings in illustration of the theme, one of the dimensions of a double-column line block and the other of a single.[1]

By the time I could send these along to the process department the galley-proofs of the nice wee middle were ready to be proof-read; I proof-read them. I then wrote a couple of winsome little captions for the pictures.

The afternoon was now wearing on; by and by it was time to

[1] Among the incidental aptitudes of my life thus far had been a small talent for draughtsmanship; I had in fact studied drawing for a while and had once entertained mild ambitions of working seriously in black and white. However, the more I learned of this business the clearer became my limitations; I was an able enough critic to appreciate the emptiness of a facile line. It was evident that while I could probably become a workmanlike artist of a second rate kind I was hardly likely to become anything better, whereas I argued that as a writer I stood a likelier chance, or possibly I thought the craft was easier. Anyhow I abandoned professional drawing – except for one brief and long-forgotten interlude: while Osbert Lancaster was away on HM diplomatic occasions in Greece I temporarily took over his Pocket Cartoon in the *Daily Express*. It was a short and anguished experiment, proving in fact what required no proof: that Osbert is inimitable.

move over to the printing department, where it was my duty to make up the page on the stone. At this point my departure from all the tenets and doctrine of reasonable union practice moved from the unorthodox to the incredible. It is a cardinal and fundamental law in the whole mystery of newspaper production that print is print and editorial is editorial, and the twain shall meet only through a ritual of intermediary communication as rigid as it is inviolable. On the one hand is the concept, the assemblage of notions or phrases or information definable perhaps as Journalism; on the other hand is the material and tangible expression of these ideas represented by innumerable little slabs of linotype metal ranged in long rectangles, which are type. The Editorial produces the source material; it can be good or bad or indifferent, either inspirational and deathless or meaningless gibberish as far as the printer is concerned; but the physical technique and expertise of actually transferring this nebulous stuff into communicable shape is the concern of the printer alone, and no alien hand must interfere. This is an ancient and proper canon, accepted everywhere – except, to be sure, where I worked in those peculiar days. When it was decided where in the page to place my nice wee middle, and where to dispose the accompanying blocks, the man on the stone would tell me: 'Away and fetch us over thon galleys, son', and I would then trot off and bring back the columns of type to be laid in the forme, full of dread lest I should blunder or stumble and drop the lot on the floor in an inextricable scatter of pied type. If this sounds a trifling or even incomprehensible act to occasion so much retrospective awe I can only say that nowhere else could it have happened; to have the editorial stone-sub manhandling type in this cavalier way can only be likened to a village priest casually calling up some passing Freemason plumber to read the Mass for him while he has a quiet jar in the vestry.

The nice wee middle having been disposed of, with an appropriate heading composed in the vernacular and rounded off, if humanly possible, with an exclamation-mark, to point up the exquisite allusiveness of its humour, the hour came to take my place on the subs' table with my six colleagues. They ranged from Mr James Borthwick the editor to everyone who happened at the time to be engaged on nothing else, including a curiously witty and cryptic casual with a club-foot, whom one saw at no other

time, and whose talent and career, amounting almost to a voca-
tion, was such an encyclopaedic and personal acquaintance with
every police station-sergeant in Glasgow that he could elicit on
the phone the most informative details of every affray, rape, or
grievous bodily harm occurring within the city limits almost
before the incident had been completed. He was by far the busiest
of our little crew. Throughout the night his voice provided a running obligato to our scratching pencils as he sat in his corner with
the telephone wedged between ear and shoulder – he had a special
cavity, or socket, embedded in the region of his clavicle with
which nature had equipped him for the purposes of conducting
telephone interviews while his hands were busy writing, or rolling
cigarettes, or drinking cups of tea. 'Ay, Jock boy, good, good; to
the effusion o' blood, eh; that's no' bad at all. Four fellas to this
one lassie up the close-mouth; fine, fine. Fish-shop afire up by
Bridgton; good, good – no fatal casualties, eh; pity, never mind,
there's time enough; we can take fatalities up to around midnight; do your best, lad; try and get me a wee slashing in the
Gorbals; it's a thin night for the town edition.'

The Saturday nights went by, and the days, and the other days.
I had lodgings in a tenement at the west end of Sauchiehall
Street, up three concrete stairs by the place called Charing Cross;
it was clean and cheerless and every night I returned there with
reluctance. It seemed to me that there must be a better way of
passing one's life, but I could not think of what it was.

Then one day Sandy Trotter, who was the editor of the *Scottish
Daily Express*, inexplicably offered me a job on his paper as a
down-the-table sub. It sounded about as menial an appointment
as the trade had to offer, and I jumped at it. It was, or seemed to
be, some sort of crevice or foothold in national journalism; what
was even more important, it paid nine pounds a week.

On the strength of that I promoted my whole life into a new
dimension, and Elma and I were married in Dundee. At the party
in a Perth hotel my father seemed happy as I had not seen him for
years. I myself seemed translated into something quite new. We
rented the ground-floor flat of a strangely ugly and splendid
house by the Botanical Gardens in Glasgow, and furnished it
with odds and ends. By day we danced around Glasgow as though
it had been Babylon; at night I would take the tram down to
Albion Street and fulfil my place in the noble calling of the

Fourth Estate by putting paragraph-marks on five-line stories about rent-strikes in Renfrewshire. And then the war broke out.

For months now my father had been growing worse; his bronchial condition tormented him and his drinking no longer brought much relief; he now seemed held in a vicious circle in that the more he drank to alleviate his illness the iller he became. I travelled up to see him every week, each time a little more distressed. One day I found him in bed in his hotel room; he had fallen down while out walking and had wrenched his leg. By ordinary standards it was a small injury, but somehow it seemed to have totally discouraged him, and I think that trivial accident marked the steep edge of his decline.

The major punctuation-mark came when he found himself no longer able to write at all. In all the years up until then, through all his difficulties and solitudes, he had always managed to turn out the regular instalments of these endless serial stories. Every year they came to conform more and more to a simple formula, but it was the formula that was required of him, and however banal and predictable its content it was always treated with the ghostly hint of sardonic originality that was the Mark Allerton touch, and the copy was always on time.

Now he found himself unable to do this; not only was he incapable of concentrating his mind on the simple situations he himself had created, but more often than not he was unable to put on paper words of any kind, and would sit hunched by the fireside with his pad on his knees in an agony of helplessness. I find this a great deal easier to understand now than I did then.

So I took to writing his stories for him. It was not very difficult; the pattern once established was fairly easily maintained, and I was able to manage a sort of continuity of theme. Between my father and I was accepted the illusion that this was 'revision', that I was merely taking the labour of transcription off his hands until he was better. The copy was delivered on time, and accepted without comment by the editors. I congratulated myself on the success of this stratagem. It was only after my father's death that I learned that the publishers had at no time been deceived. It was considerate and delicate of them that they had said no word either to my father or to me.

At the beginning of September there was a telephone message

from Dundee that my father had become seriously ill. I told Elma
– with some compunction, since it was now established that our
baby was well on the way – and took the dreary familiar train
north. The papers I bought at the station were screaming that war
had been declared on Germany.

I found him in his bed, extremely pale and unshaven and
tousled, which in itself was striking, since he was fastidious about
personal neatness. He was in a state of high excitement. 'They
have got the insane idea in their heads that I should leave here. I
cannot imagine why – to be sure I am unwell at the moment, but
it will pass; it always does. Now they have given me some sort
of a physic that has greatly upset my mind. I think there is some
sort of conspiracy in the air, and perhaps we had better watch
out. Upon my soul, I feel very strange.'

Somehow the fact of the war had registered on his mind, and
when he dwelt on it he suddenly fell into a state of depression
more acute and painful than I had ever seen him in since my
mother's death.

'This is preposterous and horrible. I had not thought to see
such an imbecility happen again – so soon; the other one is barely
over, and look what that did to us all. Take care and have nothing
to do with it, my boy. My God I wish I felt better at this moment;
there's a great deal I should write about this.'

But he soon forgot about it, and as the injection took effect he
fell into a reverie. 'I am in mind of the time when we were all
living in France; I can't remember the date; and you won four
francs on the children's *boule*. That was a great triumph; when you
grow up you will probably be less lucky. I have not been very
lucky either, but things are about to change, the moment I get
well.'

That afternoon they took him away to a nursing-home. I began
to tidy up the papers and clothes in the hotel room where he had
lived for ten years.

I went to see him the following morning, carrying the daily
papers that I supposed he would need, since always we had a
ritual of brooding and wrangling and gnawing over the papers
before, as it were, engaging in the day. Abruptly that had come to
an end, he had totally ceased to care; my father stared at the papers
irritably, as though they had been wastepaper, which greatly
moved me, since I could see now that he had decided to abandon

his links with life. He began to recount some fantasy that was simultaneously puzzling and amusing him: was it not extraordinary, he said, that he had been compelled against his will to spend the preceding night with the late Queen Victoria, and to waste so many hours debating the Reform Bill with that obstinate old woman. The authority of the nursing home, he said, had been at the same time misplaced and magical; it was preposterous but he had to laugh – he had not wanted the company of Queen Victoria, and even though he had done, how could they have so convincingly resurrected her?

'God knows,' said my father, 'things are confusing enough, what with my being confined here when I should be at work, without these bizarre intrusions. Next time it might be anyone. Or what is worse, anything.'

And then he looked up with a momentary agony that he instantly covered with a wry and touching grimace. 'I suppose,' he said after a pause, 'it is the DTs after all. I expect I am lost, dear boy.'

I sat with him for an hour or two, while he dozed in a fretful way; from time to time he roused himself and talked on the edge of hallucination: when might we expect my mother to call, were we not all going to plan a holiday somewhere? Sometimes he spoke in a speculative way about the behaviour of characters in novels he had written years before, long forgotten by everyone except himself. Even as the time went on he seemed to grow smaller, physically diminished against the hard pillows. He had taken off his spectacles, a thing he had never been known to do in his waking moments, so much an integral part of himself had they been throughout all his life; now he had rid himself of them impatiently for the first time for fifty years, as though in some way they intruded between him and his mind's eye.

At one point he broke off his reflections and said to me in lucid and suddenly businesslike tones: 'Now, my dear fellow, you'll do me a favour; will you just slip down the road and get me a bottle of whisky, they seem to be too busy here to do one these services, and it will not take you a moment. For that matter a half bottle will do; there is no need to overdo it at this stage. There is no need to bother the management of this place. I have a feeling that it is just the thing to put me on my feet again; indeed there is probably no reason why I shouldn't then get dressed and come home with you.'

He said this in such a rational and matter-of-fact way, in tones so deliberately casual and off-hand, that it was clear he understood the situation completely, while somehow miserably hoping that I did not; he wanted my collusion while trying to avoid the suggestion of a conspiracy.

I said: 'I can't; they would never let me.'

'Don't you worry about that,' he said, 'it has just been an oversight. I see no reason why they have to be consulted on every detail. As a matter of fact I rather need it; this has been an exhausting time, quite apart from the bewilderments of . . . I must get a grasp of myself; it will never do to hang around in this place. I am a bit uncertain as to why I am here anyhow; the wheeze seems to have left me for once. So be a good fellow and do as I say, and we'll be out in a brace of shakes.'

For the first time he affected an elaborately casual examination of the newspapers I had left on the bed, but I knew that without his glasses he could not have been reading a word.

It was a racking situation; all my life I would have done anything to help my father; even now I was conscious of the fact that he was aware of my dilemma, and would have spared me if he could have done.

'Please,' he said.

'I'll see what I can do,' I said like a coward.

'Do,' said my father. 'You've been a very good friend to me; it is ridiculous that we should find ourselves in this situation. Queen Victoria, how odd that they should have employed her; she is of no interest to me whatever, and I am quite sure she never heard of me. Please do your best. I shall be out of here in no time.'

When I returned in the afternoon he was asleep; the nurse told me that he had become violently restless and had been given a heavy sedative. The papers were stacked on the bed-table; he had not opened them nor was ever to do so again. He lay quite still, and very small. At one point some dream seemed to amuse him, for he smiled with real pleasure and said in his sleep: 'What *will* they think of next?'

I had to return to my work in Glasgow: the airless blacked-out train, the sense of tension and woe; the groping through the darkness of Kelvinside to the house and the companionship of Elma. Her pregnancy seemed deeply consoling.

Thus it went on for two more weeks. I travelled to the nursing-home every fourth day, and sometimes my aunt came with me – herself thirteen years my father's senior, yet now looking like his younger sister. 'Poor Willy has come low,' she said, 'and he was the kindest of us all.' Already she had come to think of him in the past, which I refused to do. He had now come to recognize us only intermittently, and though his conversation was clear sometimes almost to the point of pedantry, it was fanciful and irrelevant and fixed in the past. Only when we rose to go did he become uneasy. 'While you're around they can't send in all these people to vex me. Soldiers and lawyers and musicians, total strangers; what good they think it does I cannot imagine. The only thing is to ignore them. I cannot tell you how fatiguing it is, and I am supposed to be leaving here tomorrow quite early. O how glad I shall be of a little peace.'

This was not long in coming; he died very early the following morning. Elma and I travelled once again that dreary journey to Dundee. I went to some undertaker's parlour and saw my father in his coffin, absurdly tricked up within the planks in some sort of satin and lace embellishment; impossibly shrunk and withered and meaningless, so very ill at ease, it seemed to me, in that doll's box with the frills. For about five minutes I could not think of anything that was worse, that after a life as erratic and unexpected as his, with so much in it of merriment and misery, that there should be no one to weep for him but me.

So we went to his funeral, and already Elma in her pregnancy was having difficulty with the inevitable trudging and standing, and looked drawn and ashen in a way I was soon to remember with bitter remorse. When they had burned my father they gave me a ticket to confirm that this had been done, and purporting to identify what rose-tree in the grounds was to be nourished by his ashes.

These commonplaces have no relevance now, except as part of a cumulative pattern of loss and sorrow that brought that year for me to an extremity of personal disaster, since the months to come were to bring so much worse.

The time had clearly come when I had to reconcile myself to producing nice wee middles and third-rate drawings for the rest of my life or move into something else. I accepted this job on the Scottish edition of the *Daily Express*, of which I knew nothing whatever except that it represented some sort of new dimension to the newspaper trade. My installation as a down-the-table sub-editor was a task at the same time lowly and harassing, involving the examination, correction and verification of great numbers of very small accounts of very small happenings, any of which however had the potentiality of blowing up into something either danger-ous or embarrassing; it represented the total opposite of the late Mr Stanley Baldwin's definition of journalism. He had described the calling as 'power without responsibility, the prerogative of the harlot throughout the ages'. My menial share, on the other hand, represented responsibility without power. As I scribbled my paragraph-marks on the flow of minute reportages of council-meetings in Bothwell or stabbing-affrays in Renfrew Street, I was haunted by considerations of doom.

These arcane technicalities I would endeavour to explain to Elma the next day; she would listen with the slightly remote and smiling sympathy of one whose own considerations were not only greater and more personal but also more immediate: the baby was expected at any time.

The big event was expected at the weekend. On the Saturday morning I went to the office to do my early turn on the Sunday edition. We were paid an extra two guineas for this, and indeed all of us needed it very badly. I spent the morning in a kind of euphoric daze; I could put my mind to nothing at all; I rambled through my routine ration of random paragraphs marking time, as it were, for the call that was certain to come at any moment. Very early in the afternoon it came; we had just been given a yellow air-raid warning, the standby call, but I did not notice this. Some anonymous voice asked me to go to the hospital at once.

I took a cab, which in itself was the measure of the situation, since Saturday subs in Glasgow rarely took cabs, but I had never become a father before and I rode on air. I bought some flowers; it was May.

When I got to the hospital the Sister said: 'I am very sorry; I think you are just in time,' and began walking at a tremendous speed along a corridor until we came to a small room in which was a very high bed, and nothing else. Elma was lying on the bed, inside a plastic tent, living her last few minutes in her own private atmosphere; she was looking with great concentration at nothing, and exactly at the moment when I reached the bedside she sighed very deeply and died. The nurse said: 'What a pity; I am very sorry; she was very young, wasn't she; you just can't tell; now I think you had better go to the waiting room.' So I went to the waiting room and that was the end of it, the end of Elma, the end of my short and little marriage, the end of my short and little life. After an hour or so they let me back in again, and I put my flowers somewhere on the place where she lay. The nurse said: 'I think the raid-warning's gone; I am very sorry this happened; we shall look after everything; now perhaps you had better go and leave it to us.'

So I went away and left it to them; I was twenty-eight, and old enough to understand that hospitals were busy places.

My daughter Elma was born in May 1940; the German army was moving through the Low Countries and into France and the war had become war. This I appreciated through the crescendo of news pouring in through the tapes; I read it with wonderment and watched Europe collapse, as everything else had collapsed. They announced the fall of Paris on my birthday; the BBC had me do a French broadcast of some kind about regret, and solidarity, and determination; I cannot remember what it was all about; by now I was totally involved to the point of obsession with the technical problems of maintaining, and optimistically rearing, a two-weeks-old baby in a furnished room off the Great Western Road in Glasgow.

Somehow we managed, which is all that need be said about that. Out of that awful time was preserved and sustained, by a consistent series of flukes and miracles, the daughter who fortunately could hardly know how profoundly she was, for so long, to be the hub and purpose of my life.

By and by this process of learning the craft of the care and treatment of infant girls was interrupted by my call-up. I was given my initial examination in the middle of a period of quite absurd exhaustion; it was almost certainly out of error or impatience that they curtly rejected me. I had indeed little to offer the great crusade except an amateur ability to fly aeroplanes and a familiarity with French verse of the baser sort. The officials tersely turned me down on the surprising grounds of organic cardiac disease, with the recommendation that I should be embodied in no branch of active service anywhere, and that in no circumstance should I be exposed to an altitude more than three thousand feet. From that point various exigencies of life were to oblige me to join, in one fashion or another, in the activities of five different armies and two navies, and to pass the intervening periods largely in aeroplanes at a height of twenty thousand feet. I emerged from my medical unnerved to the point where I hardly dared cross the street, but within two years it became clear that, whatever had happened to my soul, I was at least physically indestructible. In the years to come, in Germany, Korea, Malaya, Indo-China, I was to reflect upon the curious durability of the officially infirm.

In this year of *angst* I was translated from the Glasgow office of the *Express* to Fleet Street, on grounds that I can explain only by the likelihood that exempted dullards were of more practical value to a newspaper than able-bodied draftees. For a while I laboured in Lord Beaverbrook's London vineyard, and in such straits was that organization, so depleted its resources of man-power, that by and by they were obliged to appoint me to the position of Deputy Chief Sub, than which it seemed to me no more wracking appointment exists in the machinery of newspaper production. A maximum of half a dozen of us got the paper out each night, and some of them have gone into the annals of that blackout age: Brian Chapman, Bill Knott, Basil Denny, Tim Healey, Sailor Mapleson, the incomparable Percy Crisp. The nights when I had to fulfil my Deputy role and exercise its very peripheral authority were nightmares to me – and, it would appear, to those in authority over me. In the guilty intermissions between editions when I could snatch a breather in Poppin's bar I would often discover Arthur Christiansen the editor in deep and considered argument with his assistant Herbert Gunn, debating solemnly whether either in their varied and considerable careers had ever encountered a Deputy Chief Sub as hapless and in-adequate as I. Chris would affect to recall his prentice days in Wallasey, and Gunn his in Gravesend; there had been some out-standing dead losses there – but no; it seemed that on reflection even the worst of them had shown more promise than I.

Sometimes I would almost hope that a bomb would fall upon our establishment and put us all out of our misery, and several times this nearly came to pass.

I was very much a creature of that environment; I even lived hard by, sharing a flat in Lincoln's Inn – in the building, I was told, that had indeed been the vicarage of John Donne; it may or may not have been true but it consoled me to believe it. I loathed every day of my absurd looking-glass life, working through the noisy nervous hours of darkness, drinking desultorily through the brief day that is a newspaper sub's only contact and relationship with the rest of the world. It had been clearly impossible to bring my daughter south into this half-world; I had established her with her mother's mother in a cottage in a part of Aberdeenshire that I calculated was of all parts of Britain the least likely to be bombed; and once every four weeks I used the accumulation of my hoarded days off in the journey through the length of Britain – railway rides of indescribable discomfort and delay, in crowded stifling blacked-out trains, anaesthetized with fatigue upright in the reeking corridors. The journey usually took at least a total day and night; I would arrive in time to make the baby's acquaintance once again, each time anew as she grew into a childhood that owed less and less to me. Then back again to the dark and dreary drama of a wartime London that was resentfully enduring history in a numb and lifeless mood of indomitable complaint.

In what was without irony called the art-room of the newspaper was working Elizabeth O'Conor; as I spent my nights fitting the fragmentary story of the war into the compass of a four-page newspaper so did she reinforce this operation by drawing the maps whose function was to define to a hungry nation the relative positions of Narvik and Kirkemoln, of Sirte and Benghazi, of Arras and Sedan, embellished with monstrous arrows to indicate the changing fortunes of the war. She was both kind and tranquil, she was beautiful and she was generous; she was as vulnerable as I but more composed, and nobody else did or could have done what I had supposed impossible: she took me over the barrier between the past and the present, and opened all the closed doors. When we were married it was like entering a theatre already in the second act; we united our children – my baby daughter, her baby son – and for the first time for three despairing years there seemed for me some point in establishing a root in life. We set up house in Markham Square, in the lunatic moonlit world of the Chelsea of the early 40s, inhabited by the sweet and shifting companionship of the lost years, most now untimely lost or quenched or overtaken – Brian Chapman, Dylan Thomas, Anthony Devas, Warren Chetham Strode, John Davenport, the gentle and beloved Vicky with whom I was to plod in hilarious despair through twenty years of mutually hopeless exhilaration.

Continually I supplicated the *Express* to remove me from the imbecile thralldom of the office and return me to the only job I knew: the reporter's job, the features job, anything in which I felt I stood a fair chance of fulfilment. I had no need to point out what was obvious: that I would never make executive material, that I had no gift of leadership or command, and that I knew that to the day of my death I would be obliged to count out on my fingers the number of letters accommodated in a 42-point heading of Cheltenham Bold across four columns. It took a long time, but finally I prevailed; I think my entreaties and my arguments finally bored them past endurance, and quite suddenly I found myself a foreign correspondent. It sounded rather more *farouche* than in fact it turned out to be.

Chapter Three

My ten years with the *Express* were wild, violent, diverting, obsessive, exasperating, and full of mad unpredictable movement. I joined my elders and betters as an itinerant bagman of what most of the time were dreary tidings, chasing around from one manifestation of human error to the next, feeling uneasily, though rarely admitting it that the world we saw was usually at its worst, and not infrequently because of our presence.

I began to feel that my life was spent tethered to an inclinable seat beside a perspex window, peering without pleasure at the planet below, listening with amateur anxiety to the whine and mutter of engines I neither understood nor trusted. After millions of miles I understand them no better; the theory of aerodynamics is reasonable, but there is still no explanation of how the wings stay on.

I passed through a period of concern less with the purpose of travel than with the thing itself. Its cumulative effect was not necessarily disagreeable, but peculiar: a world of schedules and time-zones, a positional transfer from Square A to Square B, a suspended animation, a trajectory.

It was not so much a case for the psychiatrist as the mathematician. The dimensions of the world got blurred and unsteady when you were careering about it at 600 miles an hour, not just occasionally but all the time, when you could change from the Arctic to the tropics in the space of a day. You began to get a vague notion of what relativity is all about. You could cross the International Date Line and have a week with two Tuesdays in it, or indeed no Tuesdays at all. I once crossed the Line on my birthday, which meant it vanished; the day disappeared completely. If I did that every year, would I never grow any older? I supposed perhaps not, but I still cannot rationalize it. I believe the physicists say that anyone who spent a hundred years in outer space would return to find everything in the world that much older, while he himself had stayed the same age. With me, it seemed like the exact reverse.

Now and again I got back to what I was by now rather desperately attempting to define as home; to that end we had moved into the imitation countryside of Sussex. There I waited a while, made tentative advances to the children, drew a picture, drank warm beer with a few ageing acquaintances, read a book on the care and maintenance of goats. In a week or so it all began again. It was difficult to insulate oneself even temporarily from other people's business in those first years of what we all rather fulsomely called peace. Very soon one's resistance weakened, one reached for the paper – a fatal gesture, committing one to another few years of bewilderment.

They scampered by: argument and effort, a receding succession of minor crises, strikes, blockades, demarches, elections, lynchings, witch-hunts, coups d'etat, famines, plebiscites, flag-showings, flag-burnings. A white man jumped out of a window in Prague. A dark man fell, holed by a toy bullet, in Delhi. The desolate columns of refugees moved across the plains, into the valleys; shrill calls for charity and blankets rang through Kensington and Lake Success while the victims continued, inconspicuously and with muted protests, to die. A good deal of chauvinist prattle, mostly incomprehensible, bounced back and forth between the nationalists and one-worlders on both sides of the frontiers. To the east some new nations, as nations, vanished; further east yet newer nations appeared. Here and there a few people clung articulately to the vestiges of faith and reason; they were generally denounced, impartially, as idealists, Communists, or imbeciles.

For a week or two I pottered about the household, with the aimless urgency of the part-time countryman. Life was one long losing argument with all the more obstinate forces of nature – a rich and rewarding work, everyone said; just the thing to flush away the vitiating taste of print. In my case there had been something unreal and miscast about it from the start. For years I had been trying to cultivate the true marks and mannerisms of the country-dweller – the earthy philosophy, the knowing phrase, the professional slouch. Yet the boots and leather elbow-patches, so functional on rural novelists and film stars in Buckinghamshire, never succeeded on me in looking other than slightly bogus.

It is the case that a certain quality of chameleon allows me to pass inconspicuously in many curious foreign environments, but perversely I could never develop a protective colouring in my own home. I always looked what I was: a seedy journalist taking time off in Sussex. It was clearly not to last, nor did it.

I went to India, China, South America. I crept around post-war Europe, diffidently, like King Wenceslas's page, in the warm footsteps of my learned leaders like William Forrest and Sefton Delmar. I went to Siam and Burma and Indonesia and the Caribbean and to eccentric and even pretentious places like Patagonia and Afghanistan, and indeed even Tibet. I went to everywhere in the world, and half the time – such was the permissive journalistic climate of those years – mainly for the simple purpose of going, and not for any end product or discovery that could conceivably have been worth the fare. I cannot think of any trade or calling that would have accorded a fairly young and earnest person like myself the same extravagant resources to examine the planet. It would not happen now. In the preface to the last of his travel books the late Evelyn Waugh wrote: 'In two generations the air may be fresher and we may again breed great travellers like Burton and Doughty. I never aspired to being a great traveller. I was simply typical of my age; we travelled as a matter of course. I rejoice that I went when the going was good.'

To this I could have said Amen, until the summer of 1946 when I had to go to the Pacific to assist at the explosion of the Atom Bomb.

There is probably no subject in the small history of my times of which I have written more repetitively than this, no consideration that came to obsess me more, no event that had a more stunning and lasting impact on my future attitudes to almost everything. Twenty years of obstinacy and emotion were founded on this, and remain so; there is no especial merit in basing a total political posture on one moment of time, but it could be argued that certain permanencies of politics, like CND, created so much later, were borne for me in that forgotten summer of 1946.

I had been living in India, striving with difficulty to come to terms with the consolations of the Independence negotiations, trying to equate the disparate austerities of Mahatma Gandhi and Stafford Cripps, trying to live on a foundation of reason with Jawaharlal Nehru and Mr Jinnah, trying to appreciate by personal experiment the wild differences between life in the Himalaya and in Madras. It was all going on, embedded in the fantasies of the Simla Conference, when I was called away again.

Ten thousand miles away to the west, on the unheard-of Pacific fly-speck called Bikini, an extravagant multitude of strange personalities was assembling for the Atom Bomb experiment. The Americans had allotted three observers' places to Britain; I had been chosen for one of them. It was a rather random distinction – the places had been allocated by ballot – nevertheless I had a very odd feeling of involvement. India had left me shaky and uncertain; I had by no means formulated my psychological attitude to American atom-bombs. I foresaw something physically and spiritually disturbing, and I was, for once, right.

Two days later I was over the Atlantic, the following day in New York, still one day later in Washington.

In all my harping on hotels, in all my obsession with the inns at which there is no room, in all my tales of non-cooperative taverners the world over, I have never touched on the absolute apotheosis of this phenomenon, which was Washington, DC. It was, bar nowhere, the fullest place I ever saw. It swarmed, it surged, it seemed at times to seethe with earnest, determined people leaping in and out of enormous cars, bounding urgently up the steps of hotels and secretariats, grasping glasses of milk with their eyes on their wrist-watches.

Through my association with the atomic operation I had enough pull to get me a hotel room on the most temporary understanding, with one night the final maximum.

The hotel was firm; first thing in the morning I was out, hangover and all, in the sultry street. It seemed that a restive queue of Admirals, Generals, Senators and Chief Executives was lined up for my room, competing for my crumpled bed. I checked my baggage and walked about among the drug-stores and men's wear departments; I bought myself a brief case so that I might be inconspicuous, and when the time came I went to report to the Navy Department and present my credentials.

There they welcomed me with an indoctrination course on

security, reference to the Federal Espionage Act, and gave me many painful injections. They led me to a room filled with maps and diagrams and handed me an envelope containing the schedules and briefing arrangements for Bikini. It was marked: RESTRICTED. CONFIDENTIAL. PROPERTY OF THE UNITED STATES NAVY DEPARTMENT. MOST SECRET.

At the time the trappings of the operation seemed even more vivid than the climax; it became an event that grew more and more fanciful and unreal, laid about with greater and greater stresses of vulgarity and display; all implications lost in a tangle of secondary issues. The experiment was called, with the American flair for theatre: Operation Crossroads.

The ship, the USS *Appalachian,* all masts and aerials and radar grids and antennae, was four days out of San Francisco, nosing through a curiously mauve Pacific towards our extraordinary rendezvous on the coral atoll nobody had ever heard of before that year.

Crowded below decks was an imposing list of experts and on-lookers, heavyweight brains of all the sciences, now in various stages of brooding introspection induced by an uneasy sea. We were the final detachment of Joint Task Force One, the last to join the intricate company of men and machines already gathered in the South Seas to watch the explosion of the world's fourth atomic bomb, the first ever to be dropped in what might be called cold blood, in a spotlight of elaborate melodrama; a monstrous scientific joust.

In other circumstances, with another background, our part of the expedition might have seemed an extremely odd junket, a comedy of American manners straight out of some sardonic Capra film. First the great train, the Crossroads Special, crawling for four days across the Continent, rumbling westwards past all the backdoors of America: Pittsburgh, Chicago, the Great Salt Lake; through the hills and over the plains: Pennsylvania, Ohio, Illinois, Nebraska, Wyoming, Utah, Nevada. At last to Oakland and the *Appalachian,* partly a warship, partly a power-station; television screens in curious corners, filled everywhere with some shrill, unfixable mechanical hum. And off we moved through the Golden Gate, crowded with the rambling troupe which was to chronicle this thing for the breakfast-tables of Dallas and Des

Moines, Nashville and New York, for the *Toledo Blade* and the
Youngstown Vindicator, Chemical Industries and the *Christian Science
Monitor, Our Navy* and the *Scholastic Magazine,* the *Daily Express*
and the *Figaro* and the *Red Fleet* . . . all prowling the decks in an
issue of long-prowed Navy caps and assorted underwear, all
talking nuclear fission or stud poker. From the moment of departure the script of the show was most clearly by Jules Verne
out of Damon Runyon.

As a demonstration of the strength and abundance of the
American Press it was truly formidable. Of the hundred and
sixty-nine correspondents swarming all over *Appalachian* from
the widest variety of newspapers – big and small, shrill and
solemn, exacting and indifferent – one hundred and sixty-one
were Americans. Britain, as some concession of right, and France
each had one place, so did Mexico, and Canada, and Poland, and
Australia, and China. And so – since she too, in those dreamy days,
still kept a seat on the UN Atomic Energy Commission – did
Russia.

Comrade Kholkov was a compact, composed and agreeable
character, who neither sought companionship nor avoided it, and
who confirmed everybody's preconceptions by playing chess all
his waking hours with the monosyllabic Mexican. Somehow it
got put about that Comrade Kholkov – who, for the purposes of
this enterprise was representing the newspaper *Red Fleet* – was
himself a Captain in the Soviet Navy. This caused some dark conjecture among our solid core of Middle Westerners, who were not
only quite incapable of assessing a ship's distance within a five-
mile margin, but sometimes claimed proudly never to have seen a
ship before in their lives. Whether their speculations concerning
Kholkov were correct was never very firmly established; whenever the subject was raised Comrade Kholkov would smile happily
and say: 'Ha, yes; indeed a very funny; my goodness, it is
terrible hot, is it? I like a good hot.'

Of this bizarre junket I have written so often and so much, both
at the time and interminably thenceforth – since no single post-
war incident so firmly attached my mind to its subsequent single
track – that I despair of not repeating myself. For years after
Operation Crossroads I was, I think, the first of the atom-bomb
bores. (In my defence it was true to say that I was, and possibly
still am, the only layman who has been obliged physically to see

three of the things actually go off.) This enterprise was a pantomime of such hilarious tragedy, compounded of every factor
from the banal to the appalling, that it remains in my mind as a
kind of slapstick nightmare.

As we drove slowly westwards across the Pacific the days
passed in a kind of congested tranquillity. The ship was impossibly
full of journalists, living in a dreadful proximity that was officially
tempered by the US Navy, according to a rule of seniority they
had devised for the occasion. I was accomodated in a cabin most
steely and functional, haunted by a high, piercing, incessant,
scream from some furious piece of electrical machinery; it never
stopped by day or night; it was like living inside some demented
electronic brain, tending to emphasize the surrealist nature of the
whole expedition.

One grew accustomed to the uneventfulness, the idleness that
must need still be ordered and disciplined by timetable routine –
the heavy meals at strange, American hours; the stream of wardroom lectures and explanatory briefings: Nuclear Fission for
Beginners, Atomic Energy Made Easy, the painless approach to
the theory of radiation. They did at least disabuse some of us of
the belief, popularly held at correspondent level, that a Neutron
was an employee in a harem.

From time to time we were Brains Trusted by the experts, a
complex business made even more inscrutable by the inevitable
failure of the microphone-gear. (It was a striking fact that this
vessel, probably the world's most intricately-mechanized for the
purpose of long-range communication, seemed incapable of
keeping its simpler domestic equipment in order; we had been
five days at sea, for example, before the refrigeration was induced
to work.) We absorbed our scientific learning in abrupt and
awkward bursts.

'Do you agree,' someone would ask through a roaring amplifier,
'that the . . . crash, crash . . . geology and oceanography would
. . . crash, crash.' The reply would come, harshly, in inaudible
polysyllables; – 'Far reaching implications . . . elemental magni-
tude. . . .'

'Thank you, Doctor.'

'. . . by the subsidence theory, postulating . . .'

On and on, over and over. So to another meal; heavy, gaudy,
utterly without savour. For years I have wondered how it is that

American food – so ample, so ingenious, so adjectival, can look so good and taste so ill. Assorted Cold Cuts, enough to feed a platoon. Superlative ice-cream, served perversely on a red-hot plate, like yellow soup. A vast joint, cut once and with a splendid gesture jettisoned over the side. A crate of vegetables, bobbing and floating behind the ship. We had not been long on our way before the word went round below the sea-lanes of the Pacific, that ours was a vessel worth pursuing; behind us trailed a growing queue of shark and barracuda. Alas for them, they followed us too long; they were at our heels when at last we entered the lagoon of Bikini; they were still there browsing contentedly on the assorted offal of a battle fleet when we moved out again, the day before science put the biggest possible stop to their indulgence.

But if there was food, there was nothing else – no bar, no official liquor at all; even for this jamboree the US Navy stuck rigidly to its dry regulations. I studied with a dismal interest my own reaction to such sudden teetotalism. It was of a purely negative kind – a lack of inspiration, sleeplessness, but above all the absence of any sort of reasonable punctuation for the day. The furtive bottle-parties were not quite enough; the exigencies of our life brought them on at dispiriting hours, usually three in the afternoon, or two in the morning, and there was the humiliating risk of being found out.

The purpose of the operation, the frightful thing they were going to do at Bikini, remained something of an abstraction. We had been increasingly well briefed in the details of the assignment; we knew when, we knew what, we knew, in a sort of way, how. But not until we reached Bikini would the thing drop into focus and become rather more than a long trip to hear a loud noise.

On and around that trifling Micronesian coral ring already were about 42,000 people, all directly concerned in the experiment. 38,300 Navy, 2,750 Army Air Force, 550 civilian technicians, 350 Army ground forces, 150 Marines. At least 220 ships were involved. For six months the place had been worked over, cleared out, fitted up, established with every possible device for determining in the most scrupulous detail what happened when an atom bomb burst over, and under, a battle fleet – a thing that could be established in one way only, by exploding an atom bomb over, and under, a battle fleet.

The motivation was preponderantly Naval; to seek information on possible changes made necessary by atomic war on design, tactical formations, and strategic dispositions of ships. To test the effect of the bomb against aircraft, both airborne and grounded; on all types of military weapons and equipment, and to determine more closely the effect of an atom bomb on live beings, an early diagnosis of which was not possible at Hiroshima or Nagasaki. Finally to learn what might be learned of general scientific value on the phenomenon accompanying atomic explosions. Somewhere behind all this, one dimly felt, there might also be a few imponderables in the way of moral issues, less easily illumined by a flash reputedly twenty times stronger than the sun.

All around Bikini, we knew, were the structures, camera towers, television points, instrument shelters, the gauges that would record the climactic moment graphically, photographically, electronically, radiometrically, oceanographically.

There were a thousand people directly concerned with this mensuration alone.

There were ten thousand different instruments in the target ships, on the islets, in the planes above, in the water of the sea around, on the floor of the lagoon itself. Some were extremely complex, and some were very simple, like five-gallon petrol-drums. (These, being curiously almost exactly the same size and strength as a man's chest wall, were to demonstrate graphically what happens to the human thorax in these trying conditions.) There was, in short, never before any single concussion where so many things were to be measured at once.

The doomed ships would be studied to see how they deformed, how fast, and in precisely what fashion. Every one of the pigs, the mice and rats and goats and guinea-pigs and so forth who were to man those unlucky ships had already had its physical condition tabulated even more keenly and grimly than had he been applying for a visa for the United States. The survivors' genes and anomalies would be studied thereafter with greater care than those of the wealthiest hypochondriac.

So far only the science writers had anything to do, the specialists who filled columns on every abstruse and recondite angle suggested by their studies. One of them, at work on a physiological theory, was tapping out an argument on the carotid arteries. 'These arteries . . .' he typed, caught himself in a mis-spelling and x'ed out 'arteries' carelessly, re-wrote and sent his message. The telegraphist, his mind elsewhere, transmitted it as 'The sex arteries'. So it reached the agency's offices in New York, where a prudent copy reader, distrusting the word 'sex', turned it into 'the love arteries'. And thus it appeared all over to the thousand subscribers to the agency's service. It was a long time before the serious specialist aboard the *Appalachian* discovered that his thesis had set him, scientifically, somewhere back among the Ancient Greeks.

Not one of us really knew any more than the albatross wheeling and dipping astern whether this was reason or folly. Somehow one began to feel, with a foreboding that had only partly a physical basis, that it would be happier to be going home.

Where the 166 meridian of longitude crossed latitude 12, that is to say dead in the middle of this endless American lake the set was ready, and 42,000 pairs of fingers were crossed for a clear day and a fair wind.

We were now into the Marshall Group. Kwajalein was behind. We were about to pass the little coral island, on the fringe of the Crossroads project, with the unreasonably jocose name of Wot Ho.

At Bikini itself, just ahead over the sunset, the seventy-five ships of the guinea-pig Fleet were anchored in their intricate pattern in the lagoon; the hundred and fifty odd aircraft dispersed on islands and carriers had run through their complex drill; Major Swancutt's crew of the B-29 which was to carry the bomb were waiting on Kwajalein airfield, presumably playing stud poker in their birthday suits like everyone else between San Francisco and Manila.

As we closed in on the scene the impression grew that half the US Fleet was doing the same. Quite apart from the mass of target-ships, still over the horizon, there were nearly two hundred vessels of the Task Force – transports, auxiliaries, destroyers, Command Ships, hospital ships, laboratory ships, instrumentation ships, water-distillation ships, refrigerator ships, Post Office ships. We were primed daily with the logistical miscellany – that for example we had assembled seven hundred thousand barrels of black-fuel oil, five hundred thousand gallons of aviation spirit; that the crowd of us was devouring each day, or hurling to the sharks, twenty-six thousand pounds of flour and forty thousand pounds of meat.

All this left out of account the miscellaneous concourse of scientists and learned characters of all kinds, each concentrating on some highly-specialized piece of research with the aid of some instrument which was either monumentally big or microscopically small. There were hundreds of such angles, and we were instructed in them at the daily lectures, classes, seminars and discussion-groups which gave this cruise the character of a rather half-baked and unruly University course in futuristic physics.

Sometimes there arose the feeling that a great deal of robust dust was being thrown in one's eyes, to conceal under a mass of jargon the fact that this was primarily an exposition of American naval and military power. The Army, to prevent Operation Crossroads being simply a hundred-per-cent Naval undertaking, insisted on dropping the bomb. For a day or two the spotlight swung away from the Target to the Missile, especially to its method of delivery; we were crammed with picturesque detail on Dave's Dream, the name of the bombing aircraft, on the colour of the bombardier's eyes, on the grotesque and shaming fact that the bomb itself bore on its undescribed casing a portrait of Rita Hayworth and the simple name: Gilda. Of such horrors was the final moment compounded.

So we came to Bikini: a typical Pacific coral atoll, several tiny islands surrounding a lagoon twenty miles long by ten miles wide. The main island, drawing close on the starboard bow, was so precisely the conventional picture of a South Sea Island that it might have been the jacket of a very old novel. Inside the lagoon, as far as one could see, were the seventy-three target vessels disposed in an intricate pattern to achieve every degree of damage: the American battleships *Arkansas, Pennsylvania, New York,* and the Japanese *Nagato.* A barracks-barge like an iron Noah's Ark lay alongside. The carriers *Independence* and *Saratoga,* aircraft marshalled tightly on the flight decks. The cruisers *Pensacola, Salt Lake City,* the Japanese *Sakawa,* and the German *Prinz Eugen,* and around and amongst them ranks of destroyers, submarines, auxiliaries, transports, landing craft, barges, and a floating drydock – an enormous naval condemned cell.

In the centre, standing out among the warship grey like a

bloodspot on a monk's robe, was the battleship *Nevada*, painted from masthead to waterline a hard, hot red. She was dressed in this brutal colour to make her a clear and vivid mark on the lagoon; she was the bull's eye. Aboard the *Nevada* it was like some great forlorn house just before moving day. Here, however, as the tenants moved out the luggage moved in. All over the red decks lay the secondary sacrifices – a 30-ton tank, a heavy field-gun, rows of the newest and smartest automatic weapons, delicate electrical and photographic gear, an aircraft or two. Down on the boat-deck, under a tarpaulin awning stretched from an aircraft wing, waited the little company of flesh and blood, standing reflectively in pens for their most abrupt and instructive dissolution. There were a few goats, with pale and cynical eyes, one or two brown spotted pigs.

A scientist beside me said: 'I feel a little like apologizing to those pigs. They belong to a reasonable and uncomplicated people, not without a certain grace. At least,' he said, 'they aren't crazy.'

On that last night life went on; skeleton crews continued to work, sleep, brew coffee on the messdecks. On Bikini Island, among the reaching palms and the stark steel instrumentation towers, they had run up clubs and offices and canteens and softball diamonds in the clearings where, not too long ago, a hundred and eighty-odd Bikini Micronesians dawdled away a placid and uncomplicated life, until they awoke one day and found themselves transplanted, not without protest, to the island of Rongerik. Now already Bikini had that improvised, tawdry, squalid look of anywhere taken over by the Services.

We went ashore and had our first legal drink for many days. The bar, palm thatched, bulging with bottles, stood on the highest point of Bikini – ten feet above sea level. It was called – and by then one was past caring – 'The Up and Atom'. It did not prevent several of us getting madly drunk.

As the cannonball sun set on the last pre-atomic evening of the Marshall Islands, Joint Task Force One began to slide out of the lagoon to action-stations beyond the reef, leaving the target fleet empty and alone. One by one the anchored ships began to flutter the red-and-yellow 'Y for Yoke' flag, the signal that the ship was cleared. Any forgotten man, abandoned by mischance in that terrible lagoon, was to reach the nearest ship, haul down the Yoke flag and 'hoist all available bunting'. No one did.

As the night came streaming over the ocean, the *Appalachian* slipped into the procession moving in long line ahead through the reef passage to the open Pacific. It was all carnival with lights, springing erratically up and down the line, the hospital ships glowing like showboats, a regatta leaving a graveyard, while the flickering aldis blinker signals kept up the interminable mysterious gossip of ships at sea.

That night we had the final briefing. Dr Compton told us that if the bomb did not go off at the proper height, and waited until it hit the surface of the water before exploding, we might expect a temporary tidal wave about one hundred feet high, not to speak of diverse other phenomena intensely distracting to the scientific mind. It still continued to cause far less conjecture than the famous radioactive cloud, which had come to hover rather larger than a man's hand around the back of everyone's mind. It was authoritively stated that the visible cloud would rise to 60,000 feet, but the invisible trail drifting down to the surface was the thing to watch out for – an awkward proposition for those who did not carry geiger counters permanently in their pockets. What danger there might be, they said, would exist from falling radioactive particles which, as was so often pointed out by the Fat Boys at Bikini, you would not know about until you came to pieces in your own hand.

At seven in the morning the first aircraft appeared, a flying-boat wheeling in wide circuits, droning round at three thousand, until abruptly it tired of it and streaked back to the south-east.

The loudspeaker system began a raucous confused chatter, indiscriminate radiophone conversations between ships and planes, filling the air with a backstage buzz of orders and counter-orders. Somewhere about in the roof of the sky already hung the bomb, suspended in the rack of the B-29 Dave's Dream, which had taken off according to plan at Ray Hour. Ray Hour was the moment of the bomber's take off. Even the moments of the day had new and special names. How Hour was the planned moment of the drop. Mike Hour was to be the actual moment of the drop, according to how many dry runs the bombardier needed to get the crimson spot of the *Nevada* trued up in his bombsight.

As the day began to grow one felt the sky filling with aircraft of all kinds, seen and unseen, manned and unmanned, bombers and flying-boats and spotters, pilotless drones from the carrier *Shangri*

La and – because by now this operation had achieved in America an importance momentarily even greater than the World Series – a bomberful of Public Relations Officers and broadcasters from the radio networks. Then high above, just fleetingly visible as a twinkling speck when the sun caught it, the B-29 began its experimental cast over the target, eighteen miles away square on the starboard beam. Far too lofty and distant to be heard, the bomber flirted for a second like a mote in the sunlight and was lost.

Over the radio, suddenly came the announcement: broadcast transmission began.

'Listen, world – this is Crossroads.'

It was dramatic, you could not deny it was intensely dramatic, a *coup de theatre*. 'Listen, world . . .'

Then soon after eight we caught the voice of the bomb-aimer in our loudspeakers. We heard the chant, tinny and remote as an old gramophone in another world: 'Skylight here. First simulated bomb release; stand by. Mark: first simulated bomb release. First practice run; stand by.'

At fifty-one minutes past eight: 'This is a live run. Mark: coming up on thirty-five miles off target, thirty-five miles. Mark; adjust goggles. Stand by.'

At eight fifty-eight he said: 'Eighteen miles.'

In two minutes, for good or ill, the thing would be falling through the empty air, its controlling drogue tight like a drum-head; two bullets face to face, twin charges of plutonium to rush headlong to the uproarious embrace, the critical mass, the meeting of ultimate release.

The loudspeaker said: 'Bomb gone. Bomb gone. Bomb gone.'

I had on my goggle-mask, so black and deep it was like staring into velvet; behind that opacity all things vanished, sea, and ships and sunlight. At the bomb-aimer's words I began to count. Then I found I was counting too fast; I made an effort to slow down. I felt the sweat dripping down my back and I was glad I had no clothes on. I felt that the time between the beginning and end of the bomb's fall was far too much. I had no consciousness of calculation, I felt that in the nature of things expectancy does not endure so long without anticlimax. When my counting had reached fifty-five the bomb went off.

It is difficult to say what one had foreseen. However keenly you wait for the stage revolver-shot it is always louder than you expect;

however long you wait for an atom bomb it is presumably a little less than you feared.

In that first fine edge of a second it might have been a sudden star, low down on the horizon. Then it grew and swelled and became bright, and brighter; it pierced the goggles and struck the eye as a crucible does, and in that moment it was beyond every doubt there ever was an atom bomb, and nothing else.

It was a spheroid, then an uprising wavering thing like a half-filled balloon, then a climbing unsteady dome like a mosque in a dream. It looked as though it were throbbing. I tore off my goggles and the globe had become a column, still rising, a gentle peach-colour against the sky, and from eighteen miles I could see a curtain of water settling like rain back into the lagoon. Somehow I found it not impossible to believe that the thing had produced a hundred million centigrade degrees of heat, ten times that of the surface of the sun, that this was the answer of the little men in pince-nez to ten thousand tons of TNT; yet it was beautiful, in its monstrous way; a writhing lovely mass. Then, just as I remembered the sound of the explosion, it finished its journey and arrived.

It was not a bang, it was a rumble, not overloud, but it thudded into all the corners of the morning like a great door slammed in the deepest hollows of the sea. Beside me a heavy wire stay un-expectedly quivered like a cello-string for a moment, then stopped.

Now, standing up unsteadily from the sea, was the famous Mushroom. In seven minutes fifteen seconds our ship's trigo-nometry gave it twenty-three thousand feet in height and eleven thousand six hundred feet in diameter. It climbed like a fungus; it looked like a towering mound of firm cream shot with veins and rivers of wandering red; it mounted tirelessly through the clouds as though it were made of denser, solider stuff, as no doubt it was. The only similes that came to mind were banal: a sundae, red ink in a pot of distemper. From behind me I heard a frenetic ticking of typewriters; very soon I found I was fumbling with my own. The reportage had begun. Many of us will never live it down.

Slowly the creamy pillar began to lean awkwardly over. Another spasm somewhere in its base forced a second mushroom bellying upwards until it too tilted and thinned and lost its sculp-tured excellence. Twenty five minutes later it too had practically disappeared, and we had all of us stumbled one more step on the path to the twilight.

There is not much point in elaborating on the development of this experiment, which by now has taken its place among the embryonic adventures into nuclear fission. In any case, I recounted and documented the whole thing in probably unnecessary detail years ago. It was established that the bomb had missed the bull by several hundred yards; that for some reason it did not explode with maximum efficiency; that nevertheless it had sunk five ships, smashed two beyond repair, badly damaged seven others, in all hit fifty-nine out of seventy-three target vessels, many of them far away. Whether the atom bomb was an immoral and perilous weapon, or whether the difference between commonplace target-area bombing and the thing we saw that day had been merely a matter of degree – we could be sure that was not the question concerning the men who were then probing among the ironwork in the lagoon. There were many who said that the bomb had not proved itself, that for so much build-up there should have been a more imposing cataclysm. Others maintained that the land, with its congested cities and tender harvest of soft flesh, was its proper target. There were those who decided there and then to skip the second test, the underwater bomb – who thus deprived themselves of all the major horror they had hoped for. And there were those eager that the bomb should not be sold short, who already called it empowering and enriching and ennobling and protective, and that was the worst of all.

Since the whole thing had been bedevilled throughout by political issues, it was naturally suggested that the Navy had been out to make the best showing for the Fleet, even to the extent of having deliberately used a semi-efficient bomb. It all helped to irritate, confuse, frustrate. A rush of inspired editorial comment tried to counter this mood by emphasizing the true facts of the first tests' damage, by pointing out the additional enormities awaited from the second; it never appeared to catch up. One got the feeling that the average American was secretly anxious to think that the bomb might not, perhaps be such a heavy obligation after all, that the 'gigantic responsibility to mankind' might not, perhaps, weigh so heavily on the conscience.

Weeks later we assembled for the second test, the submarine explosion. Already the atmosphere aboard *Appalachian* was different. What would happen when an atom bomb was exploded *under* water was a matter of profound speculation even to the heavy-weight scientific brains of Task Force One, who might know much about atomic fission in what was known locally as God's Good Fresh Air, but who continued to argue uneasily about blowing a hole in the ocean. The ships, one knew, would be subjected to a test infinitely more damaging and unpredictable than from the air-bomb. Water transmits the shock of an explosion in a much greater degree than air (the surface force varies inversely as the square of the distance; underwater it varies as the distance to the power of four) the 'water-hammer', as all submarine men knew, is the thing that gives a depth-charge its crushing effect. This time, too, there would be no falling missile, no gambling on a bomb-aimer's eye. This bomb would be suspended in a caisson at an unspecified depth, and detonated electrically; an academic study in disaster. Nobody was sure what an atom bomb would do under the sea, because nobody had ever tried. The experts were ready to say that the submarine bang was unlikely to blow a hole in the landmass that formed the floor of Bikini lagoon, and send us all boiling and spinning into nobody knew what unheard-of abyss. The chief concern now was the inevitable contamination of the water with dangerous fission-products. In the last test these had been thrown mostly in the air, and many half-lives decayed harmlessly out of reach; this could not be the case now.

For some reason on that second bomb-day my nerves were more ragged, my expectation more intense than when I had leaned against the same ship's rail three weeks before. I had been up since four, listening to the silence. Now I was again on the flydeck, listening to the radio from the trigger-ship miles away where a young Cornell physicist called Marshall Holloway was waiting to throw a switch which would induce the critical mass in the device of unspecified dimensions suspended at an undeclared depth below the specially converted and secret vessel which carried it.

It was as before. Overhead the planes at their levels, circling in their courses, crossing and drilling and waiting. 'Fifteen minutes before How Hour.' 'One minute before How Hour.'

I could see the structures of the target fleet eight miles away, standing up over the horizon line like the silhouette of a castellated city.

'Ten seconds . . . six seconds . . . four seconds, three seconds, two seconds . . .'

It came gently, imperceptibly to begin with; one's heightened senses seemed somehow to decelerate that first subdivided second until one saw, or felt oneself to see, the gradual maturing of an instantaneous thing. There across the field of the lens' view stretched the bowstring horizon of the mid-Pacific, the tautest, straightest line of nature; where this ruled edge met the sky came the flash. Then where the flash had been a ball, a gleaming hemisphere of purest white, a grotesque and momentary bubble, huge and growing huger, a dome rising from the sea. Immediately the forces inside it strained and burst through; there was now no dome but a column, a pillar of water more than half a mile across, a million tons of the Pacific Ocean leaping vertically, silently, soaring upward into the cloud base; one mile, two miles high until it hesitated, dropped lazily back like a mountainous snowman into the terrible cauldron of Bikini lagoon, by now a waste of murk and fog. In that initial moment – though one did not yet know – the battleship *Arkansas* had been tossed into the air like a tin toy, thrown vertically up and over like a caber, like a wafer. She fell back to the bottom, never to be seen again.

If the first bomb had somehow seemed a lesser thing than one had expected, this indeed was infinitely greater. There was a feeling as the enormous water-dome swelled and expanded in perfect symmetry to a monstrous bulk that it would never stop developing, that it would increase indefinitely and overwhelm us, and not only us, but everyone, even the world. Then the outward movement became an upward one, there was the ineffable grace of the column, the weary slowness with which it dripped its million tons back towards the lagoon. And when the waves ribbed over the reef and were absorbed into the smoothness of the sea, the intense realization of the enormity, not of the bomb but of the ocean, this huge expressionless Pacific which could take even an atom bomb, embrace it, and forget it while one looked on.

I left for home then; I was fatigued to the point of deliquescence. So I flew back to Los Angeles, to Phoenix, to Albuquerque, to Oklahoma City, to Kansas City, to Tulsa, to Memphis, to Cincinatti, to Washington, to New York. And from New York to London. From London, by the 6.18, to Sussex.

Sometimes I wondered where I had been, and why I had gone.

One had tried; one had travelled 22,000 miles, one had stewed and steamed, one had fought for the words against the clock. But one was only a reporter, not a historian; one had suffered awhile from the occupational delusion of importance. At home, nobody gave a damn. From the start the bomb had been promoted like the debut of some new-type roadster or refrigerator, like Doctor Einstein's Infallible Elixir For Post-War Flatulence, Uncle Sam's Protective Balm Against the Red Rash. Who was to blame if the great American and British public clapped, and hooted and finally yawned and hurried back to the attractive salacities of the new murder in Bournemouth? We were. Because Operation Crossroads was ill-conceived, ill-chronicled, because after all the hysterical trailing of coats it did not, in fact, blow the roof of the world off, most people were left with the impression that atom bombs were overrated things and fortunately not the grim responsibility they had always seemed.

The atom bomb, then, in spite of being decorated with a picture of Rita Hayworth, proved very little. It did not much more than show that warships in general do not sink under an atom bomb, even though five minutes after it they are liable to be manned by corpses or maniacs. The armchair admirals held this to be a naval victory. The protagonists of air-power insisted that atom bombs are scarcely likely to be dropped on groups of ships when there are groups of houses, backyards, nurseries, factories and hospitals within easier reach. When the submarine explosion left not one single capital ship from the target fleet that was not either sunk or in a sinking condition the atom point seemed proved, but the public, vaguely resentful that neither bomb had started a tidal wave or a mass outbreak of the gamma-ray heeby-jeebies, refused to be shocked.

At least I had memorized my piece, said my say; I knew the weight of a cubic metre of seawater; I had a rapidly blurring idea of what happens in the whirling courtship of neutrons and protons, I had listened to every conceivable exponent of the obscurer isms, down to the underwater specialist whose contribution to the sum of human knowledge was the fact that the shrimps at the bottom of Bikini Lagoon could talk. They made a sound, he said, resembling: 'Awk, awk.'

Questioned after the explosion as to the behaviour of the atomized shrimps he replied: 'They are still saying "Awk, awk", only shriller.'

It was one of the merriest of occasions, for those who took their fun out of the world's despair.

Chapter Four

By now I was in my middle thirties, an age which now seems to me desirably young and sanguine but which then oppressed me with the shadows of a totally inconclusive middle age. I had, to be sure, accomplished a great number of spectacularly ephemeral things and been to a great number of momentarily significant places. I had written hundreds of thousands, probably millions, of words of this kind or that, and broadcast probably even more. I had been elevated, or so it was said, to the tenuous title of first roving correspondent of the *Daily Express*, which at that time was the highest-circulating newspaper on the face of the earth, God help us. I was being paid quite a lot of money; about half of what was being attributed to me. I found it very difficult to understand why. I did not subscribe to the notion that it was the function of a newspaper man to traffic wholly in the eternal verities and to change the world by the impact of divine enlightenment; nevertheless it seemed to me that I was skidding about rather aimlessly on the surface of something that ought to be doing a trifle more than it did. My father in his solemn moments had spoken often about the implications of the profession of journalism; I knew what he meant but realized the fallacy of the phrase.

This was one of the many misunderstandings that are brought about by talking about the profession of journalism. Journalism is not and never has been a profession; it is a trade, or a calling, that can be practised in many ways, but it can never be a profession since its practise has neither standards nor sanctions. There are no minimum requirements of scholarship nor credentials before a man can call himself a journalist (very fortunately for me); there is no formal body to discipline those in breach of its non-existent code of rules (the Press Council can register for the worst cases a sort of tepid disapproval but not much more; there is nothing in journalism equivalent to the Law Society or the GMC); there is no cohesion of intention nor association of purpose. This may well be a good thing, since while this flexibility and permissiveness gives entry to a number of dubious oddballs it equally does not exclude many valuable and original people. It is fatuous, however, to compensate for our insecurity by calling ourselves members of a profession; it is both pretentious and disabling; we are at our best craftsmen, and that is by no means an ignoble thing to be.

I am no great propagandist of the virtues or values of the Press; nevertheless I hold its functions in the most jealous of consideration. It is certainly the case that most politicians and even more officials forget that in a democratic society the theoretical master of events is the people. This is indeed a great illusion, nevertheless it is possible to argue that the reporter engaged in serious affairs must be the people's eyes and ears; he must be the instrument associating people's government with people's opinion. Not even the most articulate and charismatic political leader can make an impact on democratic opinion without communication; he can do no more than invoke a special public attitude towards facts already made known to the public. Opinion is made, even created, by the continual pressure of a wild variety of facts, or semi-facts, which vary between the banal and the cosmic, all of which bear in some way on the human situation. How this charivaria of information is transmuted into public opinion is a most mysterious thing, since every newspaper accepts that while many of its subscribers never read the sports pages, for instance, great numbers never look at anything else. It can only be explained in terms of certain atomic experiments in physical laboratories, where effects are wrought by the effect on the mass of a constant exposure to particles, in this case facts. I have rarely heard a more elaborate and pompous definition of journalism than this, but for some reason it seems to work.

It is also the case that in what is called the American democracy the role of the reporter is significantly different from that of, say, the British. In Britain, both executive and legislative responsibility is vested in Parliament. It is accepted that the Opposition has exercised responsibility in the past and may in the future; they have on the whole access to the relevant data of affairs; their debates are carried out in a fairly public dialogue. It is the business of the British Press to reflect and communicate this, but not necessarily to initiate it.

In the United States, on the other hand, there is no framework for national debate within the government. The US Congress is constitutionally barred from executive responsibility; no American parliamentarian has the right by virtue of his office to evaluate or even know of the facts on which national policy is founded. There is virtually no dialogue between the major officials of the executive. This alone has created a situation in which the only form of national debate is the Press – not wholly by editorializing, but by the continual presentation of information and argument from all angles of every issue. The system is without shape or direction, and is on the whole in my view very casually performed; it is nevertheless the American newspaper man's extremely important share in the process of what, for want of a more precise word, we call democracy. I doubt whether more than a handful of American journalists so define or recognize that function, any more than most British journalists accept their peripheral role in society. British journalism at its best is literate and lightweight and fundamentally ineffectual; American journalism at its best is ponderous and excellent and occasionally anaesthetic. After working a great deal in both areas it seems to me that Britain cannot match America's best but incomparably transcends America's norm: we have no routine newspaper man to equate with the James Restons and Richard Roveres, who stand out like beacons in a morass of lumpen-reportage of pedestrian dullness and undisciplined verbosity. The *New York Times* is the best and the worst newspaper on earth, a daily monument to the sloppy and extravagant simplification of the overdone; the *Daily Mirror* is the worst and the best newspaper, a gymnastic in the dedicated technical expertise of the persuasive non-think. I have worked for them both, but I cannot yet determine which I like least.

I myself have always felt myself a passing indifferent reporter, since it has never interested me to write about anything in which I did not feel myself somehow engaged, however academically; I was always deeply bored at having to define occasions that involved values I did not understand. I had enough of that in the salad days in Scotland; latterly I concluded that the only advantage of maturity and a fairly high price was to indulge one's prejudices. I cannot remember how often I have been challenged, and especially in America, for disregarding the fundamental tenet of honest journalism, which is objectivity. This argument has arisen over the years, but of course it reached a fortissimo – long years after this – when I had been to Hanoi, and returned obsessed with the notion that I had no professional justification left if I did not at least try to make the point that North Viet Nam, despite all official Washington arguments to the contrary, was inhabited by human beings. The Americans could insist that they were a race of dedicated card-carrying Marxist monsters, and the Chinese could insist that they were simon-pure heroes to a man; both statements were ludicrous; as I had seen them they appeared to differ in no perceptible way from anyone else, and that to destroy their country and their lives with high explosive and petroleum jelly was no way to cure them of their defects, which in any case seemed to centre on a tenacious and obstinate belief in their own right to live. This conclusion, when expressed in printed or television journalism, was generally held to be, if not downright mischievous, then certainly 'non-objective', within the terms of reference of a newspaper man, on the grounds that it was proclaimed as a point of view, and one moreover that denied a great many accepted truths. To this of course there could be no answer whatever, except that objectivity in some circumstances is both meaningless and impossible. I still do not see how a reporter attempting to define a situation involving some sort of ethical conflict can do it with sufficient demonstrable neutrality to fulfil some arbitrary concept of 'objectivity'. It never occurred to me, in such a situation, to be other than subjective, and as obviously so as I could manage to be. I may not always have been satisfactorily balanced; I always tended to argue that objectivity was of less importance than the truth, and that the reporter whose technique was informed by no opinion lacked a very serious dimension. It can easily be misrepresented. Yet as I see it – and it seems to me the simplest of disciplines – the journalist is obliged to present his attitude as vigorously and persuasively as he can, insisting that it *is* his attitude, to be examined and criticized in the light of every contrary argument, which he need not accept but must reveal. There is a way of being scrupulous about this which every thinking journalist understands. He has at least the resources to present his liberal principles for consideration and debate, and to argue the basic importance of moral independence

– which includes, to be sure, the need to question *him*. Surely the useful end is somehow to encourage an attitude of mind that will challenge and criticize automatically, thus to destroy or weaken the built-in advantages of all propaganda and special pleading – even the journalist's own. The energetic argument for liberal thought must by definition, I should imagine, embody the machinery for its own conquest, since it presents itself as equally vulnerable.

This was a matter of consideration for me for a long time; I have to say that while it brought about some interludes of great doubt and uneasiness, it disadvantaged me much less than I had expected. It would have reinforced several theories and prejudices if I could have recorded a long history of professional persecution; in general the contrary was the case. I knew no other way of doing the work I had to do; if the newspaper trade had objected I would doubtless have starved. I did indeed go hungry from time to time, but thereafter I prospered greatly, at least intermittently. And since this was on my terms, I have to reason that this argued a greater flexibility in the industry than in me.

At the same time I have struggled for years against the conviction that my whole intellectual position was, if not false, then ambiguous. I am aware of the world in which I live, and of the character of my own life. I am immensely and continually conscious of a world of nuclear bombs, of vast hunger, of curable injustice, of a meretricious press and a cheapjack television, of perilous and apparently endless international division, of unreasonable cruelty and suffering for which almost nobody cares, and of my own silly efforts to make money to provide me with irrelevant comforts or necessities like drink and to ensure some measure of security for my family. And I know that is not the answer, because there is truthfully only one answer, which is absolute pacifism and absolute communism – not in the dreary dogmatic party-political sense, but in the sense that my father would have called religious: the sense of mortal community. Not only do I know it; I knew it all along.

Why, for example, am I not an absolute pacifist, when I know that it is right? It is the easiest thing to rationalize, and I do rationalize it, without much pride or conviction: I also know that without the use of armies and mass murder German fascism might have overcome the world and my notion of freedom – including that of being a pacifist – would probably have gone forever. Yet there is a sort of illogicality and faithlessness in that too; it is a consideration so terrible that it obstructs something possibly even more fundamental. Here, too, a multitude of intellectual dilemmas arose. All my early life a lot of passion had been concentrated on the importance of preventing war, without any real consideration of my own position if it happened. When it did, my position became irrelevant: I was found to be unfit to be a soldier, and consequently was able to suspend – dishonestly, I think – the solution to the problem of whether I could personally shoot someone through the eye or drop a bomb on his home. Since nobody wanted me for that purpose I was even spared the ordeal of refusing. Yet later, in two wars of even less direct moment to me or my children – in Korea and Indo-China – I plied my trade as a war-correspondent in the uniform of a fighting force, and while I did not bear arms I was part of a community that did, and while I killed no one – nor could for that matter have defended myself against anyone who proposed to kill me – I was part of a machine whose only purpose was that of killing people, in circumstances of considerable wretchedness. I do not yet know whether I was wrong or right about that. In both cases, had I not done so I would have been unable to protest with experience and conviction at what I had seen, but I am far from persuaded that these horrible and dangerous times were not for me the easy way out.

There is much the same equivocation about absolute socialism. This is perhaps made easier for the well-intentioned temporizers by the treachery and professional cynicism of the successful political socialists, but that is an evasion too. I work for money, and while it is not the sort of money that would interest an important property-dealer or upstanding investor it is still a great deal more than is earned by men providing a far more useful social service, such as a junior hospital doctor or a municipal dustman. It is true I give most of it away, to the tax-collector or my family, but I still keep enough to allow me to indulge the cravings for the drugs on which I depend, which are tobacco and alcohol. I sermonize about the anti-social follies and venalities of nations who cannot invoke enough compassion or common sense to maintain decent relationships among each other, and by personal selfishness and obsessions have myself brought about the collapse of an immensely happy and rewarding marriage, and the regret of someone I admired and loved. I have an almost certain conviction that the answer to everything that I feel to be true *is* true; I am profoundly doubtful of my personal application of the answer. *Video meliora proboque; deteriora sequor:* the test of a good classical moralization is that it seems to have been written for oneself alone.

Diversion 1: The Ghost

THE only authentic ghost I ever met inhabited for a little while a Greek-owned hotel in Tabora, in what was then Tanganyika Territory. For those fortunate enough to be unfamiliar with this town I should say that it is the country's sole railway-junction, and that of all the God-forgotten places in East Africa it is the most inexpressibly deadly.

I say this in no particular spirit of criticism. It is merely my opinion that if there was a rock-bottom fundament of the world, this was it.

I had been in Dar-es-Salaam; for some preposterous reason or another I had to get to Rhodesia – a neighbouring Commonwealth country, adjacent on the map. *Nothing* in Africa is adjacent to anywhere. Such roads as there are come to nothing; such railways as there are never meet; such airways as there are never come. Or perhaps I exaggerate; this was some time ago.

To get from Dar-es-Salaam to Southern Rhodesia you took ship, if you could, to Beira in Portuguese East Africa, and train on the one up-country line from there. It might take a week or two. Or you could do as I did: move west four hundred and fifty miles from Dar-es-Salaam to Morogoro, to Dodoma, all along the old slave-route, to catch the south-bound plane at Tabora.

At Tabora, however, came the big stop. For five days I waited in that deadly little place for transport across what were at the time, after all, adjoining bits of the British Empire. Five days? They smiled at my fretfulness. The unit of time here was the week. Why, Livingstone lived here. Did he talk about *days*?

The hotel was run by Greeks. The Germans had built it, years ago, in their most solid tropical-Westphalian manner. It had been intended as a *kaiserhof* for an important visit from the Crown Prince which, like almost every other scheduled event in the

African continent, failed to come off. They planned Tabora as their colonial capital; laid it out in the likeness of a mighty administrative centre with endless avenues and interminable prospects and everything two miles from everything else. They were eased out of Africa, however, before anything particular got built.

Twenty-nine years of the British mandate had let Africa crawl back quite a lot.

So there were a hundred and twenty hours of watching the rain thud down on the dun-coloured earth, of frustrating the praying mantis which always chose one's plate for its devotions, of creeping at sundown behind a mosquito-net clotted with innumerable insects.

I am not by nature a gadding, fun-loving seeker of entertainment, but I do not think I was ever so bored in my life as I was at Tabora. I do not believe that many people appreciate the real, the despairing torture of true and completely defined boredom. It is too often taken to be a simple negation, the mere absence of occupation, as in its milder aspects I suppose it is. But true boredom – tropical boredom, in particular African boredom – is something far worse: a positive, a pit, a mental misery, an almost tangible oppression, and it is my considered opinion that nobody has ever approached even the foothills of this condition who has not spent five days at what was then the Greek hotel in Tabora.

It was a gaunt, echoing mausoleum. Empty as it was, I was given a bleak little room in the annexe. I ate my meals in a bare deserted dining-room – abominable though they were I dallied over them, spun them out, tenaciously put off until the last possible moment the despairing necessity of having to find something else to do. There was nowhere to walk to. The roads led broadly, rigidly, formally, at right angles to each other, leading nowhere. Once or twice I braved the stunning heat and plodded doggedly along these featureless roads to find out what did in fact happen to them. Quite suddenly they would peter listlessly away; ahead lay nothing but empty prairie studded with rhino-bush.

There was nothing to read in the hotel. That in itself distinguished it among others. Most hotels have *something* – a dog-eared Dornford Yates, a local guide-book, the Coppersmith's and Sanitary Gazette, even an old newspaper. The Tabora hotel had absolutely nothing whatever, of any kind or in any language; the art of conveying messages by the written word might never have been invented, Caxton had lived in vain. It was as though the management at Tabora had a fierce religious ordinance against print, as the Mohammedans have against pictures. There were not even advertisements on the walls; there was nothing to advertise, and no one to buy.

After a day or two of this I began to get a gasping sort of sensation, like a deprived drug-taker; I sank as low as a reading addict can and began to scratch around the corridors and precincts of the hotel looking for scraps of newspaper, remnants of magazines that might have been used for wrapping things. In this fashion I came upon one prize, quite a useful bit of newspaper, not quite half a page. It was, on its readable side, an advertisement page. I took it back to my room and read it scrupulously, like a bibliophile with a First Folio. It was crammed with local small-ads: Wanted – a cage, suitable for Parrot. Good clean home offered elderly gent; mental deficients, etc. Required by upland Trading House, non-Asiatic clerk, literary. Being Too Thin, Nervous, Irritable – Heed These Warnings. You are suffering from what Doctors Call Glandular Deficiency. Gentlemen: Try Bannerjee's New Type Vito-Testaid. It was poetry.

There is one phrase that indelibly haunts all East African conversation, that epitomizes everything in the East African soul – the Swahili words: 'Bado kidogo'. They mean: 'Not Just Yet'. It is more futile than *mañana*, slightly more optimistic than Maybe. All will come, but Not Just Yet.

'Breakfast ready?' 'Bado kidogo.' 'Can I have my laundry?' 'Bado kidogo.' '*Is my damned plane ever coming?*' 'Bado . . .'

I am not by nature a restless or volatile person, forever demanding diversion, yet I do not think I was ever so desperate in my life: no books, no radio, no argument, no pictures, no news. It was too hot to write. I have a temperament ill-adjusted to endless contemplation. Nobody turned up.

Until, on the fourth day, somebody did. I watched his baggage arrive in a handcart, and hurried almost joyfully to make his acquaintance. I could see at once that he was the most welcome, intelligent, entertaining being in Tanganyika. From his accomplished and masterful attitude to the African boys it could be seen that he was no fourth-hand Livingstone, like me; clearly he knew the joint. Bado kidogo had worked at last

He was a middle-aged German; he ran a sisal-plantation down

the line somewhere. He spoke fluent, eccentric English. Over the odious dinner that night we came almost blood-brothers. He expressed a decent sympathy with our contemporary colonial troubles in Kenya; it would not have happened thus in the old days.

Afterwards we went to the funereal lounge and drank a great deal of Portuguese brandy from Lourenço Marques, one of the more economical local narcotics. He grew first confidential, then affectionate, then finally withdrawn and patronizing.

'My grandfather came from hereabouts,' he said, 'Indeed he helped to build it. We were a thoughtful, patriotic people. But fools.' For a while he hummed a fugitive snatch of a haunting little tune. 'I think you do not know my wife? A good young woman, but also a fool.'

He dragged out his wallet with difficulty, and there was the girl – and there too in a mounted shield was the other face: sombrely staring, moustached, preposterous and abominable.

'Heil,' said my friend absently, 'We live and we die, and we live. Your good health.'

He put the picture away – familiar and long dead: its name had been Adolf Hitler, who never touched Portuguese brandy.

Bado kidogo, said I; and I wished I were once again alone and bored.

Chapter Five

It can be deduced from the preceding lucubrations that my long passage through journalism was not without its introspective side, with the corollary that from time to time I was in serious danger of turning into a howling bore. Fortunately reporting is an exacting job, and kept me too busy to indulge myself in the philosophical consideration of my own motives; indeed it is the case that for many years I was kept so unremittingly on the trot that I had little enough time to contemplate anything at all, even supposing I had the philosophical equipment to do so. Such moments of leisure as came my way were too precious to be spent in abstract rumination; they were spent in houses of refreshment in the company, wherever possible, of colleagues whose preoccupations were much the same as my own, and whose responses took the same form. I have been dubious and critical and even arrogant about the business by which I lived, but let it be recorded that to the end of my life I shall acknowledge that the only male company in which I am content; in which I can drop pretences and relax in the conversational shorthand of completely common understanding, in short where I know where I am, is that of newspapermen. There is nothing brotherly or romantic about that; the newspaper industry may be venal and tedious and banal but my colleagues were not. Where, I wonder, should I have been over the long years across the world without the spasmodic, always unexpected, and totally reliable friendship of companions like Donald Wise, and Ralph Izzard, and Patrick O'Donovan, and David Holden, and Louis Heren, and Sam White, and Richard Scott, and René MacColl, and Stanley Uys, and Ted Levite, and David Walker, and Tom Baistow, and Stanley Burch, and a score more of their kind, at any moment liable to appear through the swing-doors of anywhere between Tuscaloosa and

Tonkin and reduce chaos to the healing anodyne of a glass and the shared misfortune of existence.

It is a curious fact that in all proper corners of the world there was always a bar that was, as far as the correspondent was concerned, the hub and centre of that place's activities. It was not necessarily the best bar, nor the most expensive, nor even the most generally renowned; it just happened to be the place to which one had to go. There is no precise explanation of how this came about. It could be the Cosmopolitan in Cairo or the Cockpit in Singapore or the Crillon in Paris or the Ledra Palace in Cyprus – and already as I write I realize that they may be otherwise today – but they were cardinal points on our map, and it was possible that in them alone one really knew where one was. Everyone supposes foreign correspondents do most of their work in pubs, and to a very great degree that is the case. There were other aspects to the job, but without George's in Rome or Charley O's in New York they would hardly have got attended to. We were homing pigeons with many a dozen lofts, and they were all called Joe's or Jack's or the Joint around the Corner. There was of course always the risk of accepting this as a sentimental syndrome; it may not have been the best approach to the solemn business of political interpretation. I do not know how it could be done otherwise. And out of it somehow occasionally came the truth, or as near to it as would have been achieved by any other method.

In this fashion I lasted with the *Express* for some years. By and by the vernal freshness rubbed away. Quite suddenly I had to leave.

A sort of a legend grew up about this affair, which for a while became a matter of much Fleet Street preoccupation. I had been abroad for a long time; my work had been constantly in Asia and in Africa. It had been so long since I had consistently seen the newspaper which employed me that I had come to think of it as something quite remote from the work I was doing; it was an establishment to which I was attached by tenuous cable-links and by little else; we inter-reacted on each other hardly at all. My main contact was with Charles Foley the foreign editor, who was not only a man of urbanity and intelligence but also a friend. He could be extravagantly exacting in his demands, but one accepted that his caprices were only part of the newspaper game, which we all played in order to justify the fantasy of our trade and to give some sort of style to our pretensions. It gave Charles pleasure to devise for me abrupt and intricate changes of location all over the world involving logistical problems of great complexity and expense, and it gave me pleasure to accomplish them, as often as not to no greater end than our mutual gratification at the solution of a problem. In the manner in which I fulfilled my function as a correspondent he made no demands at all; and my relationship with the newspaper could be likened only to that of a very remote and insignificant curate to the Holy See: I accepted their authority and paid no attention at all to their doctrine. It was an arrangement that appeared to work admirably from everyone's point of view: I continued to describe what I experienced in a fashion that seemed to me both proper and amusing, and the newspaper continued to print the results with rewarding prominence. I must have operated for a very long time in this state of vernal innocence. I reported the whole of the lengthy and tormented process of the negotiations for India's independence, for example, with every manifest enthusiasm for their success, without any real appreciation of the fact that Indian independence was of all things the one Lord Beaverbrook most earnestly opposed. I made an acquaintanceship with Jawaharlal Nehru, which eventually developed into an affection that endured until his death, and vigorously reflected this in all I wrote, without regard to or even realization of the fact that of all the many *bêtes noires* in the *Express* catalogue of anathema Mr Nehru stood highest. At no time was there any secret that any political beliefs I had were socialist, and most especially anti-Imperialist; for some reason it never occurred to me that it should have been professionally helpful to remember, if only occasionally, that I was writing for an organization most articulately dedicated to the cause of Empire. In retrospect I am still surprised that this state of affairs went on for so long. It was in fact for me an uncommonly agreeable and absorbing period, and I shall never underrate its great value for me. I wrote copiously and enthusiastically on all the themes that my employers held in scant regard. I travelled immense distances at their expense, and I was increasingly well paid for it. I rarely saw the end-product of these endeavours. My contact with the fountainhead was virtually limited to wry and wittily appreciative cables from Charles Foley; only by hindsight did I ever come to recognize their mordant irony.

Then in 1950 I returned to London and the rough-and-tumble of the English post-war newspaper scene.

My relations with Lord Beaverbrook were peculiar, even for those with a man whose relations with everybody tended to be unexpected and unorthodox. Long before this he had for some reason taken a fancy to an article I had written from Malta, about the excessive and unnecessary hardships that poor island was subjected to immediately after the war. Its sufferings were indeed spectacular; after having been pounded to rubble during the wartime siege and sentimentally rewarded by a grateful Crown with a bizarre citation for collective gallantry, Malta was thereafter apparently totally forgotten by Whitehall and left to flounder about in a multitude of privations and snubs and humiliations; its hungry population lived as best they could in caves and shanties, observing all around them only the urgent reconstruction of the innumerable Catholic churches. I wrote an article about this in the mood of somewhat self-righteous indignation that rather unfortunately later tended to become my theme-song: it was called 'You Can't Eat the George Cross'.

This met with the vigorous approval of Lord Beaverbrook, I imagine because by chance it simultaneously expressed several of his own most cherished themes – colonial paternalism, the conspiracies of the Papists, the inefficiency of Civil Servants, and a reasonable implication that the whole thing was the fault of the British Labour Government. All these things were welcome in themselves; it was not every day that they could all be embodied in one argument.

He summoned me therefore to his apartment in Park Lane, to which I went with some misgivings, since such invitations were generally the occasion of something unpredictable. By the time I arrived it seemed that he had at least partially forgotten the reason for my visit, and he spoke in a visibly preoccupied way about the breeding of cattle, a subject about which my enthusiasm is far from fanatical. When at last I steered this obscure conversation to the subject of Malta he recalled instantly the matter at issue, and produced the appropriate edition of the paper.

'Ah yes,' he said, 'a *very* commendable article we have here, most excellent in treatment. Now listen to this,' he said, and read out the introduction. It was, in fact, not bad. He then continued, warming to his subject, and read out the entire article from begin-

ning to end. I had considered it a very adequate piece of work in
its slightly ham way; as recited in those harsh and resonant tones
it achieved the sort of apocalyptic character of some doom-laden
Presbyterian sermon.

When he had finished he turned to me sternly and said: 'That is
good, very good. That is the kind of work I wish to see in my
newspapers. It is the hard, grim truth expressed through the
heart. You are a young correspondent; I hope you may go far in
our organization. Let me tell you that if you can learn to write
articles in that manner there will be a future for you with my newspaper. Take it with you and study it. Goodbye to you.'

My acquaintanceship with Lord Beaverbrook developed considerably in the time to come, but never did our relationship
altogether lose this strange dreamlike quality. Until, of course,
the end.

This book is intended to be an account of personal experiences
and not an examination of contemporary society, still less an
analysis of the function of the Press within that society. To make
such an analysis reasonably and properly one would be obliged to
write another book. One would? Scores have. The subject has
obsessed serious journalists since the days of Wilkes, and many of
them have felt the compulsion to investigate the whole *mores* of
their trade in thoughtful and detailed volumes, full of an expert
uneasiness, and only too soon forgotten. I have a number of
views on this, and prejudices too, but most of them have been
expressed extremely well by students infinitely better qualified
than I to do so. Anyone who wants to appreciate the mechanical
pressures and dilemmas of the writing newspaper man should
hasten at once to the works of Wickham Steed and Francis
Williams. I have an idea that the only people who do so are those
already only too well aware of them already. There is in any case
a great deal of humbug about it, for the subject lends itself most
temptingly to bogus moralizing and professional piety. The
spectacle of the conscientious journalist bemoaning the idealistic
shortcomings of his profession is both pitiable and platitudinous,
like that of the rueful whore. His condition may be unfortunate
but it is hardly irremediable; the journalist who feels that the
methods of the organization that pays him are a doleful burden
upon his principles can as a rule resolve his dilemma: he can stop
taking their money, and get out.

In those neurotic and uncomfortable years following the end of the war there were certainly many who were oppressed by the zeal and speed with which the newspaper industry reverted to the cruder and shadier tricks of political jungle warfare. The illusion of patriotic and humane solidarity imposed by the emotions of war and the exigencies of censorship and rationing was dissipated almost overnight by the shock of a popularly elected Labour Government; indeed even before that event came to pass the gloves had been taken off. A rational political dialogue has never been conspicuously a part of British daily newspaper work anyhow, and the Press was not so much a congeries or organs of the Right as an intuitive grouping of money and influence against the Left. Vigorously abetted by Winston Churchill, whose electoral tactics in 1945 were occasionally as base as they were foolish, and included the curiously maladroit threat that a Labour victory would mean a 'British Gestapo' led by Harold Laski, the *Express* sailed into the anti-Attlee offensive with the finesse of a bulldozer. When the *Express* coined a phrase for the Labour Party dredged from its recent historical reflexes – the 'National Socialists' – many a spirit on the newspaper reeled. Reeled, but recovered.

Despite stratagems of this nature the Labour Party won the election, and the immense majority of the daily Press took them to the barricades, and garnered its ammunition.

In the spring of 1950 the Government appointed as Secretary of State for War the austere and unlovable Socialist intellectual John Strachey. By a chance extravagantly fortunate for his enemies, who were many, it happened that his promotion was announced simultaneously with the conviction of Klaus Fuchs, the German-born Communist atomic physicist who was sentenced as a Soviet spy. The association of these events could have had a relevance only for the sickest of minds, but such a one was available. It belonged to Herbert Gunn, the editor of the *Evening Standard*. More properly it should be said that Mr Gunn's mind belonged, like the *Standard*, to Lord Beaverbrook. On 2 March 1950 the *Standard* linked the two stories in what must have been one of the most savage and bitter scare-headlines of the generation. 'FUCHS AND STRACHEY: A GREAT NEW CRISIS. War Minister Has Never Disavowed Communism.' It was the kind of attack I had never actually seen before, and it took me a couple of days to appreciate what it was bound to mean to me.

The 'great new crisis' had in some fashion been born exclusively in the newspaper offices. No crisis in connection with John Strachey's appointment had arisen anywhere else, nor was any envisaged. The paper's 'evidence' for this quite dismayingly serious deduction were a couple of fifteen-year-old quotations from Strachey's books, expressing a sympathy for Soviet Communism that he had long since repudiated. The headlines were accompanied by a photograph hardly likely to engender affection.

John Strachey was no friend of mine; I had never met him in my life. The facts about his political position had never been in any way secret. Few books had more influenced the generation of the '30s than his *Coming Struggle For Power* and his *Theory and Practice of Socialism*, which the *Standard* quoted in its denunciation. Certainly no considered political change of mind had ever been more publicly nor categorically stated than that of John Strachey in 1940, ten years earlier, beginning with a series of attacks on 'revolutionary defeatism' in the *New Statesman*, continuing through a violent controversy which convulsed the Left Book Club and its 50,000 members; it came to a peak in the book, jointly made with Gollancz, called *The Betrayal of the Left*. After this clear-cut repudiation of the Communist attitude Strachey joined the Royal Air Force and the Labour Party. When the *Standard* argued that Strachey was 'still an avowed Communist' it was not only inaccurate, it was stating the precise reverse of the truth. Nevertheless the innuendo remained: that the War Minister might be a supporter of Soviet Communism in the same sense that Klaus Fuchs was a convicted traitor, and to spread this suspicion was the palpable objective of the *Standard's* display.

It would have seemed inevitable that there would have been a barrage of indignation from everyone involved in the newspaper trade. Protests did appear in the *Manchester Guardian*, the *Daily Herald* and the *Observer*. There was a word or two of tepid disapproval in the *News Chronicle*. That was all that was heard from the national Press.

The usefulness of quotation is often dubious. It was of course true that John Strachey had written and spoken approvingly of the foundations of Soviet Communism. It was a doubtful point whether his praise of Stalin had been as fulsome as Mr Churchill's of Mussolini, or that of several noted Conservative politicians of Adolf Hitler. He had hardly gone further than Lord Beaverbrook himself, who had said during the war that Communism under Stalin won the applause and admiration of all the rest of the nations. (A correspondent in *Reynold's News*, commenting on the *Standard* story, asked whether that newspaper's proprietor had disavowed his belief in Soviet Communism, and whether, *pace* the *Standard*, was it not a matter of serious public interest that national newspapers with a total circulation of several millions should be controlled by a man whose praise of Stalin had been so recently expressed?)

That much was whimsy, but the gravamen of this new situation suddenly became a very anguished matter for me. I had had no part in the *Standard* campaign and had no feelings about the paper one way or another (although its Editor, the late Herbert Gunn, had been my friend and neighbour and, indeed, the best man at my wedding) but its proprietor was paying my salary and I could hardly ignore that. I was the chief foreign correspondent of the *Express*, which seemed to argue a measure of responsibility. That day I wrote a letter to my Editor, Arthur Christiansen, saying that I did not see how I could identify myself with the firm's technique and that I had better go.

The next day the *Express* itself appeared with its editorial support and endorsement of the *Standard's* attitude. I wrote to Chris that it was now imperative that I be released at once.

I was extremely scared. It seemed to me the height of rashness to abandon the first and only secure job I had ever had on an issue that involved nobody I knew and that was almost certain to be judged politically academic, and to incur almost certainly the hostility not only of Lord Beaverbrook but of a great number of my own colleagues, who might well feel the whole thing smelled of smugness. It seemed to me that after this things might not go easily with me in the trade, where caprice and nonconformity is encouraged only within the limits of the trivial. I did not see how I could do otherwise than I was doing, but I was greatly alarmed.

I have never been one to take big decisions on my own, and although by now I had taken this one I felt the need of some sort of reinforcement, or even perhaps of opposition that would oblige me to rationalize myself. I went home and called an extraordinary general meeting of my family: of Elizabeth and Desmond and Elma. Fergus, being only five years old, was given a place on the committee without voting rights. Everybody agreed that my resignation should go forward, as though they had any choice. Nobody but me had much idea of what it was all about.

It then seemed to me that I was now in a position where I had to go one more step forward, or the whole business became ridiculously quixotic. It was true that the only way open to me of protesting against a serious professional wrong was to get out of the business; it seemed a negative reaction. Nobody outside Fleet Street could possibly know or care whether I stayed or went; I had a little reputation as a reporter but not enough to endure more than a wisp of time. I was consumed with a sort of futile indignation against an Establishment that was obviously far stronger and more persuasive than I, and with now no medium whatever in which to express it. That night I sought my catharsis in the manner employed over the years by denouncers of tyranny or discoverers of the first cuckoo: I wrote a letter to *The Times*. I wrote it merely to exorcize a few private ghosts. I did not believe for a moment that it would go any farther than that, since – I argued – dog does not eat dog and newspapers do not publish the sour protests of other newspapers' hirelings. To my great astonishment *The Times* published the letter in full. It was to open floodgates I had never anticipated. For those who might be interested in the minutiae of Fleet Street history, I append it here as a modest footnote.[1]

---

[1] From *The Times*, 11 March 1950:

Sir, Whether Mr Strachey did or did not publicly announce his moment of disillusion with the Communists is surely of less long-term importance than this: that we have now set the precedent for the purge-by-Press, which could end at last only in a race of people talking behind their hands, knowing that the words they said yesterday, in a very different world mood, are the words they may swing for tomorrow.

Loyalty in every sense is a prerequisite in Cabinet Ministers, and newspapers have a right to examine it where they find it. At the same time one may wonder whether the best judge of political reliability is an industry whose own caprices of principle and accommodations of policy have seldom been marked over the years by a rigid ethical consistency. The loyalty-test, with the Press on the tribunal to link the names of a Minister and a convicted felon, is a troubling aspect of what – so far, happily – we do not have to call the British Way of Life.

I have never met Mr Strachey, nor, indeed, seen him outside the House of Commons; I have, nevertheless, considered the issue involved sufficiently important to resign my own professional association with the organization that initiated the witch-hunt.

                           Yours faithfully,

                                    JAMES CAMERON

42, Tedworth Square, S.W.3.

Looking back on it now, over the sixteen years which have seen so much worse, so much more awful and meaningful, so much that has collapsed in oneself and the world around one, it seems to me to have been pretentious; at the time nothing in the world seemed more imperative. What I had not expected were the repercussions. The incident, which I had seriously imagined was of importance only to me, seemed to act as a catalyst to all manner of forces and factors in the business of newspaper-making. There was a tremendous burst of publicity. A series of meetings of the Union made a great deal of the occasion, and many encouraging declarations were made. So was a certain amount of political capital, which in my mood of exasperated disenchantment was of less interest. I tried to explain that I had all along been anxious to make no more of my leaving the paper than seemed necessary to establish that my reasons affected us all; that my differences with the newspaper over the Strachey–Fuchs affair had been a professional objection, and that if the *Herald* had used the same tactics on Eden or Churchill I should have objected just as strongly, and on exactly the same grounds. And if that were so it could hardly be reasonable to put the exclusive responsibility on the management, since however rotten their policy it could not be expressed in print without the active co-operation of journal-ists, and while they were prepared to co-operate in this way, reserving their protests to mutual commiseration later in the bar, then quite clearly this dismal state of affairs could go on forever, as it probably will. It was presumptious and impulsive of me to assume this attitude, but I was glad I had tried, even later, when it made great difficulties. As far as I was concerned that was that; the affair was more widely remarked than I had expected, and the thing was over, until the next time.

Towards the end of this sorry affair I met John Strachey for the first time. He invited me to luncheon at the House of Commons, and we talked in a halting way of what had happened. He told me that when he read the newspaper story his first impulse was to take legal action, and he had sought advice on this. His lawyers, it seemed, had argued that the risk would have been considerable, that the case of defamation was by no means very solid in legal terms, and that for the Secretary of State for War to lose such a case would be disastrous, and certainly mean his resignation. In any event the publicity could do the Minister and his office nothing but harm. He was therefore persuaded to do nothing and to wait for the fuss to die down, as of course it shortly did.

I was unexpectedly fortunate; in a very short time I was offered by Tom Hopkinson a job as staff writer on *Picture Post*. I admired Tom Hopkinson, I liked what I knew of *Picture Post*, and the idea of its vast acreage of space and leisurely weeks in which to prepare to fill it appealed to me very much. This, I felt, would be the deep peace of the double bed after the hurly-burly of the chaise-longue. Here I would stay and become a tranquil commentator on the secondary aspects of life.

In that, as in almost everything else concerning my own life, I was quite wrong.

I was no sooner getting out my carpet slippers for *Picture Post* when there came the Korean War.

Chapter Six

AT the sound of the gong it would be midnight in London, eighteen-thirty in New York; the doors would be closing in Soho and opening on Broadway; eight thousand miles away on either side the world went on. Here, half-way between today and to-morrow, it was time for the morning bark from the ship's loud-speakers, with the Shantung Province to port and the target ahead, and the Yellow Sea all around.

Dawn over Delhi, sunset on Chicago, in Tokyo the Hour of the Dragon. Here it was coffee in the wardroom of the *Seminole*, 36°N, 125°E, eighty miles offshore from Korea, the Land of the Morning Calm. Back in Whitehall and Washington and Lake Success they would be reflecting on the dreary progress of the war, challenging the validity of this and the hopes of that; perhaps half a dozen well-informed quarters knew where we were and what we were doing.

For the last two days we had been nosing north on our great loop around the Cholla peninsular where the south-west of Korea peters out indefinitely in a spattering of little islands, we in our small section of the task force; the three ships *Seminole*, *Pickering*, and *Cavalier*. They were AKAs, naval auxiliary freighters. Ours was *Seminole*. We looked across at the others a dozen times a day, wondering if life was as dull, as torpid, as dubious in the others as it was in *Seminole*. It seemed to take a terribly long time to get to the place we were going to invade.

For the last ten days or more we had been waiting in Pusan for it to happen. Outside Pusan at that time everywhere in Korea seemed uncertain, repulsive, and full of menace. Of the eighty-five thousand square miles of Korea there was nothing left for us but this south-east corner, the stockade behind a hundred-and-twenty-five mile perimeter that was the final toehold of the United

Nations forces, the enclave that had become a redoubt and looked like becoming a beach-head. The maps at the morning briefings looked more and more dismally conjectural behind the dirty over-lays; yesterday's arrows half-erased, an erratic mass of smudges where the north-east front had been. Yet in Pusan there was an illusion of permanence and stability; the narrower grew the perimeter the more enormous and congested became the pile of material and store with which it was to be defended. It seemed im-pregnable, which was more than anywhere else in Korea had ever done. For that reason we knew it was an illusion; if we made a Dunkirk out of Pusan then there would be no returning.

Soon they began talking about the Excursion. It was of course a military project of the most extreme secrecy, a closely-guarded mystery of such priority that no one knew of its development except perhaps every living individual within ten miles of the har-bour, who could scarcely fail to remark the daily arrival of more and more shipping, greater and greater quantities of specialized warlike gear, heavier and heavier concentrations of self-evidently anxious men. Correspondents based on Tokyo arrived daily, wrapped in fresh laundry and with unobtainable luxuries in their packs, such as soap; they would bound in a debonair way from the plane and call: 'Okay, boys; which ship for the invasion?' Every day the multitudes of Korean sightseers drifted around the docks, fingering the crates, manifesting every variety of interest, from faintly distasteful curiosity to a lively and doubtless technical observation. Throughout the days before the invasion our mis-givings were not assuaged by the demonstrable fact that this desperate surprise mission was attended by all the hushed retic-ence of the Chicago World's Fair.

The night before we left, we went back to the camp very late (we were not supposed to eat after six) and the canteen was opened furtively for us by three Korean kitchen-boys. All three were students from Seoul; they had escaped conscription by the popular stratagem of attaching themselves to Eighth Army com-missariat, and now with a roof for their heads and rice for their bellies they were very lucky Koreans indeed, although it had meant abandoning any reasonable hope of seeing their families again. I was the first British citizen they had ever met; like most Koreans they appreciated the existence of an English-speaking country far to the other side of San Francisco, but in the vaguest way; they thought of Britain, indeed, much as Britain thought of Korea.

He said: 'But British fighting in Korea too?'

I said certainly, the 27th Brigade had been in the line some time. It was impossible to say whether this surprised him or not. I asked what had happened to his home; did he know?

He shrugged. 'The Communists come, and take. They flagging.'

'Flagging?'

'Sure. Red flagging every place. Not can return.'

But would he, if he could?

'Oh yes. I lose house – books. I not fighting person.'

'But if you went back, wouldn't the Communists imprison you or make you join the Army?'

'You think?'

'I suppose so. That is what this war is about, isn't it?'

'Oh yes. When it's over, I go home. United States take Seoul, maybe; Communists take Pusan, maybe. Then I go home.'

'You don't care if the Communists take Pusan?'

He sighed. 'You are people who hating Communists. You are people who scared they taking Pusan, isn't it? Sure, we hating Communists too, I guess.'

'But not enough to go out and fight them? You know that all over the world people have been dying for liberty, haven't they?'

'Oh yes,' he said, and went to the stove, 'We die anyhow.'

He turned his back to pour more coffee; when he looked again he was smiling radiantly.

'When your ships sailing North Korea?'

At two on the Tuesday afternoon we sailed out of Pusan, through grey water littered with broken boxes, sodden ration-cartons, bobbing cans, at one point the body of a small child. We headed due south towards the big arc that would take us north, past the beach where our last camp had been, past our deserted tents and abandoned Korean boys, the camp followers who had lost their casual masters as they had lost previous ones, as they had lost everything.

For many of us this was the first moment for a long time in which we had not been surrounded by the miseries of Korea, its frustrations, its perils, its regrets. None amongst us did not hate Korea, as sound people hate deserving beggars and mutilated things, as a man hates everything for which he has a useless pity. Most of us were tired of Korea, and frightened too, but perhaps less of what we had left than of what was to come.

That evening Captain Farrow called us to his cabin and told us for the first time officially what was the nature of our journey. There was little he could add except the destination: Inchon. And, of course, the fact that this was more than a gamble with a battalion or two, but an invasion of dimensions that in all history could be matched only once: the biggest seaborne assault since Normandy.

Inchon was a hundred and fifty miles behind the enemy's lines; it was a landing-point of excessive difficulty. There was a tidefall of thirty feet; anything wrong with the schedule would give us a three-mile stumble through waist-deep mud under the shore batteries. The enemy was known to be in force. The sea-wall of Blue Beach presented unmapped hazards.

We continued to plunge along, full of stentorian metallic commands and whistles in the dark, rolling languidly over the Yellow Sea, until we met more ships, and then a few more, and in three or four days more yet, all slowly converging on the port of Inchon.

I would never have believed how tedious it could be. It would not have occurred to me that a climactic moment of such emotional intensity and concentration of nervous activity could have been preceded by such days of numbing boredom. Of the passengers aboard three of us were correspondents; there were a dozen US Marine Corps officers and several hundred South Korean Marines, who spent their days lethargically below decks in a condition of fantastically congested discomfort, doubtless thinking of the folly of the day.

The days hung to each other's tails, punctuated only by food – US Navy food, heavy, nutritious, ample, gaudy, full of tricks and empty of taste. It was four years and more since I had last sailed with the US fleet; there were many things I had forgotten – the inescapable radio music, the rigid teetotalism, the absence of anything to break up the day beyond the meals – eleven o'clock lunch, five o'clock dinner, schoolboys' hours – and bed at last, in a four-man cabin clanking with hanging equipment: helmets, revolvers, enormous boots. As Inchon began to appear cryptically on the horizon I thought more and more mournfully about a drink, but there was none, nor would be for a long time.

Up until the end of the trip the Marines kept up their joking, the specialized exclusive badinage of soldiers before battle, the protective flippancies: this place Inchon was of all landing points the most unsuitable, the tidal mud was up to eight feet; the North Koreans were very obviously being apprised of our intentions, since Pusan was notoriously overcrowded with Communist agents, and that to assemble a fleet of these proportions in an anchorage of this size was, naturally, suicide. Everyone laughed briefly.

We came to the invasion at last. On that day of haze among the hills it was somehow like an Argyllshire sea-loch, steam-heated and washed with luminious pastel grey. In no circumstances could Korea be called lovely, or even barely likeable; yet at this moment and in this especial dusk of doubt it came more nearly to being beautiful than I had ever seen before.

The H-Hour was seventeen-thirty, which was not yet; there was still plenty of time for guesswork and fear. Then we should go ashore, for this was the big gesture, the payoff to take the Thirty Billion Dollar Police Action out of the red, this was MacArthur's final argument in his personal one-man deal with destiny. We should go ashore and take Inchon, and the war would be over in a week. Everybody said so.

Chapter Seven

FIVE years and five months before and eight thousand miles away, in Potsdam in Germany, the question of Korea arose amid the dense agenda of similar questions: what to do with the liberated territories that had no readymade independence to be restored, no Government to assume office, no especial political identity to be reconstituted – above all, no sovereignty to be reinstated. This was unfortunate. For two thousand years the peninsular had been the home of a homogeneous race of people with centuries of foreign conquest and misrule, with two consistent factors haunting it throughout – strategic situation, which was not Korea's fault, and political disunity, which was. Japan, having defeated China in 1895 and Russia ten years later, took over the gimcrack Kingdom of Korea in 1910.

Now Japan had surrendered, and here was the problem child on the doorstep. The men in Potsdam decided on a judgment of Solomon: they bisected Korea along the line of 38° North, between a Russian Zone and an American Zone, and they promised Korea independence 'in due course'.

On either side of a line that – as even the State Department was shortly to admit made 'no political, geographical, economic nor military sense' – the contrasting administrative systems grew, and solidified. The Russians sponsored Kim Il Sung and the New People's Party, which was Communist. The Americans, presented with a lunatic situation involving fifty-four registered political parties with a combined official membership three times as big as the total population, fell back on the right-wing Koreans who spoke English. Military government gave way to a landlord administration advised and buttressed with four hundred million dollars, and culminating in the allegedly noble old exile, the extreme reactionary Yi Sung-man, known as Synghman Rhee.

In the North political freedom was suppressed; in the South it was chaotic; in the North there was ambition and chauvinism and land reform, in the South there was ambition and chauvinism and no land reform; in the North there was efficiency and Government harshness, in the South there was corruption and United States handouts. The 38th Parallel grew from a temporary expedient to a boundary polarizing two wholly different forms of life. There arose an endemic condition of frontier war; the United Nations reported that in two years of peace eighteen thousand people were killed on the border. From 1945 to 1950 both sides shouted about invasion and at last, on June 25th, it came to pass.

Mr Truman announced that the South had been attacked in a 'raw, unprovoked aggression'. The Communists claimed that they were attacked while they were peacefully negotiating the unity of Korea. Their case was denounced, though not investigated. Yet when the North came over the Parallel at four-fifteen that Sunday morning they came in a force that could not have been improvised, with four hundred Soviet-built tanks, and, provoked as it unquestionably was, it was aggression.

Three months ago, and now the *Seminole* was in the bay of Inchon. Three months before, and suddenly the United Nations was compelled to stop being a collection of states with their fingers crossed, and was committed to its first serious challenge. 'All member nations shall render every assistance . . .' the primary test for a force that had no force, no army, no High Command, no common motivation whatever except that this, it seemed, was what the United Nations was for, and that the time had come.

Kim's men moved down over the new rice by the small border town of Kaesong. The faraway thud of a gun began its endless echo round the world, and in that moment wrote the mark of death, and disillusionment, on many thousand remote men who had never heard of Kim Il Sung, who had never heard of us, who had never heard of Korea.

It had been a long way to come, even by my standards, who had never been allowed to spend much continuous time in either hemisphere. The weeks had seemed endless, and punctuated only by ragged chances.

Of the four men who had died in the jeep as I was on my way three were my friends: the two British correspondents and the

Indian colonel; they exploded a mine on the Waegwan road that had been officially cleared the day before. I read the story twelve thousand feet above Siam; someone had left yesterday's *Times of India* on a seat and there it was, one more aspect of the retreat; whatever might happen in Korea there would be no meeting with Ian Morrison or Christopher Buckley or Uni Nayar; poor dead friends who had not wanted to go to the war at all.

Had I? I supposed so. At the beginning, reading the news in a train near Metz, I had known it was disastrous, but I hoped it would not be for me. But of course it was. One could not shift one's attitude to the United Nations daily; if force could ever be justified should it not be here? There were many things one knows now that one did not know then. I supposed, already half way over Asia, that one had to go, or forever hold one's peace.

By the time we had reached Korea the first debacle was over; the retreat had settled down from a helpless and wasteful rout to a kind of unstable line. But now, once again, it seemed that we might be off again at any moment. As we flew into Taegu, Bert Hardy the photographer and I, the little isolated clouds of gunfire drifted over the hillsides to the north; from the air nothing looks gentler, less obstructive or dangerous than the silent lazy puffs of artillery.

We clambered out into the blinding heat. In the first seconds it was clear that something had changed since yesterday; it is not always necessary to know a place to realize that some immediate factor has altered it; the airfield had a disrupted, despairing look. Traffic was arriving constantly along the dirt road from town; with some difficulty we got a lift in what appeared to be the only jeep that was going into Taegu and not out of it. That morning the Americans had ordered the evacuation of the South Korean Government from this provisional capital; nobody was supposed to know but of course everybody did, and already the roads were choked again with refugees – the white anonymous ragged multitudes moving off, once again, bent under their prodigious loads, the columns of dusty misery that had flowed south from Seoul, south from Chongju, south from Taejon – a pause here and there until the time came again, and on once more on the endless road to nowhere. I had had enough of refugees already; the past years had been full of them, all over the world; it seemed one could become obsessed with them.

The enemy were eleven miles out of town. Taegu was secure enough, it was said, but the ragged people did not believe it – the inhabitants of the town remained, uncertainly; it was the practised refugees who were always first away, they now had nothing to leave behind.

We found the Major to whom we had to report; he was a tall and muscular man with a broad handsome actor's face, glistening in the heat; he was sitting alone in the room reading an illustrated work called Super Comic. He put it down reluctantly, then he saw we were strangers and rose with an open-handed American gesture of greeting.

'Happy to have you here, Mister – Mister –.' But he didn't look happy; he stared vaguely around the deserted compound. 'You got us at a difficult moment, Mister –. The billets are dismantled, I guess. Meanwhile – you'd like to get a picture of the situation, no doubt. Well, gentlemen, as I see it. . . .' He took a cover marked RESTRICTED from a wall map marked CLASSIFIED: SECRET and ran his finger over a mass of lines and tabulations and arrows. 'Fluid. The Sarge will know when he comes, if he comes. It's just that we're in a very busy condition today, Mister –, I would be very happy to ask you gentlemen to join me in a coke. but I'll be darned if I know where there's one to be had. Can you imagine that for a war?' He laughed with a frank boyish charm that you felt had been cultivated over the years to match that broad honest brow, the crew-cut hair, the wonderful teeth.

We said we would be contented if we might just fill our water canteens; by now the heat had settled down like a blanket and the grey air danced with dust. Our green fatigues were patched black with sweat; even the Major's tailored sun-tan shirt clung damply to his splendid torso.

He was just about to show us the water-point when a strange thing happened: the Major stopped in mid-gesture and came to attention so violently that all his armament clattered together. A stocky middle-aged officer came into the room and the Major said 'Sir!' in a loud, non-boyish voice. To our surprise this officer turned out to be a General, and not only a General but *the* General, Walton Walker himself, Commander of the Eighth Army, senior officer in the field, top-ranking soldier of the Forces in Korea. It was not uncharacteristic of this war's circumstances that in our first hour in Korea, at a moment of recognized military crisis, of

the first two officers we should meet one should be the Commanding General, and the other should be providing us with an an-
notated map of the American dispositions, and that neither of
them should show any sign of knowing anything about our
identity at all. We had been, as it happened, adequately provided
with accreditation cards; these we were to find indispensable for
any transactions in the Tokyo PX or the Clothing Store, but in
Korea, from first to last, no one in any circumstances so much as
glanced at them.

The General was as kind as the Major; he shook us both genially by the hand and said: 'Happy to have you with us, Mister –
Mister –. Dug in all right?'

We said: 'Well . . .' and he said: 'That's just fine. Major here
will fix you up with the details. Be seeing you gentlemen, no
doubt.'

From the first there was a dismaying quality about Taegu. At
that moment, it was possible to say, few towns in Asia had a
greater immediate importance. It was (or had been until an hour
or two ago) the capital of South Korea, if you could claim a
capital for a diminishing sixth of a country that was otherwise
wholly under foreign domination. It was threatened by an enemy
who was at that moment advancing with what seemed to be outstanding efficiency, and who by capturing it could make it almost
intolerably difficult for the war against him to be waged at all.

I saw no town in Korea for which even the most fulsome guide-
book could say an honestly admiring word. Taegu was no better,
no worse than the others. Most cities, however sombre or forbidding or banal, can be recalled for some aspect of character,
some symbol of purpose or appearance. Taegu was almost memorable for its negations – it was meaningless, *lourde,* a sprawling
wilderness of tiled roofs, corrugated iron, drifting dust. It was
not even strikingly squalid nor foul in any markedly Oriental way;
it had no charm, no beauty, no notably picturesque vice; nothing
but laundries and lean-tos, and the wandering legions of white-
clad people threading among the grinding lorries and tanks.

I know how subjective my reactions to Korea were, and from
the first how deeply tinged with foreboding. From the beginning
there was the certainty that this was a doomed place, a country of
despair; one was afflicted by both the discomfort and that kind of
tenderness which, if you love Asia, means revulsion – an emotion

incapable of explanation or analysis. I loathed Korea, and to this day it lives perversely in my mind as though I loved it.

We wandered for a while through this nondescript town, which had somehow been laid out in the likeness of a broad city, with wide endless streets and diminishing perspectives and everything miles away from everything else, yet realized in a mean and tawdry way, and already in an advanced state of decay. The streets were full of heavy transports which roared along, disturbing dense clouds of grey abrasive dust. At the intersections uniformed South Koreans stood on little boxes, purporting to control the traffic with the elaborate, ballet-like attitudes affected by Japanese police, waving on all trucks gracefully, impartially, and always just a little too late. To the population of Taegu – particularly the peasant refugees, whose experience of wheeled traffic had hitherto been limited to the passage of a mule-cart every second or third week – the whole situation was baffling, the more so as the Americans had imposed their own right-hand rule of the road on the old Japanese colonial left-hand tradition (as they had, curiously, never succeeded in doing in Tokyo).

At that time, in those early days when every line and aspect of the country seemed full of unknown and potentially hostile factors he – the South Korean ally – was the biggest mystery of all. He was demonstrably for us, on principle; over his improvised barracks and public buildings, his innumerable laundries and junkshops, the signs stared in varying degrees of humble enthusiasm: 'Well Com Unitted Natons!' and 'Huray Huray for Democracy!' It was equally clear that these manifestations, having been subscribed for wholly by the local banks and Chamber of Commerce associations, in no way reflected the emotions of all the Kims and Lis and their countless relatives, who appeared to accept them in precisely the same spirit as they did the Coca-Cola signs and the wild irruption of two-ton trucks – one more inexplicable aspect of the confusion into which life had fallen.

There were around us about eight hundred thousand refugees. Even then, in conditions of comparative safety and away from the bombs, those in Taegu were a sad sight. Their costume was the uniform, indistinguishable white; they crawled along under their burdens with their eyes on the dust, occasionally making abrupt and witless darts between the jeeps and the trucks. Some of the older worthies wore the traditional Respectful Hat of the Korean patriarch, a remarkable item of costume like a very small two-storied top-hat, made of plaited horse-hair, which had clearly been designed over the generations to protect the wearer neither from the rain, the wind, or the cold, and to present him with the maximum difficulty in maintaining it on his head. The elderly gentlemen thus achieved an archly sportive, rather absurd demeanour, yet oddly poignant, as though old men should go plodding into the cave of despair wearing paper caps.

We passed the night at last in an abandoned schoolhouse – the first of many such nights. In Korea almost every building that had any appearance of design or durability was a school. That was, to me, a new aspect of the Japanese colonial methods; they had exploited Korea and oppressed it and in no way beautified it, but they had educated it, and the Korean standard of literacy testified to a certain success. Clearly their imperial methods – so utilitarian, so far from the remote paternalism of the British – nevertheless had laid an emphasis on education that would have been considered fantastically enlightened by the standards of East Africa or the West Indies. However, the obverse of this was equally obvious. Every building that looked as though it could stand up for another ten minutes had now been commandeered, and whatever had gone on in the past it was evident that all education in Korea had, for the time being, come to an end.

Our Taegu schoolhouse billet was now in a condition of double desuetude; it had been abandoned first as a school and now, it seemed, even as a correspondents' mess. The first had clearly happened abruptly; on the blackboards the lessons still remained, chalked in angular Korean characters; in the corner a litter of what must have been examination papers. There were maps and curious unidentifiable botanical drawings and patriotic slogans and very old discoloured framed photographs of ancient dignitaries in old-fashioned high-necked Chinese tunics. There was nothing else; that morning the place had been emptied of all its equipment with the rest of non-combatant Taegu; there was no bed, no blanket, no light, no food. But there was nowhere else to go. We spent the night on the floorboards, drenched with mosquito-repellent, encircled with anti-louse powder.

It was a situation of such unparalleled discomfort that sleep was patently out of the question; yet in the end I slept, and I dreamed I was back in the transport plane among the boxes of ammunition, and my son was building a castle of mortar-bombs. He had put up the walls and was hammering them into place when the plane hit a turbulence, and with the explosion I was back crouching on the schoolhouse floor, sweating and awake. There was another heavy crash outside, and then two more quite quickly; you could feel the floor bounce a little. Someone was sending shells into the station down the road. We found later that a tank had somehow penetrated within range, but it missed the railroad, and no one ever found the tank. The bugs were worse; there was no defence against them.

Things looked worse and better at the same time. Three North Korean divisions, with some armour, had struck south-east from the Naktong River against the South Koreans; Eighth Army called it 'serious'. The Air Force was now using Superforts tactically; that day a hundred and one of them dropped a thousand tons of high-explosive north-west of Waegwan, where the 1st Cavalry was staving off crossings. Waegwan, they said, didn't exist any more. All this came out on the maps in red spots, like measles, at the briefings – for our billet had gone back into business again; the flap died down and everyone came back.

We stood at the bend of the road and thumbed a lift in a truck; it was going to a place whose impossible name – Chyongmyong-myong – had become momentarily identifiable as Two Command Post. There was, they said, some success there; and attack had not merely been stopped but pushed a thousand yards back.

'You stop an attack,' said the lieutenant in the truck, 'like you stop the Missouri River with your fingers; it bubbles a bit and then you find it's got through and behind you just the same. And when you push them back, it's like doing you-know-what against the wind.'

'Then where do they go?'

'Some of them die. Some of them lie low. The rest of them put on their nighties and grab themselves a bundle and the next thing you know they've got a job dishing out chow at Eusak Rear.'

The sun seemed abruptly to leap into the sky and the heat came pouring down. And with the heat the smell; it rose off the fields almost visibly as the morning grew. Although as one's experience of Korea lengthened the first revulsion dulled, the smell remained as a background for all other sensations. This characteristic of

Korea – the hand-fertilizing of the paddies with domestic ordure – was of course by no means unique in the East, but it is a fact that here it reached an especial concentration of evidence. I have never known a country where there was a more lively and thriving commerce in human excrement, even throughout the continent of Asia, which always seems to Europeans excessively reluctant to part with its sewage. It is not, take it as you will, an irresistibly captivating subject, though Orientals will insist with eloquence and no doubt flawless reason that we, for our part, show a fastidiousness that is not only absurd, but downright uneconomic. There is no arguing with that point of view, though as a discussion I have known it pall. In Korea it was seldom far from one's mind.

The war grew around us gradually. There was no point where the line began, because naturally there was no line – except at Rear on the briefing-room map: a doubtful chalk-mark between established positions; it had no meaning on the ground. What line there was, was this road, winding up from security in Taegu northwards into the hills until it stopped, only for fear of its own length. A mile or two outside town no part of it was safe; you would meet nothing on the road, but the hillsides were full of invisible people, and when you turned back along the track there would be a barrier between you and your rear. It might be only a machine-gun roadblock, but for a while it would dislocate the whole crawling vertebrae of the column, which could move only in one plane, forwards or back, and never to the side. One drove trying to look behind; the dangerous place was always one corner away, at the back of your head.

Bit by bit the front materialized, the tanks squatted on the flats of the river-beds, the road grew dense with traffic, and soon, where it ran in a kind of cutting between wooded slopes, were the groups of men, like picnickers, crouching on the verge with automatic guns, huddling in the dust of the passing wheels among a litter of ration-cans ('The Ripe Flavor of Nutty Home-Grown Corn Enriched with Body-Building Viadose') or heads buried under the hood of a jeep. The air was alive with a tinny whispering from field-telephones and the radios of tanks, a thin erratic chattering like insects, the ceaseless indiscriminate gossip of an army. Up and down the road, weaving through the traffic, bare-legged Koreans humped loads of food or mortar ammunition on their porters' framework of wood, like men with easels on their backs.

The artillery became abruptly louder and more personal, cracking horribly from the sides and behind. The planes flew overhead as though on rails. The war was all on one side – no combat, no visible encounter of any kind; so far no reply at all to all this ironclad effort. The guns were fighting the silence; the convoy was grinding into a vacuum; the men were advancing into empty space. It could have been an elaborate and over-realistic exercise – except for the hills around, and the roadblocks behind, and the fact that it was this kind of empty country that had driven us backwards a hundred and fifty miles already, and still had us hemmed in: a yielding wall of irresistible no-man's-land.

The village where the North Koreans had been until an hour ago was half a mile up the road, or had been; there was nothing much left. It had been rocketed, what remained was a heap of ashes, a few mud walls, with one or two North Koreans sprawled among the debris in unreal tangled postures, with calcined limbs projecting in impossible attitudes. The only visible body that still bore the semblance of a man remained sitting upright in a pile of still redly glowing cinders; for a startling moment he looked not like a dead Korean but like a living yogi. The rest were carrion. It had not long happened, but already in the heat of the day the smell was unendurable. The marching men hurried past, gagging.

But by then the aircraft had arrived; we heard them screeching up from the south and looked up without any fuss of flinching – when it came to aircraft we were brave: in Korea they were always ours. There was never anything hostile in the air. If anything fell on us it would only be by mistake. It was not unknown by any means, but it was always a mistake.

The planes, unopposed in any way, treated the thing as a manoeuvre, circling and peeling off, diving and re-forming for more than an hour – at every approach the leading edges speckled with pinpoints of fire as the rockets left the wings, slapping into the North Korean lodgements across the valley with a delayed crack that was always louder than you expected. There was no reply of any kind.

The bombers followed them; the artillery followed the bombers. We stood in entranced rows and groups along the road, watching the ridges dapple with explosions and the staring white smoke of the phosphorus markers. Some men made themselves comfortable by the roadside, leaning back and lighting cigarettes, pointing out to each other this or that noticeably deft piece of flying; it was as though we were at some sort of demonstration.

A little way down, by a cluster of roofless homes, there was an old man, one of the typical old men of Korea, with a placid Buddha face; in some curious way he had let the battle catch up with him and he was done for. He sat beside a dry-stone wall, and then he lay. He had not been hit, or damaged in any way; it seemed he had been minding his own business when the war accumulated suddenly around him, and he was unable to cope with it – the noise, the burning, the fuss. We stopped a passing GI and borrowed a new water-bottle, but the water dribbled down among the hairs of the old man's beard, spaced out far apart like white wires, and he died without any confusion or excitement at all; it was the most composed and deliberate action I had seen that day, and certainly the most graceful.

At last we got back to Taegu. There was no roadblock and no sniper for us; nevertheless we jolted back uneasily enough, for the chance of a minor ambush – with the choice of dodging the fire or taking a header into those noisome paddies – would present a dilemma of hideous complexity. 'You gotta make up your mind,' said a Sergeant, 'A mouthful of shit or an arseful of lead.' You could find a certain Korean symbolism there: the bullets of the North, or the corruption of the South.

The boy who washed our shirts and swept our floor was called Kim – as indeed were two out of every three Koreans one ever met; the third was called Li. He was a youth whose charm was not too readily apparent – it did not appear when times were good; when there was plenty of food and the lights worked and there was not too much war he would sit sombrely on the stairs, full of ancestral bitterness. His face was cast in the customary Korean lines of despairing blankness, except in moments of especial difficulty or confusion – when for example, he had been kept up until four in the morning, with the knowledge that he must call us again at six – when it would break into a genial and almost radiant smile. He was able to provide canned food at unusual times, the water he brought us was always a little cooler than that from the luke-warm hanging lister-bags outside, and also no doubt even more plentifully supplied with the more toxic bacteria; he even kept a store of flea-powder, our use of which he observed with a tolerant yet cynical air, as one might contemplate the use of snake's-tooth talismans by barbaric peoples. He knew precisely, by some necromancy, the movements of all our colleagues: who had left for the 24th Division and who had endeavoured to slip one over on the rest of us by using the battalion phone; he never once offered to introduce us to a good-looking and accommodating sister. He was of course quickly called up in the fierce and urgent conscription.

Kim Chang-ki, like every other conscripted South Korean, became a soldier very nearly literally overnight. One day he was washing socks in the schoolhouse yard, the next he was in the Army, beginning a training that must have been the quickest in the whole world. I went with him.

It was never at any time possible to obtain a firm or official figure for the number of South Korean troops in the field, the ROKs; they were at most times heavily outnumbered, and their casualties were enormous. The intake was vast, the training almost unbelievably cursory. The entire period of military instruction and drill, from start to finish, took five days. The man was drafted at the age of eighteen. On the Sunday he might be at work in the paddies or the shop; by the following Sunday he was in the line; in next to no time he was either a veteran or a corpse.

Kim Chang-ki had planned, or rather hoped, to enter the *nioul-hak,* the course of law; the study and practice of law held a powerful attraction for Korean youth. Like so many Koreans with any pretensions to intellectual standards he held himself aloof from the war as an ethical or moral question; he both resented and feared it; he expressed himself as strongly against the arrival of the Communists, but it was clear that he had not fully identified them with Koreans, North or South, and having to oppose them physically he disliked as a hateful interruption of his private life. He was an inhabitant of the neighbourhood and was not, therefore, a refugee in any sense, so he had in fact some sort of private life to be interrupted.

I took Kim to the outskirts of Taegu to say his farewells to his father, an indispensable formality. Filial piety is of the highest estimation to Koreans of all degrees, and the conduct of a son towards his father, as in China, is governed by innumerable rules. If a son met his father by the way he must do him obeisance; technically a son should accompany his father both to prison or to exile. It was not uncommon, along those refugee-haunted roads, to see a man bearing his father on his back for many miles when the old man was exhausted and the chance of rest still far ahead.

We arrived at the Kim house in the heat of the afternoon; the father was at work in his field. It was the house of a peasant farmer in a very moderate condition, made of wood and clay and rice-straw, practically windowless, but part of the roof was tiled, a sign of substance. Kim hurried indoors to change from the American fatigues we had provided for his work; he reappeared in a moment in clean white cotton pajama and his best starched jacket with wide sleeves.

By and by his father appeared, accompanied by a great company of relatives and small children. He was a small man of great dignity; he still wore his working hat, the enormous dome of plaited straw three and a half feet across that makes Korean farmers in the summer paddies look like bent and moving mushrooms. He wore a thin beard, and his face looked very old; he could not have been more than forty-five.

As he approached Kim bowed low, remaining with lowered eyes until his father spoke a word or two. We all drank tea, mostly in silence – the family spoke no English and seemed to consider conversation incomprehensible to us to be impolite.

Then Kim changed back to his fatigues and we prepared to go. He made another deep obeisance to his father, who said nothing. As we walked out of the yard the father suddenly called out something, but Kim walked quickly on.

This five-day manufacture of troops from peasants, soldiers from students, could surely have succeeded nowhere else. Before anything else happened, there came the taking of the oath – a matter which for some reason no one took the trouble to publicize, though it seemed to have a very singular bearing on the political implications of the campaign. Even at that time, the ROK recruits were swearing, among other things, to 'restore the unity of the whole country within its borders', which made it clear that the Government of South Korea, like that of the North, was now committed to unification by military means. When I asked the liaison authorities how official a sanction there was for this attitude within the UN framework, they said they never knew that it was going on at all. That was scarcely surprising; there were stranger and infinitely more disturbing things at work in the South Korean administration that went unremarked, or at least unchallenged.

As a private soldier Kim would be paid at the rate of 1,000 *won* a month, about one and threepence. As a staff sergeant he would get 2,000, as a technical sergeant 7,700, a master sergeant 8,500. In the fantastically improbable even of his becoming a General he would be paid officially, 25,000 *won* a month, or ten shillings a week, which would not in any way at all reflect the fashion of his life.

He had, obviously, the most sketchy and inadequate doctrinal grasp of what he was supposed to be fighting about. Not that that was confined to the South Korean ally. It seemed a little more disturbing, however, in that the result affected him more closely; moreover he belonged to a race whose educational standards were not on the whole low. You got the impression of a world peopled with remote minds, of sudden resentments and strange loyalties, of savagery and stupidity and great lasting qualities; a great bewilderment shot through with hate. All their lives, you felt, they had hated somebody; now they knew whom it was.

For the rest, there seemed little that the American GI could wish to discuss with the Korean. From the beginning the enemy Korean was, inevitably, the Gook. Later, because of the virtual impossibility of distinguishing a North Korean from a South Korean, all Koreans became Gooks, a word impossible to apply affectionately. It was apparent that on the whole the troops of the United Nations command could feel no positive emotion about the inhabitants in whose name they were there, other than contempt, but there it was: the Koreans were not a likeable people, with none of the redeeming delicacies and artful subservience of the Japanese. Their character seemed full of paradoxes, some generically Oriental, some it seemed specifically Korean. On occasion he would, quite literally and deliberately, lay down his life, it had been done many times. At other times he – or his brother or his father or even his grandmother, dressed in the drab concealing white of the peasant – would produce a grenade from the refugee's bundle and blow off the nearest soldier's leg, himself dying almost invariably and immediately with a bullet in the head.

As a soldier he was variously capable of dramatic moments of
military endurance and resource, and of mad bursts of headlong
flight. But whatever he did or refrained from doing was, in spite
of all the rear-echelon casuistry, a UN matter; he fought and behaved in this way or that way under the olive-branch flag. It was
not always agreeable to consider; few things in Korea were.

The Communists were doing their cause no good by excesses of
a particularly brutal and idiotic kind: by binding captured GIs
and shooting them in the back and leaving them where their
mutilated bodies could be discovered and photographed, thus
providing the American Press with precisely the propaganda they
so badly needed. Less publicized, naturally, were the excesses of
the other side, who also shot prisoners in considerable numbers,
because it was in certain circumstances a bother and a difficulty,
or perhaps a danger, to escort them down the line, and who rid
themselves summarily of refugees because amongst them there
might be, and frequently were, infiltrators and guerillas. It was all
singularly loathesome.

The Koreans were uncommonly tough people. I went down to
a prisoner-of-war camp, almost without exception the men were
wounded, in some cases terribly and shockingly so. They endured,
tensely and silently, dressings and pluggings for which anyone
else would have required a general anaesthetic. One boy came in,
on his feet, with what appeared to be a black eye; he walked in
stolidly, swaying slightly. The MO's casual glance hardened into
astonishment; the prisoner had been shot in the back, and the
round had emerged from his left cheek, tunnelling entirely through
his body, neck, and face. He said that his officer had done it 'in
anger'. He was allowed to squat on the ground for his interroga-
tion; half way through he coughed, and leaned over on his side,
and presently died. The others remained quiet, sitting or lying
about the floor with the incurious Asian stare; there was no way of
asking what one would ask, no channel of communication at all,
no link in the world.

The language problem presented a barrier that no one seemed disposed to tackle; one odd aspect of the four-year American occupation of South Korea was that one practically never came upon an
American who spoke Korean. There appeared to be no acceptable
form of pidgin-Korean, and even the old occupation Tokyo-

hands with a grasp of Japanese found, in Waegwan or Taegu, that they might as well have been in Albania.

I am a great amateur and indeed collector of phrase-books, less for their practical value (which in my view is uniformly nil; either you cannot express a phrase or you express it so effectively that it elicits a long and effusive reply in the same tongue, with subsequent humiliation) than for the manner in which they seem to reveal the worst aspects both of the compiler's mind and of the language he is explaining. Anyone who has ever tried to conduct a conversation through, for example, an old Traveller's Hindustani will know how firmly and masterfully it avoids all expressions other than barks of command, peremptory complaint, and abuse. It is an ineradicable belief in the minds of those who write phrase-books that no one could conceivably find himself in a foreign land without instantly wanting his laundry done, his servants denounced, his food taken away, and his bills questioned. The only Korean phrase-book I could find erred at the other extreme.

It was called 'Sentences English', and it had clearly been designed for the cultivation of the most excessively futile small-talk. Its anonymous author might have gleaned his basic material from eavesdropping at some burlesque garden-party in the suburbs of a Midland town. There were pages of: 'Lovely morning isnt it!' 'Fine day isnt it!' 'Rotten weather isnt it!' 'Funny weather isnt it!' 'Looks like going rain (snow, wind)' 'Cold (hot, wet, dry) isnt it!' 'Getting cooler (hotter, wetter, drier) isnt it!' They were followed by more pages of equally demented detail: 'How do you do!' 'I am do fine!' 'How about Family!' 'They all well too!' – one would have thought it some grotesque Oriental satire on how the English are supposed to talk, with strange local adaptations: 'Did you see Dr Kim?' 'Yes, Professor Sung!' 'Much spending, Dr!' 'Twenty sen a gallon, Professor!'

Slightly better was a Chinese phrase-book issued by the American Army; it gave an English version of the Chinese characters, full of elaborate typographical devices to indicate inflective changes, which produced an oddly alarming effect. 'Obey or I fire!' it said: *RUH! sher BOO! TING! waw DUH MING! LING!* 'Are you hungry?' asked the book, with a clipped emphasis: *UH! boo UH!* In its glossary a Private was, rather evocatively *UHR! dung BING*, but a Staff Sergeant was, as one might imagine, *SHAUNG! SHER!* There was a brief enquiry:

'Where is a restaurant, I want to buy food', in almost onomata-
paeic terms: *SH-UM-muh DEE! fahng yo FAHN! gwahn DZ.
waw YOW! ma-ee CHER duh*. Some words almost explained themselves, as a Howitzer: *YOO DAHN! POW!*, and a husband, with
a dying fall: *shy shun*. And, perhaps best of all, a stimulant:
SHING! FUN! YOW!

But nobody spoke Chinese, and we were still in Taegu, where
there was no Shing, no Fun, and no Yow; just none at all.

Just before dawn the North began two simultaneous strikes:
against the US 24th Division defending Masan in the south-west,
and across the Naktong to the north. That evening they were
across the river in seventeen places on a fifty-mile front.

Five of our colleagues jeeping back from Yongsang ran into an
ambush at a corner near Wondong: the usual burst from a burp-
gun in a paddy field, the usual stalling of the jeep. They were
Phil Potter and Alex Valentine, Homer Bigart and Henri Turenne,
and Jean-Marie de Prémonville. Potter was hit in the calf and
Prémonville – pushing and heaving madly behind the jeep to get
it going again before more burp-guns appeared – got it in the
bottom. We had a lot of fun with Jean later, as he walked stiffly
about town with a dressing on his rear. Very soon Jean was
dead; in the next ambush Agence France Presse lost a tireless
correspondent and we lost a good and merry friend. He was, I
think, our twenty-first casualty.

On the far east coast of Korea, at the end of the tottering ROK
line, was Pohang-dong, the seaport town with an airstrip that
had been contended for consistently; already it had changed
hands three times and now, once again and maybe temporarily,
it was in our possession. It was not very easy to reach.

We managed to get a jeep from Kaymag (the ROK front was
paternally their affair); it was old and filthy and insecure, even the
South Koreans had given it up. It was driven by a young Kim
who treated it as though it were a recalcitrant mule, muttering at
it, slamming its controls with his fist, dragging at a steering-wheel
that had a ninety-degree play in it, grinding in the gears with a
penetrating scream. Every time it stopped he would get out and
leap up and down on the bonnet; this violent treatment seemed
to readjust some chronic costive defect in the machinery, and
afterwards it always started again.

For a while we drove along with an eastbound convoy, bounding and heaving over the rocky road in a thick and endless thundercloud of dust. The dust of Korea was worse than any dust normally experienced by human kind; it combined the properties of emery-powder and poison gas, for not only did it tear and rasp at the throat but at the same time introduced into the respiratory passages a concentrate of pestilential bacilli from the reeking paddies.

We came at last to a village; it was a Corps command post of the ROK sector. The school here had been taken over for the General, Kim Hong Ill. We asked if we might call on him. The General was having his siesta, nevertheless the orderly made no bones about knocking him up. We were received at once by a small and very dapper man in his fifties, who stared at us keenly. He showed special interest in our square cloth badges, and enquired sharply through an interpreter what they represented. When he was told that the lettering read 'United Nations War Correspondent' he nodded impatiently and asked what that meant; he had never before seen the badge nor heard of a war correspondent.

It was not surprising that he had not seen the badge, which had only just been issued – we understood that its design, a bright silver letter on a vivid blue ground, had been devised one evening in the Tokyo Press Club, and there was great resistance to wearing it in the field, on the grounds that it was not only too conspicuous but unnecessary, reporters in general being easily distinguishable from combatant soldiers by the extra weight and variety of their armament.

The General enquired where we were driving to; when we said to Pohang he observed, genially, that he imagined that by now it had fallen to the Communists.

'I know about Communists,' said the General. 'I have been fighting them for years. I know about Japanese, too, I have fought them as well, in Manchuria. I have been thirty years at this employment. First with the Patriotic Army, then with my old friend Chiang Kai-Shek, now with MacArthur. I am a professional anti-Communist.'

Did he foresee a date for victory in Korea?

He shrugged. 'When we have beaten the Pyongyang Communists, then the Chinese will come. Then the Russians, who as you may know are also Communists. Then the Europeans. Then the Indians, and the Japanese. There will no doubt be plenty of war.'

Up the road the countryside changed, the atmosphere suddenly assumed the indefinable cloak of hostility, with everything once again to be interpreted in terms of personal safety and doubt. The convoy had stopped behind. The land began to smell of war again, the ruins by the roadside became more frequent. As we crossed a wooden bridge the familiar ghastly reek made us look down: half a dozen bodies lay tangled by the bank in the reeds, blackened and bloated and bursting from their rags. Further on there were more, in the ricefields; the roasting afternoon was heavy with corruption. One of the strangest factors in the contemplation of Korea was the absence of birds; one felt that if Providence had designed Korea as a battlefield of this kind it should at least have provided the vultures.

Pohang, when we got there, was a sight to chill the heart with desolation. It had been napalmed flat. A European town in such circumstances would have presented a differently poignant scene; there would have been fallen walls and exposed rooms and melancholy glimpses of interrupted domestic life; in Pohang was an expanse of ashes. A Korean township offered practically no structural resistance to attack; when the rockets came it burned away, the straw roofs burned, the matting burned, the mud walls crumbled, and after a little while of this the town would be gone. There were few ruins in Korea. A Korean ruin was a pile of ash and charcoal; about the only things that did not burn were the cooking pots and some of the bones. Pohang was flattened acres of black cinders, from the air it must have looked like a thumb-print.

We drove through it very carefully, and for some time it seemed as though there was not a living soul left. Then we saw a strange thing: one solitary old man, alone it seemed in all the blackened emptiness of Pohang; he was raking and groping among the ashes of what must have been his house, actually sifting his home through his fingers. Now and again he would find something which he laid aside: a tin can, a nail or two. He was like the last man in the world, the relic, the shape of the future.

There was one exception to this black gritty destruction; on the other side of town was one stone building that remained standing

– of course, the school. We made our way very nervously inside – there were no traps nor mines and it was remarkable, among the wrack and ashes all around, how little damage had come to that large classroom. There was nothing to look at in there, except a few books. One book, perhaps, in particular.

Korea was full of sad things, but for some reason few of them had quite the same lowering effect on me as this worthless school-book. It was an ordinary exercise-book of coarse paper, part of some English-speaking class. I think I might be tempted to embellish it, improve the symbolism, but I have the book beside me as I write this; I kept it carefully ever since that day, feeling that one day I might have its psychological pattern analysed, or even maybe explained, by some technician in the devious conditions of the human mind.

It was obviously a phrase-book – a very different kind from the others I had known. It was home-made, the English and Korean equivalents were written in a schoolboy hand with a thin pen. On the cover was written 'Comon Sense'. Throughout this random and casual record ran a thread of negation and hopelessness that I feel to this day must be significant of something.

The first page was headed: 'A peace of good advice.' From then on it consists of words and groups of words with their Korean equivalents. It is the choice of words . . .

advice. His manner is advisiable. You should be gentlemanlike.
argue – debate, altercate, dispute, war.
My stomach is full of food.
annoyed – ugly – embarrass – trouble. Troble?
opposite – opposition – contrary.
What is contrary of 'good'? This is.
I opposited to your opinion.
It is proper that I ought to advise you to go to hell.
to damp one's order. hate – hatred – resentment
Few can live to one hundred Year of age.
There are no man who can live to 100.
I have no place to go to
I have no house to live in
Though he is a fooll, he is filiel to his Father.

Though Korea has been Told to be freed from the japanese government, she has not yet her independence.

free – freedom – freedom of speech – correspondance teaching
Under the condition that I will lend you money on the con-
dition that you would cut you Flesh in one pound in time of
non-payment
Fixed Mind
confused Mind. disaster – end – result
The Confusion of Korea will or sure to end in her ruin
I like my wife especially when she give me good wine
white Color worker
When he is sober he never speak.
Vice. Show me your Vice.
By no means. I will not go with you any Masters
Wear. War. Worn people. War sufferer. War torn people
out of Work. I am job-less.
the Seoul – capital of Korea has been. Character is poor mans
capital. Seoul is become of the entry the U.N. Committee to
Seoul.

This terrible emphasis on the negative, this preoccupation with
all the sorrowful and vicious conditions and emotions, seemed a
despairing thing. And the book finished abruptly, so oddly in
character that it might have been contrived:

Personal History
Kum Sung Ree
born on March 10 1928

Permanent domicile: No. 92 Kum Chung the city of Chung ding
Present address: No. 22 Yongsang-dong, Seoul city
Education: entered the Cung-ching Elemantory school in
April of the 1939 year of Suki. Finished the Sixth year of the
1939 year of Suki. Finished the Sixt
Finished

So back through the ashes, down the road, over the bridge in the
gathering dusk, past the cryptic peasants in the fields and the
remnants of people in the sedges and by the roadsides. We passed
nothing on the road but a van, with two disconsolate American
soldiers in it – they had a poor job: a Graves Registration Unit;
they were looking for bodies of United States troops. Any that
they found they wrapped in tarpaulin and put into the truck, so
that they at least would get a burial and not, like everything else,

disintegrate slowly and merge with the rest into the rotting ruin of Korea.

Somewhere behind us there was a rattle of shots, and the sound made a compound with the smell and the growing darkness and the shadowy hills, and I prayed for the collapsing jeep to hurry us away.

What in fact is the boundary of pacifism? I can imagine I was then nearer to being an orthodox pacifist than I had ever been before, yet there were unreasonable reservations – it is not a new feeling, only the knowledge of something that I should have managed to integrate before, if I had had either the courage or the experience. And yet I can remember moments in the past – Nanking, Spain, Belsen, the early revelations – when I felt very nearly bloodthirsty and did not consider the feeling ignoble. Clearly the answer is wholly simple, and almost wholly discreditable – it was all right in theory; now I was up against it in a violently personal and nauseating way. I rationalized my cowardice and disgust into a complex ethical explanation for being scared to death. Was that the reason?

Throughout the acerbities of Korea, the dullness and regrets, the hazards and tedium and sometimes the despair of Korea, the thing one looked for, as a convict for remission, was the occasional visit to Japan. It was far from simple to arrange administratively and seldom easy to justify professionally, and when in fact one had contrived the excuse and the means the trip was highly perilous. One gave up taking note of the numbers of transports that had nosed into the country by running an engine at take-off, that had disintegrated off the runway, or those that had exploded like Stefan's, or the one in which Frank Emery and Charlie Rosenkranz and Ken Inouye of INS had died the other day leaving South Japan. Still, there was no other practicable way and – until you had done it often enough, and lost enough nerve, as happened ultimately – it was worth it.

So there was the airstrip of Taegu again, no longer a place of excitement but of settled calm, with everyone moving about very slowly in the heavy sun as though they had been there for years. A brisk trade was going on outside the control room in captured North Korean weapons of Russian manufacture; a soldier had two fine burp-guns and a long old-fashioned musket in the back of his truck and was negotiating with a businesslike group that included, remarkably, a padre. There was a paper on the board which said: 'Notice to Air Force: Trick Beards Will No Longer Be Worn On This Station.' While we waited for our plane to appear there was a disturbance in the air and a combat aircraft made what seemed to be an agitated approach; as it touched down an unexploded rocket-projectile detached itself from the starboard rack and went bounding and leaping down the runway, coming to rest at last happily some distance away.

'Another misfire,' remarked one of the members of the small-arms syndicate, glancing over his shoulder. 'Something wrong with that release mechanism, I guess,' and returned to his examination of the burp-gun.

'What happens to it?'

'To what?'

'That rocket. It isn't a dud?'

'Maybe. Never can tell. Armourers' job.'

By and by a couple of men in baseball caps went out in a jeep to look for the rocket; they cavorted away sitting, in the American fashion, all over the jeep rather than in it, their jaws working rhythmically.

I waited for an hour or two in the shade, until some men who had been dozing quietly all around suddenly jumped up and called out: 'Get aboard, you men; wake up, passengers; what do you think this all is, keeping the transport waiting?'

We were all offloaded at Itazuke, which was still six hundred miles from Tokyo but wasn't bad, because there was a rest-room and chairs and a coke-machine and magazines full of brassiere-advertisements. They told me to stick around and wait for a call.

I waited for three hours. The NCO who had looked at my travel-orders came over and said: 'You British? Fine country you got over there.'

I said: thank you very much.

'Sure, I know it. Stationed out there in '44 – guess you must know the place: Warrington, Lancs? That was some place. Yes, sir, finest place in all England – pretty, too.'

A little while later he came back and said: 'I know a guy lives over in Britain. His home town's Twicken-Ham. Guess that's real countryside. Sure like to see that cottage. Running water too, I guess they got out there, radio and all. Pretty good, out there in the country.'

From time to time he would come over and say: 'You ever been out to the Black Dog in Warrington? Gee, often wish I was right back there, in that Dog. Had a swell set-up.' He talked on, here in Itazuke, midnight in South Japan; he was full of his strange nostalgia for Warrington.

A GI lay sleeping on the floor nearby, the back of his head pillowed inside the liner of his steel helmet. The first time you see this done you think it must be purgatory, but it is not uncomfortable. About midnight the GI woke up and said he was going home on compassionate leave; his father was dying.

'Home?'

'Wisconsin.'

'That's a hell of a way.'

'You can say that again.' He looked young and blond and old and tired altogether. 'Still, I should worry how far. It isn't Korea. If my poor old man knew it, he done me a favour. Say, I should buy you a coke if I'd got any scrip, but I don't draw a cent till Tokyo.'

I said I had a little scrip; I could spare a couple. He refused, but I was very insistent; I wanted for once in my life, at the cost of two bucks, to make a dollar loan to an American. I said: 'We'll chalk it off against the two thousand billion.'

At last the plane was due to go; it was a big empty four-motored transport, and the GI and I were the only passengers. We made beds out of the parachute gear and lay down; it was wonderful. Somewhere over Japan I got up to look out of the port – down below there was a dark and terrible glow, obscured by what seemed to be lines and drifts of opaque fog: the crater of a volcano; grim.

Tachikawa at three in the morning, the end of the line. It was still twenty odd miles into Tokyo, and no transport going until dawn; all over the enormous waiting-room men were sitting and lying and snoring. There was free coffee at a stand in the corner, where an attractive middle-aged American lady was handing out paper cups. When I spoke to her she smiled, as though it had not been the fag-end of a sleepless night.

'Did your boys get in yet? The British troops in?'

'Yes, they're there.'

'My, that's splendid. We're all sure they're going to be a great help. Now just on account of your being British I'm going to fix you a little treat.'

In a few moments she handed me a paper cup of warm water with a small cotton bag tethered with string floating buoyantly on the surface.

'There, isn't that what you British boys pine for, a nice cup of tea!'

I had built up long hopes on the journey for a powerful cup of good coffee, but there was no asking for it now, and very soon a sort of brown stain seeped from the little bag into the warm water, and I toasted the lady in it for her kindness.

Soon after dawn I got a lift into Tokyo; for once even that deplorable city looked wonderful. At the Club they were having breakfast: real eggs, real orange-juice, real toast. The board bulletin said: 'An intensified attack was made yesterday against Masan, commanding the coastal road to Pusan, and was repulsed. Air Force fighters made tactical sweeps over the north-east sector, causing 29 enemy casualties . . .' It was wonderful too; from a fighter they could count 29 casualties on the ground, to a digit.

Later that day I plied my trade, writing against time until the noise drove me out. The room backed on to a building occupied by the Soviet Government Information Bureau, which was a strange establishment, sombre and forbidding and blank from the outside, yet given over to what seemed to be an uproarious internal social life. The inhabitants sang at all hours – not necessarily at the all hours associated with song; they would be in full cry at curious times like three in the afternoon, and they could keep it up all night. It was far from inharmonious; in certain circumstances it was remarkably good; but it was murder to concentration. I packed up and took a cab to the Chigodo-ku district where a friend had a room and I worked again – sitting on the tatami mat with my typewriter on the floor between my knees, in the calm and concord, the gentle desirable peace of a Japanese hotel.

Japan enchants me. Japan has the instant effect upon me of making it imperative to write of it, to convey something of that strange nervous atmosphere to those who think of the country in terms of Madame Butterfly on the one side or Pearl Harbour on the other . . . as though it had not in fact been done a hundred

times before, as though oneself was the first to be beguiled by the
subtle flavour of the place. Just a little more study, I felt, just the
experience of one more month and it could be done. Of course it
never will.

Korea was for the moment far away. And Toyko was like all
cities defeated and occupied, only here the schizophrenia was
hideously exhibited: the split mind of the city that accepted equally
the horrors of the Ernie Pyle Cinema and the delicate grace of the
Meiji Shrine, that bowed cryptically before the spiritual barbarities
of occupation procedure, maintaining its secret decorum in a
private poverty. Tokyo was twice ruined; first by bombs and
burning petrol, and next by the Way of Life. That second was a
destruction gentler and more kindly meant, and infinitely more
cruel.

I went back through the damp monochrome streets of this
gigantic sprawling town – its flimsy fabric pulverized by bombs,
restored now from the ashes in the image of an Oriental Milwau-
kee: a block or two of solid half-hearted skyscrapers engulfed by
the most interminable shantytown in the world. Japan is lovely,
Tokyo is abysmal. Back down the main street past the Doolittle
Baseball Park, past the monumental Dai Ichi building, the holy of
holies to which each morning the General would repair past a
genuflecting mob; an eagle profile among the shaven skulls and
bristling sentries. Back past the dark sombre moat that lay around
the dark sombre walls, that lay around the dropping willows: the
pervading grey mystery of the Imperial Palace. Back among the
clacking of the *geta* on the pavements and the pad of polished
boots: the old enchantment fast in the grip of the drugstore
civilization. And back into Shimbun Alley and the squalid but oh,
so long-awaited luxuries of the intrusive west – Whisky, boy-san;
and a fried egg sandwich; do it twice and do it quickly; tonight
will be time enough for the raw fish, the bean curd and seaweed.

But when I persuaded Michiko-san to let me take her to dinner
– or rather to take me – it was a place ten miles out and when we
got there it was a desolate commandeered hotel with tables and
chairs and Maryland fried chicken and canned beans, and a loudspeaker anchored to the American Forces Program, as false and
ersatz and savourless as the Pre-Digested, Oven-Baked, Farm-
Ripened American food-surrogate we were obliged to eat.
Michiko-san indicated with a kind of humble pride the knives and

forks, and the potted palms, and the picture of the General and the ice-water jugs. It was at that point I decided not to fall in love with Michiko-san – it was clear she had not done all this for me, but because she liked it.

General MacArthur had been to Formosa, he had completed his discussion with Chiang Kai-Shek; now he was back they were still wondering in GHQ why such a simple thing had caused such comment.

'It has been widely reported in Tokyo,' said the English papers, 'that the British Government felt that the General's visit was not in the best interests of the United Nations – or at least that the UN should have been consulted.'

The extravagant impertinence of this attitude took some time to sink in. When it did, the Dai Ichi drew its majesty together and by and by produced a statement, issued and distributed through the UP. 'It is inconceivable that the British Government should attempt to arrogate to itself, under guise of membership of the United Nations, the slightest warrant and judgment on the propriety of the mission of an American officer in compliance with the orders of his Government.'

Yet the malapert and intransigeant voices continued to argue: the American officer was also the Commander-in-Chief of the UN Forces in Korea; did not one take precedence over the other? How often during the war was that question of corporate responsibility going to crop up, with its tiresome intrusions of principle? General MacArthur went to Formosa as an American soldier and a United Nations officer; however that may be by the time he returned the order of precedence had been reversed in the minds of many people who were already making angry complaints against the South Korean regime not because it was South Korean, but because it was most demonstrably United Nations.

In any case, the British diplomatic representation in Japan had not been able to gain access to the Supreme Commander's presence for more than a week.

The Japanese, at least, made no trouble. Formosa was something in the bank; the main thing was a firm, clear, undeviating line on Korea. Nothing must be allowed to compromise this; it was not every country that had ever achieved such an economic windfall. By the second month of the war the US was spending a million

dollars a day in Japan. Korea, with its demands for ancillary services, supply, transport – was a godsend; the Prime Minister
publicly called it 'an Act of Providence', and again thanked the
General for it, which was an embarrassment but it didn't matter.
The stagnant Japanese shipping industry was booming; rails and
roads were thriving. The Prime Minister kept urging the country
'to express enthusiasm'. Some people did, guardedly. The Socialists limited their part to 'spiritual co-operation', and there was a
considerable amount of hedging of bets, in the form of rice
hoarding.

This time I was allowed forty hours only in Japan; a quarter of
the time I slept, one-eighth of the time I spent in the bath, and if
Paradise exists on earth it is probably a Japanese bath after weeks
of Korea. Nowhere matches the fleshly bliss of it – the rapture,
the sloth, the water so hot that to enter it should mean a syncope,
yet never quite does – to be soaped beforehand by pretty smiling
young women who are so nearly sexless automata but just that
fine and admirable degree not quite. To lie drained of all initiative
and ambition on the *futan* in the empty room and think, if one is
able, of the reeking schoolhouse yard in Taegu and the hanging
hose-pipe with the perforated baked-bean can at the end. And to
forget tomorrow.

The plane for Korea left at the customary airplane hour –
four-something in the morning; one usually stayed up in the bar
until the jeep came, regretting the spent dollars that could no
longer buy some of those desirable, and in Korea unobtainable,
bottles of bourbon. I got to Haneda in time; there was a two hour
delay; at six-thirty we were all paraded, stiff and clumsy like dolls
in a great variety of life-saving harness, and at six-thirty-one I was
bumped off – eased from the step and told we were overweight.
There appeared a group of porters carrying a vast refrigerator
which they manhandled on to the plane. It went, and I stayed.

Since there was nothing else going to Korea from Haneda I
must needs make my way the thirty miles to Tachikawa; it was
said there was always something going from Tachikawa.

Wait and more wait; a lift and another lift, and Tachikawa. Yes,
there would be something going to Taegu, but not yet. Wait,
wait some more in a chair for another five hours, and at last the
blessed despatcher shaking one's shoulder.

And finally, humping one's haversack through the door into the hot afternoon (I had started the vigil at 3.30 a.m.) somebody calls: 'Hi, Mac.' It is the GI from Itazuke. 'I got bumped off my stateside plane. Guess I'll get off yet, if my poor old man can hang on awhile. Give my love to Korea,' says the GI. 'And, Mac – here's the couple bucks I owe you.'

What a wonderful, terrible people.

Back to the schoolhouse; it was like coming home. By now I felt that half my life had been somehow associated with this bleak and austere building, with its broken balcony, its decaying woodwork, in sound alternating between a cheerless echoing emptiness and a turbulent congestion, full of urgent barks and sudden laughter and the sounds of bitter contention. Throughout the day it was deserted; at night it was something between an Approved School and a play by Chekhov.

I got back as the fellow-boarders came trooping back from their labours in the field, in squads and groups and a few furtive isolated individuals who had clearly been on to a good, which is to say exclusive, thing. My colleagues were in many ways the most memorable part of the UN organization. They cultivated an intrepid and mettlesome appearance, loaded with helmets and carbines and with daggers protruding from their boots; several had intimidating beards. The effect was very passable to Hemingway, as of tough but fundamentally sensitive men newly returning from dangerous enterprises behind the enemy's lines. The cynicism of that analogy, however, was hard to maintain, because the plain truth was that that was in many cases precisely what they had been doing. They hurried purposefully in, cast their martial impedimenta from them, and set to work in what appeared to have been a class for infants, forcing their soldierly frames into the only available furniture, which consisted of miniature desks constructed for diminutive Korean children.

When things were best for news – which is to say worst for everything else – we lived in a rather hideous proximity, among a litter of old socks and portable typewriters and .45 revolvers and half-opened cans of peanuts. Such circumstances beget unreasonable prejudices, and many a man will be forgiven for his irrational resentment of the maddening idiosyncrasies of his neighbours. So must Arctic explorers react to one another. Out of this confessed fellowship we all emerged rather badly, with passionate denunciations of the most trifling and idiotic points of behaviour; the bursts of acrimony passed swiftly, as with children. What lingered was the memory of bitterness on the deeper planes, of occasional revelations of doctrine casually and terribly expressed – of a climate of hate that had filtered through from the tormented country outside. It was not by any means universal, for the correspondent was not the Command; there was just enough to provide the mind with its first sowing of foreboding. So many of us believed, and I am sure sincerely, that in our precise persons was vested the preservation of liberty and political honour; it was a thing you marked on the map and described in the banal phrases of The Ordinary Soldier, whose one qualification as an authority was that he had his home in the circulating area of your newspaper.

Only a few seemed to take the remotest interest in the country in which we were, whose liberty was, it seemed, the theory in question.

The nights were intolerably long; the curfew prevented any sorties from the billet without the chance of a bullet in the stomach from a nervous ROK guard. Half the time the electric light disappeared altogether. In the long steaming evenings, lying sweating on the cots, endless arguments expressed our doubts and frustrations, not wholly as professional reporters but – to such straits had correspondents been driven in this barren town – as people and citizens and, as we sometimes said, democrats; at least nominal supporters of the United Nations cause.

There should not have been any doubts about it, but there were. The gesture had been made by statesmen who were doubtless working for the best, with a full sense of its huge responsibility – the implementation had been handed over to a different crowd of people altogether. Politically it had stopped at the Security Council. What were we, in fact, trying to do with Korea? No one outside GHQ Tokyo seemed to know what our immediate objective was, other than self-preservation and the building up of a defensible beach-head, let alone our long-term political aims. If indeed we had any of those they were the one part of the United Nations project in Korea that was a really close secret. If the question ever arose it was instantly buried under the ready meaningless phrases: Integrity, Containment, show the Reds we can't be pushed around. It was like arguing at school.

For all that psychological uneasiness and mental confusion it was fatally easy to blame the Americans, who were everywhere here in all their contrary aspects – their ready friendship, their generosity, their conviviality; at the same time their emptiness, their dependence on juke-box amenities for existence in a foreign land, the basic spiritual arrogance.

Yet that got one nowhere, and introduced a dangerously misleading argument into the real issue, which was that someone had moved physically into the defence of the collective principle, and the Americans claimed to be fighting – however much one deplored the cause and the means, and doubted the effect – to reaffirm a principle that an international body had held to be essential. Perhaps it should have happened before. Manchuria, Ethiopia, Spain, Czechoslovakia – there had been plenty of occasions when men of goodwill had urged this course of international action, and seen the results of holding back. Now here in Korea, surrounded by what officially was not but which most demonstrably was an East-West confrontation, we had to concede that we were committed equally with them, and however we might now resent the obstinate American attitude to China, to Formosa, we had presumably known about those attitudes when we gave our support.

Similarly we knew, I suppose, that the United Nations under MacArthur's command would inevitably tolerate abuses and condone outrageous distortions of the basic UN theme. At this point only the individual could complain – and that was where trouble lay for some of us, who considered that a man could denounce these wrongnesses of method not because he was morally *against* the United Nations, but because he was seriously and not just sentimentally *for* it.

From most points of view Korea, as a war, was bound to be bloody and revolting in a singularly intimate way. It distinguished itself by barbarities and violence on both sides of an especially corrupting kind; there was without doubt some moral virus in the Korean atmosphere that infected even men of moderation and decency with a strange irrationality that led to gross aspects of human behaviour. That was inevitable; it is axiomatic that modern war is in itself debasing, atrocity begets atrocity and beastliness breeds beastliness, and the psychic climate of Asia lays an irresistible emphasis on the unimportance of cruelty. That was particu-

larly evident in a campaign waged in and among and on top of a
large population of whom only a few were actively concerned one
way or the other; where the refugee problem tended to be solved
in the most direct and uncompromising way, and where the
physical structure of the towns and villages was most susceptible
to total destruction.

So far that is a simple pacific argument against war, any war. It
was something I was to see only too amply and bitterly reinforced
years later in a not dissimilar arena in Viet Nam, where in rather
different circumstances not very far away another set of military
technicians, having been presented with such a war to wage,
waged it in the way they considered most efficient, and to hell with
the politics of it. The fact remained, however, that the politics
did go to hell and the military method failed, too.

From the first moment it was clear that, since Korea had been
selected for this new experiment in international affairs, Korea
was doomed.

The most ironclad and mechanical army in the world, with unchallenged control of the air and the sea, completely failed to
crush a poorly-equipped multitude of peasant foot-soldiers. The
motorized army used about fifteen per cent of its manpower in the
line, which meant on the roads; the others, having little or no
maintenance or ancillary services, used ninety per cent, and in the
hills. There remained the towns and villages. The policy of 'total
interdiction' was simple: the soldiers must be preceded at all
times by air and artillery attack on a scale that assumed terrific
resistance. If a village stood in the line of advance it must be
obliterated *before* examination; the elimination of communities of
civilians was inevitable because amongst them there might be
sympathizers, if not active participants, of the other side.

That was the point: one disapproved of seeing nice old men
with bundles put down with a bullet in the head; but likewise one
disapproved of seeing nice old men reaching into their bundles
and fetching out a handful of grenades. It turned the stomach to
see commonplace little villages blasted and burned to ashes because they chanced to be in the way; it was similarly upsetting to
see a hostile mortar company advancing behind a screen of white-
clad refugees. The worst thing of all was to accept that these
emotions were equally worthless – that it was ludicrous to assume
that you were governed by some set of conventions, since by now

the thing had begun and must run its course through every possible aspect of savagery, and neither age nor youth nor sex, nor
goodwill nor repentance could save you if you got in the way of
the machine.

But when that policy failed it left not much to work on. In
those anxious short-tempered arguments in the messes and the
billets and on the roads, the problem seemed hard to face by the
thoughtful and the stupid alike. To one or two, indeed, the solution was luminously clear: we had the Bomb. Fate could not harm
us, in the end, when we had up our sleeve the infallible Einsteinian
incantation: $E = mc^2$.

It was logical, only a fool could deny that; the simplest extension of the napalm bomb. It would – militarily speaking – have
been only a little more horrifying, and almost as ineffective. And
where, accepting one, is the line to be drawn? At the line of the
most publicity, perhaps – accepting the old-fashioned flame-
thrower and the phosphorous grenade, accepting the extravagant
consequences of a brew-up in a tank caused by a hollow-charge
projectile, and flinching at the napalm jelly-bomb because it, for a
while, is new, and perhaps especially ghastly, and especially suitable for burning out mud-and-wattle villages. Or – as we argued
ceaselessly in our steaming schoolhouses, among the little desks
and the forgotten exercise-books – should we draw the line at the
field-gun? or the rifle? or the crossbow, which could also cause a
nasty hole, though it was true in only one person at a time. Or
have the lily-livered anti-Atom-Bombers to retreat to a line drawn
at the very starting-point, at war itself? In which case, why were
we here? Or, being here, how could we ever return and reconcile
our hatred of this scene with our pretentious talk about collective
action and democratic will and the immorality of aggression?

By the time we got home Taegu had changed once again. The
fighting was about five miles away by now; the sandbags were
going up at the road junctions; our schoolhouse was dismantled;
GHQ had gone. Our telegraph and phone had been cut off; even
our beds were packed away in a truck. There was nothing for us
to do but go too.

A long casualty train was about to leave for the south. Inside it
was black darkness, full of restless painful sounds, the mumbling
and suspirations of the wounded. They lay in racks; the train was

a corridor of suffering; here and there a man rolled about and swore as the morphia wore away. We sat where we could among the litters; it was too dark to write and there was nothing to eat; there did not seem anything to talk about. The troubles came in waves; when one soldier began to groan and cry out something was released all down the train; it rose around in a ripple of audible unhappiness. It was ninety miles to Pusan, and it took us ten hours.

In Pusan the hospital was just better than the train. It had four hundred beds in it and it was two hundred and fifty per cent overloaded. It was not really a hospital; it had been – of course – a school. It was a factory of plasma, of litter-beds, of makeshift wards. In the theatre the operations were going on three at a time.

Outside in a tent were the North Korean prisoners: rows of litters on the ground.

'These guys can't stop counting their luck,' said the American orderly corporal. 'They figured they were to be shot. Now they're alive, they reckon they'd like to stick around in this dump for ever. Or so our Gooks say, who can talk to them.'

A hand came out from a stretcher and plucked at his trousers. The prisoner spoke softly and excitedly, pointing to his leg; the bandage was too tight and his thigh was swollen and discoloured. The orderly at once bent and re-dressed the leg, with a deft gentleness, a kind of practised tenderness.

He said: 'See how the son of a bitch bastard gets on now.'

Back in the hospital a nurse passed with a saline bottle; she was smart and spotless and aseptic and pretty, like a nurse in a movie. That was the first woman I had seen in Korea. Apart from Koreans, of course.

Our camp was half a dozen miles out, beside the sea, a sort of tented overflow or appendage of Eighth Army Rear; it was like living in the annexe of a crowded hotel, full of offices and canteens and communications rooms crowded with restless chattering instruments. Far pleasanter was our canvas compound by the beach. Over the weeks it had accumulated a certain comfort and permanence, with wooden floorboards and cots with mosquito nets, and a tap not far away at which the crowds of Korean boys who attached themselves to all such communities could queue to fill our helmets with washing-water.

In Pusan there was nothing to be done about the war. The news
was in the north. Some conscientious correspondents flew off at
daybreak to the fronts, returning at midnight, swaying with
exhaustion, to file their paragraphs. The cot beside me was used
by such a man, a gentle little French writer; he faded almost visibly
away, and the more drawn and fatigued his countenance the more
vivacious and jaunty his demeanour. He carried a huge Colt revolver, the chambers of which he had purposely filled up with
clay, so that it could not fire.

'Ainsi,' he said, 'je vais de pair avec mes collegues du meilleur
monde. Cependant, je ne veux de mal à personne.'

There was one amenity: beer could occasionally be bought at
the PX. We would keep the cans in a bin with blocks of ice – we
had made friends with the sergeant embalmer at base; he would
arrive at sundown with a truckful from the morgue.

'Very quiet up at the business today, gentlemen,' he would say.
'We got more ice than we need. Now if you'd been asking me for
a favour last week I'd have had to say no. But I'll look after you
boys – just so my customers don't suffer, you understand.'

Most days we travelled into Pusan to consult our various
oracles, to renew contacts, or simply to pass the time. Pusan was
by now the administrative capital, indeed the only South Korean
town with any organized daily life. It was wholly devoid of glamour, it had not even the minimum pretensions to architectural
design, and there was little to do once you got there. The bazaar
went on for miles, rickety and dull – somehow it was the Edge-
ware Road of Korea; windows full of hair-oil and old magazines,
bits of machinery; all the third-rate spurious stuff piling up like
rubbish at a breakwater.

Then one day we were on our way through the station compound at Pusan when we came on the sight that more than anything else in that unlovely country made us realize that the
corrupting hand of Korea had reached out for us at last.

This terrible crowd of men was worse than anything I had so far
seen. I had come up against such groups and herds of prisoners
before, of a condition and appearance that would have been
startling anywhere but in the East; this was the first time that a
lull in active work had given me a chance to enquire, and examine,
and photograph.

This grisly mob of men projected the war in special terms of human abasement. There were about seven hundred of them, and they were political prisoners of the South Korean Government – they were not prisoners of war; their uniform was a filthy and indescribably ragged kimono. After so many weeks in which there had been so many distressing and troubling things to be seen this might have made little impression on me if the condition of these men had not been quite sensationally appalling. They were skeletons – they were puppets of skin with sinews for strings – their faces were a terrible, translucent grey, and they cringed like dogs. They were manacled with chains or bound to each other with ropes. They were compelled to crouch in the classic Oriental attitude of subjection, the squatting, foetal position, in heaps of garbage. Sometimes they moved enough to scoop a handful of water to drink from the black puddles around them. Any deviation from their attitude brought a gun butt on their skulls. Finally they were herded, the lowest common denominator of human degradation, into trucks, with the numb air of men going to their deaths. I was assured, by a willing attendant anxious to make a good impression, that most of them were. Sometimes, to save inconvenience, they were shot where they were.

It is hard to convey the despairing impression this made upon me. These prisoners were of course not convicts, nor prisoners of war; they were political hostages of the South Korean administration for whose integrity the United States and Britain and the United Nations were at that moment fighting. They were not North Koreans, but South Koreans in South Korea, whose crime – or alleged crime, since few of them had been accorded the formality of a trial – was that they had been named as opponents of the Synghman Rhee regime, the one-man oligarchy called with Asian irony the Liberal Party. They had, for a variety of reasons and by a variety of people, been denounced or accused, not necessarily convicted by any process, of being unreliable, 'potentially Communist'. Many of them had been in captivity long before the war broke out at all. Their treatment had been manifestly barbaric; this was self-evident even if I had not had the complacent assurances of their guards that such had very properly been the case.

The spectacle was utterly medieval. Around this gruesome market-place gathered a few knots of American soldiers, photographing the scene with casual industry. A matter of yards away stood the US headquarters; the officers wandered curiously around. Five minutes away stood the sequestered villa that housed the United Nations Commission in Korea. This had been going on for months. Nobody had said a word.

Of all the melancholy considerations of the Korean war this, to me, was the most dispiriting. I took my indignation and protests to the Commission, who received me in a very civil fashion, and said in effect: 'Yes, it is all very disturbing; nevertheless you must remember that these are Asiatic people and congenitally different; their standards of behaviour are different from ours. Clearly it is most undesirable, but the situation is especially difficult . . .' It was an attitude of supine and indefensible compromise. Further than that they made it clear: however technically this was a war of the UN, in practice I must appreciate that it was a United States Army affair, which meant the US Supreme Command, which meant General MacArthur, and he was in Tokyo.

No one, I said, could deny that, yet nevertheless in all the pious announcements, in all the international attitudes, and likewise in the minds of men, this was a United Nations show if it was anything, and if the bell tolled in Pusan, it tolled for us.

To try and make such points was, in such an atmosphere, to ask for misunderstanding. I attempted to explain that it was because I considered the United Nations principle important that its cause could best be served by exposing intolerable abuses. I considered that if circumstances compelled the United Nations to support a regime that was discredited and disgraceful then our function was not to condone that Government's excesses, however tacitly, but to see that they did not continue, now, under the UN flag.

It made no difference, of course. The South Korean police methods continued to be the gossip of the rear-echelon HQs – the beatings-up, the crucifixions, the attachment of genitals to the terminals of field-telephones. And long after, when the tide had turned and the offensive begun, even *The Times* newspaper was recording: 'All the complaints against the People's Government of North Korea could be levelled against the democratically elected South Korean Government. Acts of persecution and reprisal have been committed under both. The only difference is that at present men and women accused of being Communist or of collaborating with the People's Government are being killed or imprisoned under the United Nations flag . . . In South Korea the defence of the local brand of democracy has been no less vicious than have the atrocities committed in the cause of Communism.'

It seemed to me that there was something so tremendously wrong there that it went immeasurably deeper than the defections or inadequacies of local Provost-Marshals, or the see-no-evil complacency of professional United Nations officials on the spot. I tried very hard not to be emotional or unrealistic about it; it was no secret that wars in general are bloody and disgusting; that it would be naïve to expect a dirty business like battle to be successful through lofty philosophical methods alone. But, if completely blackjack methods were to be used by the UN forces, remote from any military emergency, openly and indeed proudly; then, leaving the moral issue quite aside, I felt it was a form of psychological idiocy that ill became a war ostensibly undertaken in the name of a collective international principle; for however bogus that may have been, that was its argument.

But by now there was no time left for pompous reflections. The words had gone round about the Excursion. The gear was piling up, the ships were standing by. Then suddenly we were off; Pusan and prisoners and futile argument were behind; Inchon lay ahead; we thought progressively less about generalities. It was to rebound with some impact on my own life later, but not yet.

Chapter Eight

THEY told us we should be going in for the landing at seventeen-thirty.

We lay in a channel between long flat bands of grey silt that were slowly being engulfed by the tide; very soon the tide would be full and then we could go in. If we failed to go in then we should not go in at all; if some of us got ashore and the others did not we could be neither reinforced nor rescued. The coast lay ahead with the sun still on it: low hills, and the roofs of the town, a drift of smoke; enemy country. Over to the left was Wolmi-do, a little island linked to Inchon by half a mile of causeway; the Marines had taken it already and it burned sulkily.

In the wardroom they were serving coffee and cakes, of all things to start an invasion on; the stomach contracted at the thought, but we drank the coffee because there was nothing else to do. We had learned the drill, or hoped we had; the Marine had said: 'When you gentlemen hit the beach you better run diagon-ally for one-fifty yards and then get your goddam heads down behind a tussock, and wait till somebody does something.'

'Till who does what?'

'Till anybody does anything, for Christ sake. What am I, a fortune-teller?'

'Roger.'

We had checked our gear and put two sets of laces in our boots and tested our lifejackets; there was no conceivable thing to do until we had to get over the side down the scaling nets and into the boat. Where was the boat? We were not to fuss about that; it would be there. For the thirtieth time we went up and peered over the rail at the crowded walls of the fleet. It was an extra-ordinary sight: the ships lay now assembled offshore along the channel more densely than ever before; Inchon had surely never seen any such concentration of vessels, of all types and of all sizes, for all purposes, swinging round to the incoming tide as though for some strange review, with the sun sinking gently and beautifully on our port bow, and the enemy shore ahead.

Then the challenge, when it came, was really too loud, the effect too abrupt; it was not reasonable to fight a war so noisily. We had waited too long – however you anticipate the stage revolver shot it always makes you wince; so I suppose invasions are always more startling and uproarious than you expect. The guns began erratically: a few heavy thuds from the cruisers, an occasional bark of five-inch fire, a tuning-up among the harsh orchestra. At what point the laying of the guns merged into the final and awful barrage I do not know; so many things began to take place, a scattered pattern of related happenings gradually coalescing and building up for the blow.

All around among the fleet the landing-craft multiplied imperceptibly, took to the water from one could not see exactly where, because the light was failing now – circled and wheeled and marked time and milled about, filling the air with engines. There seemed to be no special hurry. We could not go in until the tide was right; meanwhile we lay offshore in a strange, insolent, businesslike serenity, under whatever guns the North Koreans had, building up the force item by item, squaring the sledge-hammer. The big ships swung gently in the tideway, from time to time coughing heaving gusts of iron towards the town. It began to burn, quite gently at first. What seemed to be a tank or a self-propelled gun sent back some quick resentful fire, but it soon stopped. Later we found that one ship had thrown a hundred and sixty-five rounds of five-inch ammunition at the one gun: the economics of plenty.

Then we saw the floating tanks, and the Amptracks, the grotesque sea-going masses of amphibious ironmongery; they crawled out of the hull of the mother-ship; she spawned them out in growling droves, a grotesque mechanical parturition. They were surrealistic and terrifying – ludicrous and dreadful at once; like a flock of rattling tortoises they lurched out of the womb of the ship and began to crawl over the surface of the water, their treads spinning, with the heads of their little men growing from their carapaces.

As the light faded the noise rose in key, soared in volume; the intervals shortened between the explosions; from over to the south the aircraft came in – steady formations, everything very neat: the approach, the dive; the plane pulled out of the dive but the rockets continued. The din was hypnotic, something out of a laboratory.

It was time to get into our landing-craft – and even dread of shellfire made it no easier, scuffling and dangling down the vertical net in the rising sea, awkward and fumbling among the rolls of lifejacket, the helmet swinging and bumping on the nose; the final uncertain drop into a crowded heaving steel box full of edged things. When the diesels shouted and ground, and we were leaping over the waves towards the shore, the concussion of shells and bombs was no longer a noise but a fierce sensation, a thudding jar on the atmosphere, on the hull of the boat, on the body itself.

The waterfront of Inchon began to disappear behind a red-shot screen of smoke; it seemed somehow to vibrate. Staring at it, as every minute a new volcano of smoke and scarlet gushed upwards, one felt that it *must* be too much, that by now life must have ceased to exist there – and yet it hadn't; in that shuddering blazing place people were somehow sheltering, surviving, hiding, and waiting – for silence, for respite, and for us.

Staring at it, too, we did not notice the long low ships under whose lee we were passing, until they – the Rocket Ships – let go, and then we knew that everything else had been endurable, and possible, but that this was too much. This was the most appalling uproar of all – the rocket-squadron burst at our ears into extravagant pyrotechnics, with a new and ghastly sound, the sound of a tremendous escape of gas, the roar of a subway, a demoniac thing that sent its groups of projectiles arc-ing into the beaches, grinding a solid groove of noise through the air, and when one prayed for it to stop just for a moment it howled out again.

At last, as the hundreds of troops began to surge towards Inchon, row after row of craft in line abreast, like a cavalry formation, with what seemed to be powerful express trains roaring overhead, there came the stage when individual sounds ceased and the thuds and crashes united in a continuous roll of intolerable drums. The town, and what remained of its quarter-million inhabitants, was gaudy with flame, and with more explosions leaping out of the flames – one more inconsiderable little city,

one more trifling habitation involved by its betters in the disastrous process of liberation.

Now the twilight was alive with landing-craft, tank landers,
marshal craft, swimming tanks, things full of guns and bulldozers
and Marines – US Marines and ROK Marines, and X Army
Corps – forty thousand men in Operation Inchon, twenty-five
hundred to be put ashore with the tide. Tall boats and squat boats
and bad-dream amphibious inventions – and in the middle of it
all, if such a thing be faintly conceivable, a wandering boat
marked in great letters: 'PRESS', full of agitated and contending
correspondents, all of us trying to give an impression of determination to land in Wave One, while seeking desperately to
contrive some reputable method of being found in Wave Fifty.

We headed into a heavy bank of smoke, and there we were.

No beach, no diagonal run, no tussocks – just a sea wall. By
some extravagant miscalculation our Press boat reached it just
ahead of the Marine assault-party; they were there remorselessly
behind us, making retreat quite out of the question. The wall was
a sixty-degree incline of masonry, rising seven or eight feet up
above highwater mark, with a concrete parapet. My feet were
numb; I lost my grip on the slippery wall and slid down to my
waist in the sea – for a moment there was much more terror from
the roaring LCIs that were slamming into the wall than from anything on the other side. I scrambled ingloriously up the stones
and over the parapet and instantly fell flat on my face into a North
Korean defence trench, most happily empty of North Koreans.

There seemed to be a field ahead, and a tidal basin, and beyond
that the town still surging with smoke and jarring to the bombs;
a place – it must have been – of stark despair. We were ashore.
The fact that in our flurry we had reached an unscheduled area,
that we had in fact hit entirely the wrong beach, were considerations that moved us only when we were made aware of them some
time later.

That was the landing. There were many mysteries about it, the
greatest of which was that we had been allowed to do it at all. We
would know more later. Then, and for some time, there was no
debate about our survival, and the rest of the evening surged past
in a confusion of thankfulness, doubt, speculation, pity, and
relief.

Later, in the real darkness, I was being ferried back to the fleet; I was among the big ships again; I was groping and sprawling over a swaying staircase up the side of the command-ship, and my helmet lost at last over the rail.

It was the USS *Mount McKinley*. It was the *McKinley*, and I knew her. Once upon a time I had been in her company before – four years back in another sea and another age: outside the Pacific atoll called Bikini, and inside that coral circus had been an Atom Bomb. I had seen the Atom Bomb, and *Mount McKinley* had seen it, and now we had seen Inchon, and somewhere – in the racket of that night, in the fatigue and emptiness and emotion and endlessness of everything – there seemed to be the edge of a wheel that had come full circle.

When I realized that I was in *Mount McKinley* I had remembered that I was in the wrong ship, since I had come in *Seminole*, and that all my luggage was aboard her, and there was no way of knowing where she was or of getting there if I did. I never saw the *Seminole* again.

That day, then, the biggest landing force ever assembled since the last war – bigger than North Africa, bigger than the biggest amphibious force of the Pacific war – was at Inchon. There were two hundred and sixty-two ships – a hundred and ninety-four American, twelve British, three Canadian, two Australian, two New Zealand, one French and one Dutch; thirty-two were US ships leased to Japan, and fifteen were South Korean.

Why the North Koreans did not resist more effectively we did not know, unless the obvious reason were true: they had too few troops there and could not disengage forces quickly enough from the south. That they did not mine the channel, that they did not scrape together even a squadron of planes, however decrepit, to sprinkle bombs on that crowded roadstead, that they did not send fireboats or saboteurs down that dense lane of shipping on the rushing ebb – that in fact they behaved with a helplessness and irresolution they had never shown before: those were matters that no one at the time could explain.

But that was the landing, the hammer-blow to the heart, the opening of the gate to Seoul. The rest was to come at next day's light – the consolidation, the flattening of ruins, concealment of corpses, tending of wounds, the sifting of friends from enemies, the quick from the dead, the simple from the suspects.

We went in again at dawn; it was like motoring through a regatta, and the silence was like a blanket of lead.

Up the road from Red Beach the bulldozers had swept a swathe through the debris, the collapsed walls; here and there some fires still burned. Cables and power-lines drooped all over the ruins.

There was quite a lot of Inchon still standing; one wondered how. There were quite a number of citizens still alive. They came stumbling from the ruins – some of them sound, some of them smashed, numbers of them quite clearly driven into a sort of numbed dementia by the night of destruction. They ran about, capering crazily or shambling blankly, with a repeated automatic gesture of surrender. Some of them called out as we passed them their one English phrase, as a kind of password: 'Sank you!' 'Sank you!'; and the irony of that transcended the grotesque into the macabre.

The pacification and securing of the town was the task of the South Korean militia; this they undertook with violent and furious zeal.

The lines of bemused people were driven from place to place; old men and ancient crones, baby toddlers were lined against the remaining walls and threatened with the butts of guns; every now and again a ROK patrol would see a straggler groping helplessly down the street and cut him down with a quick volley. We passed the open door of what must the previous day have been a small laundry; ten minutes later we re-passed, and three bodies lay sprawled in the corner, two men and an old woman.

Outside the town there was still some desultory fighting. Here and there prisoners waited crouched on the ground with their hands round their necks; they were naked. The dead were arranged by the roadside, the wounded lay in groups beside them, and American medical corpsmen were moving methodically among them. One of them moaned quietly, like a dog; he was a collander of bullet holes; once again a Korean mutilated to a degree that would have meant death to a European – yet continued to live. The doctor came over to give him morphia; he crushed the needle of the omnopon capsule three or four times against the Korean's arm without making a puncture.

'It sure is the damnedest thing,' he said. 'The Gook has genuinely got a thicker skin than any other guy, in a strictly physical sense.'

The soldier suddenly sat up briskly and began to explain something rapidly to the doctor. He spoke urgently, shaking his head. 'Let's have the interpreter,' said the doctor, but the Korean attempted one gesture too many with his shattered arm, and died in mid-sentence.

I got a lift back to Red Beach in an Amptrack; it was like riding in some gigantic clockwork toy. Down through the town; the queues of civilians still stood against the walls, and in one corner a ROK sentry stood guard over a dozen little children, they were four and five years old, their hands above their heads, gaping in bewilderment.

The Beach had indeed been a beach once – a day ago? – and now it was a churned-up, tormented quagmire, a lunar landscape of mud ground into pits and gullies by the tracks of the machines. From far away to the east there was a little rifle fire, and occasionally an aircraft whined low overhead, above the smoke and the dying fires. Inchon itself was silent. By and by an LCI came splashing into the shore and slipped its ramp down in the mud.

The seaman in charge said: 'Where to, Mac?' and we looked out at the concourse of ships a mile or two away, standing by the silhouette of a castellated city. We didn't know. Any one of them would do. I remember *Mount McKinley* was officially the communications ship, but I had nothing to communicate. Nothing that could be said in three hundred words of efficient cablese, that would tell anything or explain anything. I remembered that the wardroom there was warm, with chairs to sleep on and copies of *Time* and *Colliers* and *Life* and the *Saturday Evening Post*, all the sources of solid certainty and conviction, the firm omniscient dogma unclouded by moral doubt or fear.

'To the *Mount McKinley*, please.'

'Roger.'

It was like taking a taxi, taking a launch from Southend – that, with two hundred and sixty-two ships of eight nations ahead, and the broken smouldering town behind, the old men clapping and the little boys with their hands up.

Chapter Nine

THE day the United Nations forces crossed the Parallel I was not there; I was not in Korea but on my way home, in India. I went to the bungalow of the Prime Minister, Jawaharlal Nehru, who had been kind and hospitable to me before. It seemed necessary to hear something that might possibly disinfect the mind for a while from cant; every desperate thing that had been going on had gone on in the name of this or that conception of honour and justice; sometimes the dismal deeds had been less hard to bear than the pious talk surrounding them.

They had always said that Jawaharlal Nehru could take the curse off moral platitudes by the curious method of believing in them. For that reason, obviously, he was called Red by the reactionaries and Reactionary by the reds: a commonplace situation for men of goodwill, nevertheless remarkable for a Prime Minister of four hundred million people. The indecisions and inconsistencies that were to shadow his later years were still remote; he was in command of body and mind, and I had many times been grateful for his kindness to me.

He came out to the verandah – looking older and more fatigued, as well he might; life could never be simple for a politician who self-consciously assumed to himself all the paradoxes that threatened Asia. Because his attitude towards Korea was that of settling by negotiation, of treating with China, of limiting the destruction, he was attacked by the Americans as misled, unscrupulous, and dangerous. Because he opposed Communism in India as tenaciously as he had opposed Imperialism, the Russians assailed him as a fellow-traveller of the Right. To many less articulate people he suggested a point of view that might be sentimental, even unrealistic, but which at least made ethical sense. Coming home as I was from Korea, with the smell of Inchon still sour in the senses, still slightly punchdrunk from the crossfire of vilification from East and West, it seemed a refreshment to meet again a man so equally poised between the world's respect and abuse.

'Every action has its reaction. It's the old natural law, nothing extraordinary about it: a good action will result in good and a bad one in bad – maybe not immediately, but some time. When you enter the realm of warfare and the military mind there's always the impulse to go to the last limit, and possibly betray the object you're fighting the war for. Wars are fought to gain a certain objective – war itself isn't the objective; victory isn't the objective; you fight to remove the obstruction that comes in the way of your objective. If you let victory become an end in itself then you've gone astray and forgotten what you were originally fighting about . . .

'It's *always* wrong to assume you can succeed by pursuing military means to the utmost and the last. Every major war there's ever been has shown that – the last one created plenty of problems just for that reason.'

Nehru lit another cigarette, stared over his trim and watered lawns. 'One can never say what circumstances may bring about. One tries to heal the cleavage but – by taking sides one might precipitate the thing one wants to avoid.'

The conflict within Nehru was more than that of all the millions of liberal men everywhere who found themselves in a dilemma for which they felt partly responsible and from which they saw no immediate escape. Nehru was too many men within himself; it is my belief that he had inherited from Harrow and Cambridge too many petrified aspects of old-world non-conformism that could never really survive the pragmatic exigencies of revolution. Nevertheless, I greatly loved him.

'In India, now – we have spent our lives trying very imperfectly to follow the spirit of a great leader. He talked of non-violence, and here we are now in charge of Government, and Government keeps Armies and Navies and Air Forces and indulges in violence pretty often. What do we do about it?

'One thing is absolutely clear: no argument is going to work in Asia if it goes counter to the nationalist spirit, Communism or no Communism. I'm not talking for it or against it; I'm just saying that's how it is . . .

'I am Prime Minister of India and I haven't the faintest notion

what India or Asia will be like in twenty years. I know what I
want it to be . . . If in the modern world wars have to be fought
(and it seems they do) then they must be stopped at the first
possible moment, otherwise they corrupt us, they create new
problems, and make our future even more uncertain. That's more
than morality; it's sense.'

By contemporary standards, as one found them in Tokyo and
Taegu and the Imperial Hotel in New Delhi, that was heresy, if
not sedition. On that verandah, by the lily-ponds, it sounded
remote and sad. It was little enough, and generalities are generalities. It just reminded one momentarily that somewhere between
the excesses and threats that hemmed us round there was a point
of view that put a higher value on principle than expediency; one
had almost forgotten there was such a thing.

That night I took off from Palam and headed west, back to the
consoling frivolities of Europe. For a while the core of history
lingered under the starboard wing, then it slipped away.

Once more I returned to trouble. The article I had written about
the excesses of the Synghman Rhee regime in South Korea had
preceded me home. It had been written with the best restraint
and care of which I was capable; I had done my best to drain it of
emotion, and it was documented in detail. Since even the most
arid words can be pejorative in such situations, I had made sure
that they were substantiated by a considerable file of photographs. There could, I believed, be no disputing that this was an
objective record of an intolerable condition, the exposure of
which could not possibly be opposed by anyone of goodwill,
least of all by a journal of the liberal and humane pretensions of
Picture Post.

It appeared, too, that my editor Tom Hopkinson was in
accord; we talked the matter over many times and with measure-
ment and care, we considered the material in all its aspects. This
took some time; it could not be said that we rushed immoderately
into publication, and meanwhile we were both doing all we could
to interest appropriate and influential people in the matter to the
end that we might not have to publish at all. We sent the whole
dossier to Kenneth Younger, who was then leading the British
UN delegation at Lake Success; nothing happened. Finally we
agreed on a layout which in the circumstances was the most tactful

and unsensational possible. We used only those pictures of the desolate and wretched prisoners that would establish their dire condition without unnecessary shock; my article was written and re-written over and again until it became almost bleak in its austerity. It said, after all, little more than had already been published in both *The Times* newspaper and the *Daily Telegraph*. The completed feature was titled, simply: 'An Appeal to the United Nations'. It argued that if there were a just cause for making war in Korea, then it were better not to corrupt that just cause; that if the Communist radio from Pyongyang and Moscow denounced us daily for atrocious political behaviour in the South our best answer would be that they were lying, whereas the existing state of affairs manifestly proved that they were not. It all amounted to a vigorous plea that if our indomitable South Korean ally, Dr Synghman Rhee, saw fit to sustain his regime with methods of totalitarian oppression and cruelty, it should not be done under the imprimatur of the United Nations flag. All things considered, it was a journalistic essay of elaborate moderation.[1]

What then ensued became another Fleet Street scandal of a depressing and for me almost ruinous kind. It is probably hardly necessary to recall its melancholy development which, formally based on a conflict of serious principle, was in reality governed by considerations of personal purpose very far removed from the jails of Pusan.

The edition containing the United Nations appeal had been plated and had got as far as the rotogravure presses in Watford when – inexplicably suddenly, it appeared – the proprietor of the magazine, Mr Edward Hulton, was informed of or became somehow aware of the nature of the feature, which in the ordinary processes of publication had already passed through his hands some time before, and demanded its immediate removal.

The motivation of this melodrama was never made exactly

---

[1] Most appearances to the contrary, I did not live my life wholly on hindsight. However, ten years were to pass before that offensive and dangerous little despot had the rug pulled from under *him*, when finally his own people rebelled against the clamant crookery of his rigged elections and the tyranny of his administration. For a while they were lavishly shot down by the firearms supplied to him by the U.S. for the defence of freedom, but the Americans were at last reluctantly aroused to the embarrassment of their 86-year-old problem child, now revealed as a senile delinquent. He died in the end in exile, never having – naturally – rescinded his declaration that I was Undesirable, which was probably the only mutual sentiment we ever shared.

clear. Whoever had drawn Mr Hulton's attention to the fact that his magazine was about to publish an appeal to the United Nations, and indeed an implicit criticism of the Americans for their endorsement of an arrogant tyranny, had done it with such timing that his intervention was certain to achieve the maximum publicity. It is not the simplest of matters to remove a magazine spread from the presses at that advanced printing stage; however, it was done, but not before somebody had secured a proof and had been able to pass the copy on to the *Daily Worker*, who naturally led the paper with it. Thus was achieved the precise negation of my purpose.

Within a couple of days the affair had blown up into an occasion of serious professional importance. When the furious row with the management paused for breath, Tom Hopkinson had been fired and I had resigned. What manner of disagreement and rancour had been building up in the past between Tom Hopkinson and the proprietor I did not know nor seek to know, but Edward Hulton's announcement was unprecedented in its brusqueness and rejection of the usual euphemisms. Tom Hopkinson, it said, 'had been instructed to relinquish the position of editor of *Picture Post*, following a dispute over the handling of material about the Korean war and other matters'.

That morning Tom called a staff meeting and made his own announcement. It was one of the oddest gatherings I had ever attended. It lasted the entire day. The entire personnel of the magazine, about twenty of us, from the editor down, were seething with anger and an almost incredulous resentment. At one point a deputation of us insisted on confronting the proprietor personally; we found him in a condition of high emotion and unable to make any sort of persuasive case for his behaviour. My note of resignation had gone in; virtually every member of the staff who had anything articulate to say announced his or her intention of following me. The argument was still going on into well into the evening.

By now Fleet Street had its teeth well into the story. That week *Public Opinion*, which was controlled by *Daily Mirror* interests, commented: 'Mr Hopkinson was about to publish the evidence when he was interrupted in a public duty by his dismissal by his proprietor, Mr Edward Hulton. The despatches from Korea which *Picture Post* had published up to now have been distinguished by two things, their obvious integrity and their technical brilliance. That this valuable combination should be snuffed out by a peremptory managerial decision is more than a matter for regret; it is a denial of a genuine but highly inconvenient comment on a situation that involves several thousand British troops and at least ten million British taxpayers. Mr Hopkinson's dismissal may solve for the moment a highly awkward editorial situation, and although the usual diaphanous expressions of tepid friendship have been exchanged between the executioner and the decapitated, the issue at stake remains unaltered. Many years ago the men of goodwill could not be so summarily deprived of their posts as public commentators at the whim of irresponsible persons who employed them, and who had profited by their talents and their integrity. That these things should occur now is a surly comment on our society.'

The West London branch of the National Union of Journalists passed a resolution 'pointing to the dismissal of Tom Hopkinson from the editorship of *Picture Post* as yet another example of the fact that the only real freedom existing in the British Press today is the freedom of proprietors to suppress news and views as they please.'

The *New Statesman* said: 'During the last ten years Mr Edward Hulton has won the reputation of an enlightened press proprietor who realized that the contents and integrity of his papers were important as well as their circulation. His most conspicuous success has been *Picture Post*, which proved under Mr Hopkinson's editorship that a popular and financially successful weekly could avoid the stereotypes of propaganda and handle awkward subjects in an honest and objective spirit. The occasion of Mr Hopkinson's dismissal was significant. The disagreement between editor and proprietor arose over an article by Mr James Cameron describing, as *The Times* correspondent and others had already done, atrocities committed in South Korea, and urging the United Nations to end this disgrace. The result was not, as Mr Hulton seems to have hoped, to withhold this unsavoury information from the public. Indeed the *Daily Worker* printed much of the information – the truth of which is not denied. The *Daily Mirror* made sure that it received the widest publicity. Mr Hulton's action provides unanswerable propaganda for the Communists.'

It can be imagined that for my part I could well have done without this sort of professional sensation at that time. Less than a year had passed since my rather spectacular row with Lord Beaverbrook. I had been badly shaken by that, and craved a little tranquil obscurity in which to get on with my work; the last thing I wanted at that moment was to be pitched into another controversial situation. I felt extremely bitter with the *Picture Post* organization, where only a brief time before I had felt so relaxed and confident of its mature and reasonable direction. The Beaverbrook fracas had been, it is true, of my choosing, but this new unpleasantness was most certainly not. However, one or two more of these journalistic crises would make me virtually unemployable, it seemed to me; one could hardly blame the publishing organizations for concluding that I was either quixotic to the point of being a permanent liability, or merely slightly out of my mind.

As the days went on the high-minded and resolute indignation of the *Picture Post* staff began, naturally enough, to wane, and the united front of the first meeting to disintegrate into doubts and second thoughts. Ted Castle, who had been Tom's assistant, accepted the editorship, which confirmed in many people's uneasy minds the feeling that a general walk-out now would be both irresponsible and slightly ridiculous. Many of them did indeed maintain a considerable loyalty to Tom, and to a lesser degree to me. Tom had already gone, doubtless by now to his own great relief. I was still lurking on in a sort of undefined limbo; another staff meeting decided to tell the management to ask me to remain, and this they did. I extracted from the board another announcement to the effect that their killing of the Korean article in no way reflected on my own judgment or motives, and that the facts were not now held in question. So for a little while longer I, too, remained for a while on *Picture Post*; it would have been a little less inglorious if I had done otherwise.

I did not wait to see the magazine out, however. This debacle was the punctuation-mark of its honourable career; from that day on it was doomed. Its proprietor issued yet another statement around which already clung the scent of defeat: 'There is no intention to change the tradition of *Picture Post*,' he said, 'whereby the staff have full freedom to develop their creative abilities and rely on their own judgment. It is my intention to maintain the political independence of *Picture Post* . . .' In fact *Picture Post* soon painlessly surrendered all the values and purposes that had made it a journal of consideration, before the eyes of its diminishing public it drifted into the market of arch cheesecake and commonplace decoration, and by and by it died, as by then it deserved to do.

Diversion 2: The Wizard

IT chanced that the first story I ever sent to the *News Chronicle*, shortly after I had become one of its briefly happy band, was from the Kingdom of Laos, Land of the Ten Thousand Elephants, the inconsiderable part of South-East Asia that was then, as now, part of someone else's war.

It came to pass, then, that I found myself in a place called Luang Prabang, the Royal capital, and for those not familiar with Luang Prabang it can be placed only by saying that Siam was behind, Burma over one shoulder and Viet Nam the other, and China straight ahead. It was uncommonly lovely. I had come in some time before with an airlift of the French Foreign Legion, to which I had improbably and almost accidentally been attached. At times I have been temporarily and lovelessly engaged with all manner of forces by land and sea; I recall this unit of the Legion as by far the most unattractive of all. It was composed almost wholly of Germans, generally rather tipsy, and given to singing *Tipperary, Wir Fahren Gegen England,* and *Aupres de ma Blonde*. I suspected them to be for the most part defecting war criminals. In their care was the preservation of the French Colonial Empire, already much frayed around the edges.

It was an unfortunate moment to arrive, everyone said, since Luang Prabang was now believed to be surrounded on all sides by the Communist armies of the Viet Minh, who were – though this I happily did not appreciate – then rehearsing for the final siege of Dien Bien Phu. I mention this only to hint that my encounters with history have not always been as irrelevant and dotty as may appear.

At all events there we were, on the banks of the great, slow, tepid, cocoa-coloured Mekong River, which carries the silt of South-East Asia from the heights of Yunnan two thousand miles to the China Sea, oiling past the drowsing buffaloes, snaking through the mountains. In those mountains, some ten miles away, were 300,000 invisible and by all accounts indomitable Viet Minh, drawing a little closer all the time. There was not much to be done about it. It was, for one thing, ferociously hot.

A picture of Luang Prabang at this crisis in its destiny would have shown a township overcome with an unconquerable drowsiness, relaxed in changeless siesta all day long. Here and there a few eight-year-old monks played desultory games on the pagoda steps; now and again a bemused Legionnary would reel back to his tent muttering quiet blasphemy; from time to time a turtle would rise lethargically to the surface of the river, sigh, and subside. For the rest, everyone slept. Meanwhile the Viets pressed on.

The reason for this tranquil acceptance of the situation was surprisingly simple: the good people of Luang Prabang were completely confident in their security. Not, you may be sure, because the French had told them so, since the French had told them very much otherwise. The fact was that the Wizard had told them so, and everyone believed him. This Wizard was the head necromancer on the staff of the monarch of Laos, King Sisavong Vong, and he had been in the business a long time. He was very old, and blind, but he was recognized as an outstanding local prophet whose forecasts were invariably reliable. Daily he cast the hen's entrails, announcing with passive confidence that the invading Viet Minh would come to within exactly eleven kilometres of the town; they would then stop, and would then withdraw. This was in every sense good enough for Luang Prabang, which thenceforth put the war out of its mind. Morale was high, and when Laotian morale is high it relaxes into torpor.

Daily the Wizard studied form, examined the omens and read the stars, and always the answer came up the same: the Communists would approach to eleven kilometres and no more. Far away in Hanoi the French Command shifted impatiently, but its forces in Luang Prabang only rolled over on the other side, having greater confidence, and perhaps with reason, in the Wizard than in General Navarre.

By and by the air reconnaissance helplessly observed the advanced Viet Minh positions in the hills some eleven kilometres from the garrison. For a while they remained there, doing something inscrutable, then they withdrew. In fact they vanished. The siege was over.

This of course confirmed the Wizard in the top flight of sooth-sayers; he gained more face than ever before; and when he ended his days shortly thereafter, old and full of years, there was a smile of crafty wisdom on his ancient blind countenance.

It was some time before we discovered what in fact the Viet Minh had been up to all the time. They had been harvesting the opium crop. Laos was one of the great opium-producing states of South-East Asia, and the crop that was worth 500 piastres a kilo-gram in Luang Prabang would fetch 2,000 piastres in Hanoi, 3,000 in Haiphong, and more than its weight in gold in Hong Kong. So while our embattled township dozed the war away the Viet Minh had been busy with the harvest. They cropped 70 million piastres worth of opium – about £1½ million pounds worth – and when they were finished they retired, and sold it to the Chinese in exchange for the guns with which, some time later, and in deadly earnest, they destroyed Dien Bien Phu.

The Wizard, of course, his artful old ashes now at rest, had been on a certainty all the time, since, as a leading agent of the Com-munist organization of many years standing, his information was infallible, because he had prudently reinforced his hen's entrails with reliable short-wave radio communication with the Com-munist General Giap.

Anyhow, as General Navarre said when the tricolour came down in the end, the Wizards are always on the side of the big battalions.

Chapter Ten

SOMEWHERE over the coastal rain-forest the ordinary world ran out, left behind in the endless green tangle of French Equatorial Africa. For hours it had been diminishing in reality, losing itself in a random natural confusion: too much growth, too much water, too much sun. What remained when the aeroplane had drummed away among the thunderheads was the bank of the Ogowe river, deep in mangrove and palm – a few huts, a ferry, and beyond that, it seemed, nothing.

That was Lambaréné. Somewhere up that cocoa-coloured waterway was the Hospital. I stood on the slip and laid down my bag in the ochre dust, and watched the river slide heavily by. Even from Lambaréné it was a long haul up that broad avenue of river crawling into the Gabon to where the Doctor lived, fulfilling his insistence on remoteness, self-containment, his resistance to progress. There had been some word of a canoe. The driver who had brought me to the embarcadère climbed sweating back into his truck; his black hands made a languid friendly gesture. 'Attends, pagayeur va venir.' He backed away up the track leaving me standing, a forlorn wilted character in crumbled linen trousers and unsuitable shoes.

The day had started hours before in Brazzaville; a grey warm dawn and the lowering unmerited sense of hangover brought by all equatorial mornings; a plane that rocked and bucketed erratic-ally here and there, zigzagging over the weekly run that had to serve so many settlements. Half a dozen planters disposed them-selves sombrely into seats screwed haphazard in the cabin; there was a colonial official with an improbable Assyrian beard and a sense of grievance; somewhere among the previous night's fare-wells he had lost his briefcase. There was a pale priest in a stained topi who muttered soundlessly and told his rosary with energy, as

well he might, as we lurched into the heavy air. The rest of the
plane was filled with boxes and crates and awkward unidentifiable
sections of agricultural machinery. At the last moment two
Africans appeared laden with baskets of fruit, a string of staring
purple fish; the man was demure and bourgeois in black alpaca
jacket and his string tie, his wife magnificent in wild dramatic
prints, embroidered robe and headcloth. She settled down
apologetically at the back; it was like watching some sensationally gorgeous butterfly effacing herself in an engine-room.

To Dolisie, to Pointe Noire, to Mayumba, to a sequence of
plots excavated from the forest, invisible until the plane would
lurch down through the solid hump-backed air and there would
be the strip of red earth, the scattered group of palm huts, the
baking little office with the flapping Air France poster and the
weighing-machine that no one had used for years. At Tchibanga
the colonial official got off, grumbling, and an African rode
straight up to the plane on a bicycle and embarked, bicycle and all.
At Mouila we took aboard a woman with a black goat, which
stood balancing daintily and rattling its pointed hooves on the
aluminium floor, ruminating amber-eyed and sardonic among the
straw baskets and the tractor parts.

At four in the afternoon we leaned over the jungle and bumped
down at last to the most deserted strip of all, a long empty room
with green and growing walls – Lambaréné. No one else got off
but me, and the heat jumped out of the earth like a blow.

For how many years had the name of Lambaréné meant something to me in terms of other people's experience? It was where
Schweitzer lived; was the symbol of whatever consideration or
emotion Schweitzer evoked; there were people who spoke of it as
a sort of shrine. They were customarily the people who had never
been within two thousand miles of it; I knew people nearer at
hand – in Brazzaville, in the Congo – who reacted very differently,
sometimes because they claimed to know more but more often
because cynicism is a modish attitude in all colonies, but especially in French colonies. Anyway, this was it at last.

When the pirogue came it was a long canoe carved in one piece
from a hollowed log; the boatmen sat at the stern; amidships was
a tiny stool. I began to ask for the Hospital but clearly the boatman knew; we were in the stream, cutting through the brown
river like a pencil.

The brown current rip-roppling along the sides of the hollowed log, the rain-forest sliding behind and replacing itself, damp and green shadows, vegetation at war with itself; too much of everything. I suppose the whole thing was beautiful in a way, but I am a creature of narrower reasoning; nature I love only when disciplined and employed in some service; this exuberance of growth was full of a sort of sublime and careless menace. Dr Schweitzer knew it; that was why – one supposed – he was here.

The little stool in the dugout canoe became first uncomfortable, then very nearly intolerable. The panting distress of the boatman ground through the back of my neck into my conscience; why is it in Africa one is always conscious of the physical efforts of Africans? Doubtless he did this journey every day transporting fish or vegetables; in any case, of what the hell else did his life consist? He at least was not obsessed with the complexities of crossing a continent to make contact with a myth.

Round the broad bend of the river it opened up abruptly; there was the Hospital, the village he created of his own wish and built practically with his own hands. It was a rickle of wood and corrugated iron, a gimcrack colony of sheds climbing erratically up a slope among the mango-trees; an air both confident and forlorn. The pirogue cut diagonally across the river and drove crabwise down on the beach. Somewhere in there at last was Dr Schweitzer – philosopher, musician, theologian, doctor, and holder of the prize of peace. It had indeed been a long way.

The Ogowe is eight hundred miles of dark and tepid stream north of the Congo – not a river but a system of rivers, four branches each as big as the Rhine, interlocking and embracing great lakes and islands among the forests of the Gabon. Along the delta lives the riverine tribe of the Galoa and the enfeebled remnants of the once warlike Pahouin. When Albert Schweitzer was born in the Alsation Vosges, Dr Livingstone was dying by Lake Bangweulu, Paris was falling to the Prussians, William 1 became Emperor of Germany, and along the banks of the Ogowe River on the Equator not more than a hundred or so white men lived or had ever lived; it was known as the Impenetrable Forest. Of this Albert Schweitzer knew nothing at all, nor for some time.

The choice – the famous choice, recorded so often and in so many forms – came years later: Albert Schweitzer elected to abandon celebrity, fortune and glory in more fields than any contemporary had ever simultaneously mastered, so that he 'might not have to submit to the necessity of becoming a Reasonable Man'. What it exactly meant no one knows to this day, except that it had a certain intrinsic wonder of its own.

By that time Albert Schweitzer was a Professor of the University of Strasbourg, a Doctor four times, a celebrated organist and builder of organs, a humanist of repute, and the husband of Helene Bresslau. He wrote, or was to write, on Bach, on Saint Paul, on Jesus Christ, on the Philosophy of Civilization. It is a fact that he appeared capable of anything, even of renouncing it all. He had, it seemed, made a pact: he had permitted himself thirty years in which to cultivate all the talents in his possession and bring them to maturity so that for the rest of his life he could bury them all in the direct physical service of other men. That was the dedicated role.

Everything in the early life of Albert Schweitzer has by now been documented, studied, speculated and argued over by scholars, devotees and sceptics, by those who see in this phenomenal pattern of life something either too good to be true or too true to be good.

He himself had written all there was to say of the Lycée at Mulhouse, of the University of Strasbourg, of the years of dedication to the music that permeated even his studies of philosophy and theology. The extraordinarily catholic scope of his endeavours was obviously made possible only by a tremendous sense of personal organization and self-discipline, an extraordinary force of intuition and exegesis. He studied the organ under Munch in Strasbourg and Charles Marie Widor in Paris; at the same time he learned Hebrew so that he might read the Scriptures in the original text; he did his military service in 1894 – a most peculiar picture: Schweitzer soldiering with a Greek testament in his pack. In 1897 he finished his thesis – a profound adventure indeed for a young man of twenty-two – on 'Schleiermacher's Notion of the Last Supper, as Compared With Those of Luther, Zwingli, and Calvin.' He left Paris for Berlin, returned to be himself appointed pastor of Saint Nicholas, Strasbourg.

He took his *licence* in theology with a thesis on 'The Problem of the Last Supper as it Emerges from the Studies and Research of the Nineteenth Century' while he was at the same time writing his major work on Bach *and* mastering the mechanics and technique of organ-building – *and* at that moment becoming a student of the Strasbourg Faculty of Medicine, thus weaving one more strand into the complex pattern of his life. Then in 1896, shortly after he became twenty-one, Albert Schweitzer made his celebrated and momentous decision – to study, to drink of every aspect of knowledge and practice for just ten years; from that time on to commit his life to Africa. It was an uneasy thing for me to consider, there on the hot banks of the Ogowe, that it was this caprice, or inspiration, taken just fifteen years before I was born, that had in effect brought me there today.

Life is full of arrivals: the new town and the strange faces, a change of language between meals, a different set of problems and uncertainties brought in with the shabby suitcase. What I had expected from the Hospital I am not sure – there had been a fanciful illustration in one of the endless books on Dr Schweitzer, all graceful palm-trees beside a sort of lagoon; there was an old photograph in a French magazine of the Doctor feeding a deer in a forest. I had some vague anticipation of a cabin beside the water's edge, overhung perhaps with creepers and the growth of forty dedicated years.

What I saw as the pirogue sidled across the bay of the Ogowe was a village, a settlement climbing up a slope, wooden walls and terraces of corrugated iron, hutments in rows among the mango trees, like some kind of mining camp or frontier post. It was a place of surpassing ugliness.

I was hoping intensely that the arrangements were in order, that some word of my coming had preceded me. I have the temperament that naturally foresees disaster; I pictured a scene of exquisite embarrassment when I was asked my business. For a lifetime, at that remote period, Dr Schweitzer had contrived to keep the world from Lambaréné; now it had begun to intrude, the Nobel Prize looked like making an end to solitude. I felt myself acutely part of that intrusive world. And *if* I should be unwelcome – now, at this stage of the complex journey – then I had not the remotest idea what I should do, nor how I could depart gracefully, or even ungracefully, for that matter the pirogue was now only a speck far away on the broad sunset river. I began to hump my bag up the slope.

A few Africans were moving around among the hutments,

carrying cans of water and stems of bananas; they looked at me curiously. One of them said 'Bo'jou'' and quietly took my bag from me, walking behind. I had hoped he would lead the way – somewhere; but he waited for directions.

As I climbed the wooden steps to the verandah of the first row of huts a middle-aged lady emerged carrying books; she was dressed in speckless white, with a white topi. She looked at me with complete composure – I was dripping with heat and wan with fatigue; I suddenly saw my clothes stained and clumsy and wet from the pirogue. I realized sadly that she had not the slightest idea who I was and that only too evidently I had not been expected. I began to explain the stratagems that had been contrived from Europe to introduce me; she listened with experienced compassion and said: 'You will forgive the Doctor if he doesn't receive you immediately; he is tired.'

In my hut was a bed, a chair, a basin; wooden walls; a kerosene lamp. The place smelt of damp leaves and abandoned fruit. Somebody, I felt, would tell me when something more was expected of me. I lay down for a moment on the iron bed, and fell asleep.

I had come to see Albert Schweitzer with no qualification to meet him on any terms at all. I am no philosopher, no musician, no doctor, theology is a science comparable in my knowledge with the quantum theory. Such random experience and knowledge as I had accumulated were, as I was very soon to learn, exactly those the Doctor would consider least valuable, if not positively corrupting. It is surprising that, for a while, we became friends.

It had been given to few men to be their own ancestor, to achieve a kind of symbolism in their lifetime for no reason anyone could exactly define. In some sort of way Schweitzer embodied everyman's idea of the dedicated life, of great gifts ingrown and abandoned; the man of all the talents who had finished here, of his own choice, doctoring Africans in the equatorial forest.

It was a career that thrust itself on the world's attention by retreating from it; that by its ingenious simplicity had transpired the most complicated speculations. But virtually nobody, then, had met Schweitzer at home. And of course, the nearer one approached the legend the more it was muted.

I had never been very fond of good men; when I consider

throughout my life among which of my acquaintances the more congenial and possibly rewarding hours have been spent I have to concede that they have been among slight men and inglorious, philistines and tosspots, intemperate and worthless skipjacks, men of whose work I never read a word. The reason for this is not easy to determine, since my own nature is not that of a rake or hellion – perhaps it is envy. But if ever there was a man I had wanted to meet it was Doctor Albert Schweitzer; he was the end of the emotional trail; of whom else could it be said he was a good man? In those days the adjective was not questioned; the legend was unchallengeable. When I became the first to challenge it, long afterwards, it was the first heresy.

That evening I woke abruptly: I had slept through the bell; everyone was waiting for me; an inauspicious start. I hurried down the verandah to the dining-room, and there I saw Dr Schweitzer for the first time in my life.

He was big; I had not previously thought of him as so tall; a heavy man in crumpled drill trousers and a short sleeved shirt, and the rest according to the legend – the bush of disordered hair, the undergrowth of moustache, the aggressive nose, the eyes of an old man. He hurried across the room to greet me with such momentary enthusiasm I felt he must be mistaking me for somebody else; but he was impatient for dinner.

'We are delighted to have you here,' he said, and wrung my hand. 'It is such a long way. You must meet . . .' but there seemed to be too many people to meet all at once; I had not realized the size of the Schweitzer staff: there were some twenty to dinner. His French was heavily coloured with a fine rotund Alsatian accent; he was a peasant and proud of it.

We ate communally at a long table in a refectory built on the spot where the old Galoa chiefs had lived, musing on ever more ingenious ways of strangling their redundant wives. We saw by oil lamps; an African servant handed round food. The Doctor ate only fruit and vegetable, but considerably: great quantities of mango and avocado and soya-bean, and above all a specially huge variety of boiled banana. When I first saw these vast soggy fruits appear I thought they were some kind of fish.

'Eight of these sustain a man for a day,' said the Doctor, 'and now the natives agitate for sardines and canned peas. That is, of course, progress.' (Like everyone else in French Africa he used the word *indigène*; not so warm as 'African', less contemptuous than 'native').

He did not speak English. The table-talk was indiscriminately French and German, but there was little of it. I noticed that whenever the Doctor spoke the table fell silent, though he spoke rarely.

After a while I tried to speak of the many shadows of despair that haunted Africa, and which seemed somehow that week to obsess me more than usual, but at first he would not pursue the subject.

'I am a man of limited experience,' he said, in a manner that I took to be satirical, 'I feel at a loss with people who know the world. I have never even been to Brazzaville.' He looked up quizzically, waiting to have this whimsy challenged, 'A man *must* occupy himself with what he knows and lived among. I would suggest that there are far too many people hurrying around having everybody's troubles at once. Yours must be a distressing occupation; rather useless.'

Later he said: 'Internationalism – surely it is asking too much of the human capacity to make rules that apply everywhere. Rules – the world is run by rules, instead of confidence. There is no confidence left in *people*. I am thinking of things like labour organizations – laying down conditions internationally, my dear sir, when it's downright impossible to legislate over fifty kilometres, things differ so from place to place. I assure you I am right. In the forest here, now they can cut timber only when the river is full enough to float it; when that happens they work day and night, by lamplight even; three days of it. They do a fortnight's work in three days, and take a fortnight off. Reasonable? Of course. But your Internationalists would consider only the fortnight, not the three days. Maybe I'm too old; I remember when there weren't rules, only justice.'

Quite suddenly the meal was over; he reached across for his Testament, put on his spectacles, and read from the Acts of the Apostles: there in the forest the old story, and St Paul was wrecked upon Malta.

Then he left the table and crossed the room to the piano, and that cracked chord from the ancient instrument was the first note of music I ever heard from the hands of Schweitzer. We sang: '*Reste avec nous, Seigneur, le jour décline* ...' The piano was in a terrible state; no stringed instrument can hold out against the

murderous climate of the Gabon; nevertheless it was played by
Schweitzer. Then he prayed: '*Notre Père, qui est en cieux* . . .'
among the hiss and rumble of the rain. It sounded strange, and
sad, in Africa.

Someone rang a bell. The Hospital days were timed as in a
ship, by bells. But Schweitzer time was exactly twenty minutes
behind Lambaréné time, through some precise solar calculation
of the Doctor's.

'We must work by the sun,' said somebody, 'here on the
equator the days and nights are, of course, the same length.'

'No,' said the Doctor suddenly, 'far from it. There is a difference
of very nearly eight minutes, summer and winter. One can do a
great deal in eight minutes. Do you know what I want for a
present?' he asked me, 'a Sèvres vase, but filled with time.' The
idea delighted him for a moment. 'From the President of the
Republic – a jar of time!'

But then the thought reminded him of his writing; he fell to
silence, and soon disappeared. He would work until midnight.
He would rise at six. Every day, day after day, for forty years.

'On the first morning,' said Dr Schweitzer, 'I ask you if you slept
well. On the second, I say "Good-day". Thereafter, let us reserve
the right to be sombre at breakfast.'

My lodging was part of a wooden row called, without irony,
'Sans Souci'. From where I sat working in the mornings – shortly
after dawn, as very soon the awful heat bore down and crushed
the will to think as it did the will to move – I would see him
through the mosquito screen, shuffling up the path towards the
leper village with his great umbrella – in a hurry, as usual; there
was never enough time, he argued, for what had to be done:
things to mend, people to cure, animals to feed, books to write.
He spent much time protesting how little time there was.

The hot rain beat down endlessly, vertically; occasionally the
sun burst through like a hammer. The humidity mouldered books
and mildewed clothes; by evening every smooth surface carried a
film of dampness; one spent one's nights in a dew of sweat, by
morning the sheet was wringing. I am used to tropical heat, but
the breathless heaviness of the Ogowe during the rains, imprisoned on three sides by the great walls of forest and on the
fourth by the steaming breadth of the river, was inhuman. And

Schweitzer had endured it for some forty years – indeed defeated it – he was then almost eighty; some said he was probably the oldest living man in French Equatorial Africa. European colonial functionaries take care to be restored to France in early middle age, and the indigène is an old man at forty. But the Doctor's wife had surrendered; she had worked in the Hospital in the first days, when the only surgery was a henhouse and they operated by candlelight, but she had had to go back to Europe, defeated at last by the murderous sun.

The Hospital was a shock; I had been prepared for some professional unorthodoxies, but not this glaring squalor. The Doctor had fenced off all mechanical advance to a degree that seemed both pedantic and appalling. The wards were rude huts, airless and dark, plank beds and wooden pillows; every one infested with hens and dogs. There was no running water but the rain, no gas, no sewerage, no electricity except – again in character – for the operating theatre and the gramophone. To be sure, French Equatorial was not the Belgian Congo, whose spotless and aseptic hospitals were then maintained by the resources of the Union Miniere; this was the Gabon, where every compulsion of fetishism and superstition urged the primitive African not to go to hospital at all if he could help it. Certainly he could not be persuaded to go alone; he was obliged to bring his wives and their children, his goats and his poultry, in a comfortable congestion of brown flesh and feathers. Yet many another jungle hospital had done better than this – I thought momentarily of Anthony Barker in Nqutu in Zululand, spreading his infinitely slenderer resources over every professional advance he could contrive . . . But then, it was argued, Lambaréné had Dr Schweitzer.

I said then that the Hospital existed for him rather than he for it. It was deliberately archaic and primitive, deliberately part of the jungle around it, a background of his own creation which clearly meant a great deal more philosophically than it did medically.

Somehow one had expected a great humanist to propound the accepted arguments of liberalism. Schweitzer, who claimed to have spent his life in the personal labour of giving, considered that he had no need to squander his intellect on clichés; he had the right, perhaps, to disconcert the orthodox progressive.

'The great conflict of our time is personality versus collectiv-

ism.' He had said that in the United States a few years before, for
the Goethe centenary. 'Collectivism in its various forms has
deprived the individual of his individuality. All the troubles of
the world come from that. Mankind has been persuaded to give
up its natural relations with reality, and to seek the magic formula
of some kind of social or economic witchcraft.'

All the time I felt that he was expecting me to talk politics;
there was a watchfulness about him. There was the usual repertory
of commonplaces expected of journalists: Communism, Atom
Bombs, the decline of human responsibility, apartheid, the parliamentary system . . . the routine seeps out, varied in minute ways
from country to country. It was easier to drift around with the
Doctor fiddling with broken locks and loose boards, fraternizing
with the countless animals.

Life abounded; in the yards and the compounds, up the forest
tracks, deep in the low grass and high in the trees; the river had
its fish, its crocodiles and its hippos; high in the skies a heron or a
pair of ospreys . . . It was impossible to open a book without
finding some minuscule expression of life escaping from a crevice
and crawling away across the page; life on wings bombarded the
window-screens or whined shrilly around the ears. You could
destroy life and other life took charge – crush a beetle underfoot
and within moments the corpse was sliding across the floor to
some terrible obscurity, impelled by regiments of voracious
ants...

There were the three chimpanzees; I came to know them well.
They were young and nimble, yet with that over-anxious,
ancient-of-days expression of their kind; they would play for
hours around a sapling outside my door, climbing and falling and
wrestling with the exaggerated and over-emphatic tumbling of
professional acrobats; it was impossible to believe in their
naïveté, so obviously did they show off to any passer-by. They
developed for myself first a powerful curiosity, which caused them
to peer forever through my window, wrapped around each other
in intricate patterns, and then, I rather believe, a certain affection,
or at least tolerance, at which stage they would knock on the door
to be admitted. I came to feel very warmly about the apes; there
were times when the responsibility of my inadequate relationship
with Dr Schweitzer oppressed me so that I returned with relief to
the chimpanzees. They would sit for hours on the floor beside my

doorway, embracing each other, with their six dark sorrowful eyes fixed intently upon me; if I turned a page or crossed my legs they would stir quietly, nudging each other. To change my trousers in these circumstances became almost an embarrassment, so intensely was the process observed. There was one genuinely startling moment: I was working beside the window, grinding out from the typewriter whatever contemporary nonsense was required (in fact a fragment of this book) when I glanced round and there were the monkeys in a row, by the doorway, beating out a ragged tattoo with their fingers on the floor; a very reasonable imitation ... I could have nearly cried: two more typewriters were all I needed for the conclusive experiment: given time *would* they have written the first two acts of Hamlet?

One such experiment I could at least begin. The chimpanzees showed interest at the mechanics of writing; more so at the process of drawing; one evening when I was sketching in the plantation I felt those questing reflective eyes on me again, and a group of thin leathery fingers reached out gently for the crayon. It occurred to me that whatever the chimpanzees did with it could scarcely be more futile than what I was doing myself, and I surrendered it. The effect was gripping. To begin with the chimpanzee darted and slashed at the paper in an uncontrolled way, tearing the sheet, sometimes missing it altogether; surprisingly soon a kind of intention came over him, and on the third or fourth fresh leaf he began to draw. There is no other word to describe what in fact the ape was doing. He held the pencil awkwardly and vertically, like a chisel, and his first reaction to the creation of a line was very odd indeed: as it appeared under the pencil he grabbed at it with the other hand – it had not been there a second ago and now it was; obviously it was some sort of worm that had emerged from the pencil, and he tried to pick it up. Very soon he appreciated the uselessness of this, and seemed to derive a wild satisfaction from the process of covering the paper with lines. It became, in fact, drawing; without the slightest question it was drawing in the truest sense; whereas in the first seconds he had attacked the paper at random, now he understood the very first principle of draughtsmanship: that the paper's surface had boundaries. He kept his scrawling within the rectangle, and that is a thing I would not have imagined within his powers. Naturally he drew nothing in a representational sense;

his drawing was all the purer because it was an end in itself; the process was what mattered, not the result. He would begin the top of the pad and drag a heavy line across the paper, controlling its conclusion before he ran off the edge; soon he learned to vary his mark with a bend or a flourish. He could not grasp the possibilities of relating one line to another, but there was no doubt that he appreciated his power of varying the shape of a line within itself. His attention soon wandered; by and by his nails began fretfully to scratch at the paper; it ended in tearing the pad apart. Yet he was an artist in his way.

My association with the chimpanzees was unofficial, even clandestine; once the Doctor caught me taking a walk with them hand in hand, gathering fruit – he was displeased, and chased them off. '*That* is the way to catch dysentery, if you like,' he said, and I was never sure whether his solicitude was for me or for the monkeys.

One day in the plantation he suddenly pulled me aside; a column of soldier ants was crossing the track; it seemed they had the right of way. During the rains these creatures can be formidable; they march half a dozen abreast in precise military order, and can be menacing to any small creature that falls in the path of their advance. Nevertheless, this multiplicity of life had to be protected from footfall. A little later, however, the Doctor stooped to gather a handful of fallen palm-nuts for Tekla, his wild pig; he did not observe that the orange nuts were crawling with ants until they began to bite him. It was a pleasure to see how smartly and with what vigour the Doctor knocked them flying, without regard to their finer feelings.

He expressed the dilemma: 'You can't have respect for life and confine it to one aspect of life, say the human; you must accept that every other kind is capable of experiencing well-being and fear and pain, and has a natural dread of destruction. There are really no philosophical rules about it . . . Philosophy has tended to dodge the question of whether life-dedication must include *all* living things at *all* times; extending the circle of responsibility so far creates too many conflicts, makes it more difficult than ever to create ethical rules that are practical as well as satisfying.

'We are constantly being forced into situations which oblige us to cause suffering, sometimes death. The peasant couldn't really bring up every beast that is born on his land, it would not be practical. If you rescue an injured bird, you have to kill insects with which to feed it. We sacrifice many lives for one; what we have to remember is that it is a purely arbitrary choice.'

But if animals, why not vegetables? In his own essay in self-analysis *My Life and Thought*, Schweitzer wrote: 'The farmer who mows a thousand flowers in his meadow to feed his cows must be careful on his way home not to strike off heedlessly the head of a single flower by the roadside, for he thereby commits wrong against life without being under the pressure of necessity.'

It was an intolerably scrupulous theme, the attitude that once even made the Doctor describe his pathological work as 'the mass-murder of bacteria'.

One day we were supervising the construction of a new leper village. It was with a striking absence of the routine saintliness and loving-kindness that the Doctor spurred his *indigènes* to work, abused and upbraided them for their reluctance and indolence. He stumped around the more slothful sections in his vast soft black boots, projecting his great menacing moustache. 'Marche! Depèche-toi!' he shouted. 'Fais ton devoir, sans discuter!' – and the Africans would break momentarily into a semblance of movement. 'Toi – cours! Travaile comme un blanc, quoi!'

He said: 'Those who talk sentimentally about the Africans require just a few months controlling them personally. Unless one watches them *all* the time they do *nothing*.' It was, I am afraid, demonstrably true. 'They are uninterested in being resourceful, industrious, economic, or provident. Nor must you argue – they are better orators than you, always. Au travail, toi!' he cried to a group of lepers with shovels, apparently paralysed in mid-gesture. They began to make feeble scraping motions in the dust. 'That's better.' As we moved off the Africans relaxed, gradually, into immobility.

'Before I came to Africa I used to hear traders and missionaries insist that one must always strictly maintain the authority of the white man – like every decent European I felt it was a rigid and unnatural theory. Now I believe that only by demanding certain external forms can you demonstrate kindness and sympathy. You know the formula – I coined it – "I am your brother, that is true, but I am your elder brother". The Negro is not necessarily idle, but he is a free man, consequently always a casual worker. When he has done enough to satisfy his immediate needs, he stops –

never mind the future, still less anyone else's convenience. We *need* this new leper village, it's for *them* . . .'

Fifty yards away one of the women staff was standing beside a group of Africans; two were supposed to shovel earth into a box which two others were supposed to carry away. They moved with a deliberation I should scarcely have thought possible; it was like watching a slow motion film. Sometimes the work slowed down to the point where movement, if it existed, was imperceptible; it was like studying the hour-hand of a watch.

I said: 'With one small bulldozer you could do a month's work here in less than two hours . . .' but she held her hand before her mouth and glanced anxiously around: 'Bulldozer! Please do not say such words; the Doctor might hear . . .'

But he didn't; he was busy up the track, making people work.

On my first day the Doctor was scandalized because I appeared without a tropical helmet. I protested that I had spent months hatless in every tropic there is and taken no harm, in Central Africa and South-East Asia and the Caribbean and India and South America; it made no difference; the Doctor was adamant about hats, and insisted on sending for a topi.

'In any case,' he said, 'if you are determined to become ill, become ill elsewhere, where some other doctor will have to treat you.'

As we walked back along the track he picked up a fallen mango from the ground, whipped a pocket-knife from his trousers, and carved it in a flash. '*That* is the only way to eat one of these, and keep clean.'

I recalled that the first mango I had ever eaten had been given to me by Gandhi, on an Indian train between Delhi and Kalka. I spoke of Gandhi, feeling the allusion should be appealing; everything suggested a parallel approach to the humanities.

'There,' said the Doctor, 'was the classic tragedy. Gandhi was killed in the end by the very forces of the past he had spent his life trying to evoke. A great educator, misled into politics.'

At the word politics he shook his head. 'Man is a clever animal, who behaves like an imbecile,' he said.

Later we walked beside the river and he caught me on a careless phrase and said: 'But you *can't* legislate internationally. Men are narrow. There would be – for example – no ridiculous dispute over who governs China, if there were not these perpetual attempts being made to rationalize it in the United Nations. The

Government of China would be there or it wouldn't; everyone concerned would argue empirically. How can you have such questions voted on by Arab states and little South American countries?

'First we had the League of Nations. Ethiopia. Well, I was never for Mussolini – the essence of the commonplace, the vulgar, and the wretched – but still less for a country that was run by bandits, and still is. Italy had faults, but as a colonist she was not a bad educator. *Now* look at Libya – a country that can't live and can't die. *Rules* – why will people try to reach so far?'

Yet it was Albert Schweitzer who not long before had approvingly quoted David Hume, to the effect that human beings are strings vibrating in harmony with those in sympathy everywhere – 'des cordes vibrant a l'unison avec celles qui resonnent'. He said: 'You can't make terms with the Absolute. The world is a paradox anyhow, in conflict with itself; horror in magnificence, absurdity among the intelligence, suffering in joy.'

By now we had come against an open-air kitchen; the heavy pots dumped carelessly had bent the fire-bars.

'If people would only learn to lift things and not drag them around,' said the Doctor, 'I shouldn't be plagued with so many breakages *here*, for a start.' And he went off shaking his head, with the animals around his feet.

There was no reasonable way of summarizing the Doctor's philosophical attitude; I think he himself would have defined it as that of a man who, having examined every major philosophical system and detected the artifice within each, henceforth refused even to attempt to create new rules. He argued that he was never attracted by the methods of pure speculation, his interest has always lain in the application of history to morality, as every philosophical decision of his own had been translated into action, rejecting the formalism of the 'professional philosophers'. His system of thought had been, he said, built on gigantic research; in his *Philosophy of Civilisation* he began with the Greek and Roman philosophers, moved through Renaissance and post-Renaissance to Kant, Leibnitz, Spinoza, Goethe, Fichte, and Hegel, concluding with Neitzsche and Schopenhauer. This vast survey equipped him, then, to examine the questions of ethics against the background of the history of ethics, simplified by Schweitzer in the simple statement: 'All that nourishes and encourages life is good; all that destroys and mutilates it is evil.' His interest in Indian philosophy was stimulated by its stress on man's relations not only with man but with all living things. He had considered the origins of Brahmin mysticism, the intricacies of Jainism (whose tense preoccupation with the salvation of life involves, sometimes to this day, almost fantastic expedients of behaviour, such as breathing only through gauze masks to protect invisible insects); examined contemporary Hinduism and the Bhagavad-Gita, studied Rama-krishna and Vivekanada and Tagore. Its conclusion was, by formula, the limitless nature of ethics. He defined it: 'Ethics is the acknowledgment of our responsibility towards all living things.' And somehow he could be contemptuous of Gandhi.

Any bookshelf that holds the works of Dr Schweitzer proclaims an almost fabulous unity of thought. Of his publications as theologian and exegetist the major five – *The Mystery of the Kingdom of God*, *The Quest of the Historical Jesus*, the *Psychiatric Study of Jesus* (which was his 1911 medical thesis), *Paul and His Interpreters*, and *The Mysticism of Paul the Apostle* – were all written between 1900 and 1913. That is to say, before he went to Lambaréné, and before any of the philosophical works. There are nearly two thousand pages of analysis, record and comment, all written by a young man simultaneously hard at work in many other fields: a physical effort that was by any definition prodigious.

Then at last to Lambaréné: the resounding retirement, revealed by a spotlight that was not, at least at first, of Dr Schweitzer's creation. And at *that* point values changed, philosophies were strained, the argument was distorted on too many planes at once; Dr Schweitzer found his popular apotheosis and lost his peace of mind.

In his long autobiographical essay *My Dear Timothy* a little while ago Victor Gollancz wrote: 'Do you know about Schweitzer? He is eminent as a philosopher and theologian, and plays Bach superbly; but people think of him chiefly as a man who, while still in his thirties, went out to Lambaréné in French Equatorial Africa and, from then till now, has doctored a few hundred Africans. That is all: he has doctored a few hundred Africans ... There are hundreds, even thousands, who have cured men and women, or relieved human suffering, on a far greater scale. And yet I should say that Albert Schweitzer is loved – by the relatively small number of people to whom his name means anything – in a way no other person is loved who is living today . . . He would not pretend that, theoretically, he has solved the problem. He leaves it, in a sense, unsolved. He tells us that, in human conditions, we cannot help doing wrong – doing it not once or twice, but times out of number . . . We have to strike a balance; we are involved in relativities. But let us always obey, Schweitzer says, two imperatives. First, never let us pretend when we are doing a wrong we are not doing a wrong . . . let us not call such behaviour ethical; let us call it unethical, and confess that we see no way of avoiding it. Secondly, let us never do even the smallest wrong unless we are certain that it is quite inescapable . . . Schweitzer's theory is criticized by many as inadequate, as inconsistent. His critics may be right: though he seems to me, who have no technical competence in the subject, to get very near the truth, with his recognition of the final insolubility under human conditions – of something remaining over which impinges as self-contradictory . . .'

One day he came, for the first time, to see me in my room, clean and spartan and about the size of a country gentleman's wardrobe – the sort of room I like, being well accustomed to a life without possessions. The towel, the jug were marked with the initials 'ASB'. Everything of the Hospital is so marked 'ASB' – Albert Schweitzer Bresslau; from the first days of the beginning he appended his wife's surname to his own; they used the monogram when they arrived in 1913, and the letters became recognized on crates and boxes all over the West Coast as meaning Schweitzer, Lambaréné.

'Do you mind it's being small?' he asked. 'This was the last part of the establishment to be built – it didn't quite join up with the rest of the block; do you see the flaw? We kept that as a memento.' Down in the sous-sol of an early building this preoccupation of his was scratched into concrete posts – 'A. Schweitzer, ingenieur . . .' 'Alb. Schw., maçon . . .' 'A. Schweitzer, menuisier . . .'

One day luncheon began with a reprimand; the Doctor was concerned at my having walked alone up the forest track past the settlement: did I not realize the danger from gorillas? This was a bad place for gorillas. I said, with rather fatuous lightness (since I did feel guilty) that it might be possible that by now the neighbouring gorillas had themselves developed the rudiments of Respect for Life.

He replied with acerbity: 'Doubtless if you communicated to the gorilla that you were a member of the British Press, he would stand aside; if by chance you had no time to do so he would first break your arms, then your legs, one by one: following that he would tear off your scalp. Gorillas I know.' Then he quickly gave me a boiled banana to show there was no ill feeling; he was light-hearted that day.

But on the whole I was less interested in gorillas than in Africa, in the racial thunderstorm that I felt building up all around, that I felt should oppress everyone as gloomily as it did me. There was no especial sign of racial tension in Lambaréné. Or was there?

'Colour . . . until recently no African here was allowed to buy imported liquor. Now they can. Step backwards. They have citizen's rights now, but no citizens' responsibilities. They destroy most things they touch . . . The more the personal responsibility falling on the white man the more likely he is to be trapped into becoming inflexible and hard with the natives. We are here to help them; it is not our job to get results from them, so it is easy to be self-righteous about the attitude of those who have. How many of those who speak savagely and bitterly about the African came out here full of idealism, and have been crushed into weariness and hopelessness by the contest?

'You ask me whether the *indigène* can ever develop to responsibility without us, and the answer is No, he cannot. Others disagree. The United Nations Trusteeship Commissions and so forth . . . they think in terms of *politics*, sir – do they ask who plants the trees so that the African can eat, who bores the wells so that he can drink? No, they say "How are they progressing towards self-government?" Self-government without resource, without thrift? Democracy is meaningless to children.'

In the afternoon torpor I went to my hut with a paper Dr Schweitzer had given me, written not long before, on 'Ethical Problems in the Evolution of Human Thought' – the very thing, I thought, for such a day.

'Christianity induced the Stoics to consider love itself as one of the virtues: Seneca, Epictetus, the emperor Marcus Aurelius . . .

But the reform without precedent in the history of mankind was accomplished in the discovery that the principle of Love is informed also by Sense . . .'

The parrots stirred desultorily by the windows; a man with a bandaged foot trailed over the compound; somewhere down below his wife was having a baby; from time to time she called out, far away, breaking the stillness of the equatorial afternoon. The palm-fronds rasped in the first hint of the breeze; the rain would be on us very soon.

I went along the track past the graveyard – it didn't look like a graveyard, with the home-made headstones and the lemon-trees haphazard all around; it looked like something the children had made for fun – and up to the leper village to see Mademoiselle Erna. Mademoiselle Erna had come from Denmark a year ago to work with the Doctor among the advanced cases of leprosy – young and blonde, pretty under the great absurd pith helmet, among all that horror, swabbing leprous ulcers and handling people whom a sickness had turned into decaying ruins. The lepers sat on a bench and unrolled their bandages, violent purple – sometimes when the bandage was removed there was practically nothing left beneath it. When there was part of a foot, or of a hand, Mademoiselle Erna painted it; once the swab on the end of the stick went clean through a palm and out the other side, like a nail from the cross. The man winced a little. 'It doesn't hurt as frightfully as you would think,' said the Nurse. 'Lepers lose so much nervous sensation. But it hurts, for all that.'

I went back along the track, and sat down for a cigarette. There was a schoolboy feeling about this; no one else in the community smoked. The air danced with colossal butterflies; I saw some as big as books, in strident and violent colours. A family of pig came snorting from the bush and a procession of big ants drove along a branch, endlessly – up the trunk, along the branch, round a twig, down the trunk again, going where? The air was full of the crepitation of crisping of countless millions of unseen insects. Sometimes an African plodded by, nodding 'Bo'jou', m'sieu'' I observed that the Doctor had somehow contrived to get hats on them, too. They wore them rakishly, with feathers on top.

How much had the legend diminished? There was the theory that somewhere in this monument to sacrifice rested a core of spiritual pride – the mystique that maintained the Hospital as a slum because it was thus that Schweitzer had always seen it; that denied to his patients and his staff the minimum of amenity because his mind was elsewhere; that refused offers of mechanical ploughs and motor-boats and refrigerators because such things were not enmeshed in the great emotional impulse of that early choice.

It was the last night, at our supper the Doctor suddenly announced a thing that none of us knew anything about: he was to be on the radio that evening, in a couple of minutes. We all trooped down the path to the room of one of the other doctors who actually had a set; we were just in time to catch the announcement from Radio Brazzaville: '. . . for the first time . . . the winner of the Nobel Prize . . .'

Then it came, in the lamplight, the voice of a very old man – absurdly, unnecessarily so; it was a bad recording on tape, a cruel parody. As he listened the Doctor's wild grey head sank lower and lower between his broad shoulders, almost to his knees. '. . . the conflict always between sentiment and reason . . . and the supreme truth, of course, is love . . .' It tailed away.

'So,' said Doctor Schweitzer, and stood up. We went back into the dining-room. For some reason he seemed in the mood to stay up. He said: 'Is the gramophone working?' and somebody began to fuss with switches; we were unused to switches.

'This radio . . .' said the Doctor, 'essential to plan the discourse. Einstein once asked me to go along and hear him make a broadcast, a popular definition of his Theory . . . If I had not already known something of the matter already I would not have understood one word, not one word. He improvised. No manuscript. Impractical.'

It seemed to be a special day, because for the first time since I arrived we put on the gramophone – Albert Schweitzer on the organ of Gunsbach: César Franck's Chorale in A Minor. Outside in the darkness the frogs were coughing; two newly-orphaned goats cried thinly. From time to time through the music came the crash of a heavy fruit falling on the tin roof, the ceaseless rush of the night rain. The music ended.

'Tellement jolie, la basse,' murmured the Doctor. He waited around for a moment; then he walked out.

When I left next morning the Doctor came with me in the pirogue all the way to the embarcadère at Lambaréné – I do not know why, it was a considerable distinction, for he rarely leaves the Hospital. We had two pagayeurs, and when we were out of the dead water by the bank and into the current we spun downstream. It was part of the Doctor's approach to things that he regarded all journeys as momentous, as matters for heavy preparation if not misgivings; it had been necessary for Mademoiselle Matthilde to make me up a small sack of provisions against emergencies – mangos, bread, several of those massive eight-day bananas. That, I thought, clutching the bundle, would give Air France something to think about when the time came.

We slid down the great breadth of the Ogowe between the mangroves, and I got ashore at the embarcadère – a few huts, a ferry, and beyond that it seemed, nothing.

'Goodbye,' said Doctor Schweitzer, and returned up the river to the Hospital, where he belonged; and I to the truck, and the airstrip, and all the other things where I belonged.

When I returned to England there was much pressure to write a book on the visit, which had, it seemed, been the first. I did not; I am uncertain why. Among the wistful fancies that had haunted the reveries of biographers and journalists for years with a guilty and unreasonable itch was the definitive exposure of Dr Schweitzer. There, it had been felt, would be the really outstanding essay in tastelessness, the truly resounding iconoclasm. The endurance of the Schweitzer legend was a permanent challenge to explode it, or at least to question it; to examine with some sort of objectivity the man who through half a century conned the world into an adoration in which the mere investigation of his pretensions was a sort of heresy.

It was not hard to know what had for years been argued only by a few: that while the original achievements of Schweitzer were considerable and his sacrifices notable, yet his accomplishments were negligible; his mission an illusion; his hospital in the Equatorial forest medically valueless, or even dangerous, existing solely as a frame for his immeasurable ego; his own philosophical contribution to the advancement of Africa rather worse than negative.

Everything lay in the decision of timing, and this I mistrusted.

When I stayed with the patriarch in Lambaréné it was long ago, before the Doctor began to discover and enjoy the reverent pilgrimages of journalists and TV teams. Then did the theme become popular: that the Schweitzer hospital was no place of light and healing but a squalid slum, from which the Doctor excluded all the advantages he was forever being offered simply because he did not personally understand them; that his immense personal vanity insulated him from anything less than sanctimonious worship; that his celebrated 'Reverence for Life' contrasted bitterly with the cruel loneliness imposed on his own wife and daughter, just as his arrogant contempt for those around him contrasted with his cultivation of the rich dilettante women who affected to nurse at his shrine. To that could be added that it was the Doctor who proposed to me his opinion that the most salutary influence on the African race question had been the late Dr Malan; that he had never in forty years taken an African to table, and that indeed in no circumstances could he contemplate even the possibility of an *indigène* being seated in his presence. There was at the time the baffling suspicion that he was pulling my leg; only later I knew he was not.

I reflected much on these things, and came to the decision that while the life of Dr Schweitzer was indeed a paradox with very unwholesome undertones, to argue so would almost certainly be defined as unreasonable sensationalism and probably rightly. Numbers of people were presumably deriving some sort of value from the inspiration of the Schweitzer mystique, and if the price of that were to let this strange old man perpetuate his peculiarities, then it might be dishonest, but was not particularly harmful.

It were possible that in redressing the balance of unreasonable devotion one could be ungenerous to those aspects of Schweitzer's life that must command admiration – the almost inhuman industry of the young Alsatian who *did* become a distinguished scholar, theologian, musicologist, and all the rest; to surrender such a rare virtuosity for the sake of a dream was not a small thing, albeit the end was so little.

Diversion 3: The Passenger

THE practitioners of my trade are of two kinds: those correspondents who are always on the spot, as it is called, and those who await the alarums at home, in the manner of a fireman. There is also a third category: my own. When there came the Hungarian uprising of 1956, for example, which was held to be the great drama of contemporary European history, I was in a Greek steamboat called the *Semiramis* half-way through the Dodecanese, which is about as ill-contrived a springboard for activity as could be imagined. I had one foot on the quay at Crete, poised for a rousing day among the Minoan ruins, when the radiophone from London put paid to that. So back I went all the way to the Piraeus in a gruesome nameless little ship with an unmentionable cargo through an autumn storm.

By then, with Budapest ablaze, the Balkans were in what can only be called a ferment. Aeroplanes were out of the question. At Athens I got myself with difficulty on a train bound north.

For those who have never taken the Balkan train from Athens to Belgrade at a time of high political uproar, my serious advice is: do not. The train was very full. I do not know why everyone in tranquil Greece appeared to be trying to go the hard way into Yugoslavia, but that appeared to be the case. The train plodded up through miles of mountainous night, through Macedonia to the frontier at Devdilija, where a man came along and changed me some drachmae for dinars at a ferociously disadvantageous rate. He asked me if I had any gold, diamonds, dollars or drugs; when I said I had not he wished me bon voyage with a cynical smile.

The train was jammed to the eyebrows. Every train those days was jammed to the eyebrows. Most of the time it seemed too heavy for the engine. Occasionally we were overtaken by long freight-trains carrying cows, field-guns, second-hand cars, loads of hay, and very old women. We ground up through the hills to Skolpje, and then to Lestovoc, and by and by to Nis. Nis is the Clapham Junction of South-East Europe. People have been stuck there for ever. We stayed only three or four hours, while I tried to find out what was going on by studying the newspaper *Borba*, which is far from easy for those who do not read Serbo-Croat.

At last I managed to reach the dining-car, where I shared a table with a sinister man called Popovic. (I scarcely need disguise his name, since in many trips through Yugoslavia I rarely met anyone called anything else). By now we had been in the train for some twenty-four hours. M. Popovic spoke adequate French, which was a relief after so much Borba. He was a Yugoslav of the dissident, nonconformist kind; it seemed he deplored the Communists.

'Mais mon cher petit monsieur,' he said, even before the coffee. 'Vous me croyez bête? I am a business man, that is to say a serious revolutionary, not a bureaucrat.'

I said very little to that, because if experience has taught me anything it is that friendly chats with articulate anti-Communists in Communist states usually lead to plenty of trouble. By now we were passing Mdlenovac, and letting down for Belgrade.

'You see,' he said, 'the past is gone. I should tell you that I am by origin a Montenegrin and inevitably despise these Serbs. My father was an aristocrat, or at any rate he had quite a large farm. I have no time for these peasants.'

We drank long life to Montenegro. I wondered if the phone was still open between Belgrade and London.

'You are staying in Belgrade alone?' said the man. 'What an infamy.'

I said he was not to concern himself. He said: 'You may be sure that the Hotel Moskva is full, the Majestic is full. The Metropol, the new one with the taps, that is also full. So,' said M. Popovic, 'you stay with me. Here is my address. I am without prejudice. I am also quite rich, for a Montenegrin. I own a bottle of English whisky.'

In the middle of the night the train pulled into Belgrade station, which is always as stimulating an experience as arriving in Stockton-on-Tees. I bade au revoir to my friend. 'How sorry you will be,' he said, 'that you spurned Popovic.'

He was right; there was not a vacant room anywhere in Belgrade except on the top of a certain dreaded hotel, the best and most expensive part of which resembles the punitive quarters of Pentonville, and where no one in history has been known to stay more than one night.

Next day I went to the address M. Popovic had given me; it turned out to be a branch of the State Bureau for Hides and Skins, and nobody lived there at all.

Meanwhile there was the revolution in Hungary, though you would barely have known about it from the Belgrade Press; so I drove for hours through fields of red pimento, like a scarlet ocean, to Subotica, and the frontier at Horgosz. There seemed nobody much about, so I went on towards Szeged, where they threw me out. Next day they threw me out again, and burned my Yugoslav hired car. The third time it did not matter much, because Suez had begun.

I was sitting at a table on the Boulevard Marshal Tito waiting to go back to Cyprus when I saw M. Popovic coming down the street talking to another sinister man with a built-in briefcase. He saw me and came over, looking round his shoulder like a conspirator.

'If you are, as you claim, a newspaper man,' he said, 'you might be interested to know that there has been some unpleasantness in Hungary. I have my sources. You should not ignore Popovic.'

He hurried off before I could ask him about the Hides and Skins, and then it was time to catch my plane. I never met him again, but I have a feeling that I shall.

Chapter Eleven

It was just ten years after my departure from the employment of Lord Beaverbrook, who had survived this blow with no apparent diminution of his fortunes, that our paths, as they say, crossed again. It would perhaps be more accurate to say that the very small and winding right-of-way along which I was quietly plodding suddenly and briefly found itself crossing an autobahn. The encounter did not last long, but it had a quality of rather low comedy about it that was rare for me in those days. A great many various and ribald transcriptions of the incident were subsequently put up in and around Fleet Street, some more entertaining than the facts and some less. This is what the shade of Lord Beaverbrook would I am sure approve of my calling the Authorized Version.

Since my somewhat explosive and rancorous severing of relations with the *Express* my association with Lord Beaverbrook had been, predictably, tenuous indeed; the harsh truth is that from that day on we had never clapped eyes on one another. This was a deprivation I was readily able to sustain, and I cannot believe that it caused much loss of sleep to Lord Beaverbrook. We both of us doubtless had preoccupations other than this trifling estrangement; he with affairs of state, high finance, and God; I with the rather more exacting cares of making a living. While Lord Beaverbrook's botherations apparently endured, my own had momentarily slackened; after all the vicissitudes consequent upon the Korean affair, I had finally beached on the anodyne shores of the *News Chronicle*, where I found myself unexpectedly so relaxed and even happy that for some years I gave no thought to anything else.

When in the winter of 1960, then, I began to receive a series of telephone-calls ostensibly from Lord Beaverbrook, I assumed them, naturally, to be in the nature of a practical joke by some of my waggish ex-colleagues, though the motivation of the prank eluded me. I was in no mood for jokes, and consequently replied to these phone-calls by coarse monosyllables and hanging up the instrument. This went on for some time. One afternoon thereafter I was surprised by the arrival outside our house in Tedworth Square of a rich car containing a respectable man in a bowler hat who, on admission, claimed to be on the staff of Lord Beaverbrook, which I had no reason to doubt. The burden of his mission was: that for some time his Lordship had in fact been ringing me up on the telephone, and that I had responded in a cynical and unbelieving way, and that he, the emissary, had come to say that in precisely five minutes his Lordship would be on the phone again, in person, and would I kindly accept the call with a decent attention, as it might be to my advantage.

My first reaction to this extraordinary piece of news was to feel that nothing Lord Beaverbrook could possibly have to say to me at this juncture could be in any way to my advantage, and might indeed be very much otherwise, since he had by no means any reason to bear me goodwill. It would have been a satisfying future, denied to most newspapermen, to have hung up on him again. However, I was now consumed by curiosity as to what mad caprice could have urged the Lord to restore contact with me, of all people, and when the phone rang I was there.

Addicted as he was to the telephone, Lord Beaverbrook was notoriously a man never to use it for casual small-talk. He saluted me in the old abrasive way, and moved immediately into his theme. I had recently published a book called *1914*, which purported to describe the political and social atmosphere of that peculiar period of the European scene. Lord Beaverbrook, himself no mean historian of that epoch, had read it. He had thought little of it. A considerable opportunity had been missed. My analysis had been inadequate, not to say superficial. I could do better than this. As he growled on it was as though the clock was turning back and I was once again receiving apostolic reprimand; I could almost have believed that I was once again on the payroll. Lord Beaverbrook had the faculty of making anyone believe that nothing about the First World War could conceivably be set down on paper without his imprimatur, and for all I know that may well have been the case. I still could not understand why he should have been putting himself to so much trouble to berate me about a matter of so little consequence.

He had, it seemed, a much more useful and important proposition to convey to me. What I must do, now, was to take lunch with him on the morrow.

I had not the least desire ever again to involve myself with a personal contact with Lord Beaverbrook, which I knew could be perilously hypnotic. Nevertheless my curiosity, as I say, was now so acutely aroused that I could not possibly say no. At the last moment, however, I guarded myself – I suddenly remembered how, in my past days as one of the boy wonders of the Beaverbrook stable, similar impulsive invitations had arrived and been dutifully accepted, only to find that at that moment the Lord was in residence in Jamaica, or Canada, and that acceptance involved a trip half way across the world.

I said: 'If you're in Montego Bay I'm not coming.'

But of course he was not in Montego Bay; he was no distance away; he was only in Cap d'Ail, just a stone's throw from Nice; I could get there in a moment. He would make all the arrangements. I went.

Lord Beaverbrook lived in a rather splendid house near Villefranche, to which I was conveyed from Nice airport in a Rolls Royce motor car. It was hardly my travelling style, but I much enjoyed it, since I am greatly warmed by luxury at someone else's expense. Lord Beaverbrook met me at the villa with a kind of cordiality that was in itself a tour de force; it was as though our ferocious row of ten years before had never been; we greeted each other in a fashion of most curiously oblique familiarity: I might indeed never have worked for him, yet somehow we had a working relationship that required no definition. I had the impression that the old gentlemen had completely forgotten the circumstances of our terrible row, which may well have been the case.

The reason for the meeting was disposed of in half an hour: I had written a rather second-rate book about 1914; nevertheless it had clearly been good enough to suggest that I was capable of better things, and better things meant pursuing the course of history a couple of years further along. In 1914 Lord Beaverbrook had played no noticeable part in British politics, whereas in 1916 he had been a figure of notable significance, and had indeed been *deus ex machina* in the whole political embroglio that had destroyed the unlucky Mr Asquith, and had – perhaps for the last time in his life – been a man of moment, a buzzing and whizzing backstairs instrument of national affairs. If I could waste my time – he argued – writing about the pre-Aitken era of 1914, I could surely extend the theme to writing another book about 1916. On that particular political interlude no greater authority existed than he; furthermore by a judicious sequence of purchases he had come into possession of all the relevant documents; they occupied vast storage-space in one of his lesser properties in Shoe Lane, and would be revealed to me if I cared to extend my researches into yet another book.

I was greatly interested in this proposition, less for the notion of personally exhuming the intricate double-dealing of the war-before-the-last (which, after *1914*, had come to bore me beyond words) but because I could not understand why Lord Beaver-brook, whose own published volumes on that period had, I would have thought, completely exhausted the subject, should want me to scrabble again among those tired old bones. I understand now the curious compulsion that made Lord Beaverbrook want some-body other than himself to record once more his queer and con-voluted relationships with Bonar Law and Lloyd George, and of those days when Sir Max Aitken was a serious power in the land. I knew I could never do it as well as he himself had done it, in *Politicians and the War* and *Men and Power,* and he knew that I knew it; nevertheless it was clear that he wanted it done. At his best, no more persuasive counsel in the world existed than Lord Beaverbrook. After half an hour's discussion, I agreed to think the matter over.

'You will of course stay the night,' said Lord Beaverbrook, and since at that hour there was no imaginable way of doing otherwise I gladly agreed. 'There is no question of a party', he said, quite sternly, 'Just a couple of guests.'

I asked innocently and even casually whom he expected, and he said: 'We are expecting only Winston Churchill and Onassis. I shall see you later.' He then sat himself in the odd and fascinating mechanical chair that by some interesting feat of engineering con-veyed him effortlessly upstairs to his bedroom, leaving me to reflect on the extreme unexpectedness of life.

Now it was the case that even then, fifteen years after the end of the war, I had never in my life seen Sir Winston Churchill in the flesh. As far as I knew I had never been under the same roof as this distinguished person, and the thought that this sort of momentous encounter should be brought about in such a curiously casual way was clearly the sort of thing that could happen only in the household of Lord Beaverbrook. Sir Winston and he had, of course, been cronies for forty-five years or more; there were many who said that Lord Beaverbrook was his last surviving intimate. To see the once-great wartime Prime Minister for the first time in such circumstances seemed to me extremely piquant, and I went to my room in some concern to reflect on it.

A couple of hours later I was bathed, changed, refreshed, and returned to the drawing room. Nobody else had yet put in an appearance. By and by the butler appeared, and asked me if I would take a telephone call. His manner seemed to me peculiar, suggesting a kind of controlled outrage. This became comprehensible when it turned out that the call was from London, and from – the words emerged with difficulty from his lips – the *News Chronicle*.

I should explain at this point that during the whole of this bizarre interlude I was in fact still on the staff of the *News Chronicle*, which was, albeit in its own ineffectual way, a direct competitor to the newspaper of my host. It should have occurred to me that my position at that moment was, to say the least, equivocal: that the chief foreign correspondent of one newspaper should be for no immediately obvious reason hobnobbing with a rival proprietor. I had made no secret of my whereabouts. My relationships with both the *News Chronicle* and Lord Beaverbrook were simultaneously so elusive that the oddity of the situation never entered my mind.

On the other end of the line was Mr Norman Cursley, the then editor of the *News Chronicle*. He was in a condition of some emotion. Only that afternoon, he gave me to understand, had the British Prime Minister Mr Harold Macmillan summoned the London editors into conclave in Downing Street, on the eve of his departure for his tour of Africa. He had taken this unusual step, it seemed, to break the news that while he was indeed leaving for Africa on the morrow, there was a possibility that the trip might have to be cut short abruptly to enable him to attend the funeral of Sir Winston Churchill, who had just been laid low by another stroke. This was grievous news, but – and here came the reason for my editor's call – since the former Prime Minister was allegedly at this moment staying in the Hotel de Paris in Monte Carlo as the guest of Mr Onassis, and since Monte Carlo was a mere step up the road from where I was staying, it was not unreasonable that my editor should ask me to keep an eye on the situation, which seemed to have the makings of some drama.

To this I could only reply, as best I could over a flagging telephone-line, that while my loyalties lay steadfastly with my newspaper, or words to that effect, nevertheless I had been given to understand that both the former Prime Minister and his host, Mr Onassis, were expected for dinner this very evening; indeed at any moment.

I had no sooner explained this eccentric state of affairs than a sudden confusion arose: the outer door of the house opened to admit several manservants, bearing among them the recumbent form of – observing that famous countenance for the first time – what could be none other than, of course, Sir Winston Churchill.

It was a strange and uncomely way in which to see for the first time a human being of such renown and consideration, the man who, by an association of so many adventitious qualities and chances, had been for a large part of my adult life the most significant figure of Anglo-Saxon politics, and for some five years of history at least the most celebrated public figure in the world. And here was he being borne in to dinner by footmen.

I was then overtaken by a moment's serious uneasiness. It could be, I felt, that I was in the presence of a happening of outstanding moment; by the standards of journalism a matter of climax. For a moment it seemed to me that Sir Winston Churchill, ripe and full of years, had fulfilled Mr Macmillan's curious prophecy to the editors by passing away immediately on Lord Beaverbrook's doorstep. This would have been a tragic occasion, to be sure, and one likely to be loaded with excruciating embarrassments for me. How, I asked myself, could I now initiate the delicate process of telephoning this story of international importance over Lord Beaverbrook's own instrument, but to a rival newspaper? The situation appalled me. In those days I still clung to some of the vernal romanticism of the trade: I foresaw myself seized, overpowered, manacled in a Riviera oubliette, lest I should scoop Lord Beaverbrook on his own story of his own guest from his own home.

While these considerations passed through my mind, standing

helplessly in the hall, the crisis was abruptly resolved: the prostrate figure of Sir Winston Churchill came emphatically into being, gesticulating and muttering in a fashion most indicative of life, and within a few minutes was established in a drawing-room chair and manifestly the man who had come to dinner.

I had passed the previous twenty years in a total awareness of Winston Churchill; he had been for me integrally part of the political composition of my times. It is true that for some time I had ceased to share in the idolatry; it seemed to me a poor service to a superlatively vigorous and inventive mind that every one of his splendid semantic experiments should be invested with infallibility. I had always greatly admired his writing and his oratory, in small doses (it had seemed to me inspirational that any politician could have tumbled intuitively on the fact that the literary style most suited for the beleagured British days was the Augustan), but, in common with much of his respectful audience, I regretted his adherence to the stage when the war was over and the task was done. Nevertheless, it had never fallen to my lot to meet this phenomenal man before, and I saluted him with reverence.

He was not, I think, aware of this; having been deposited in his chair the old gentleman was clearly content to let circumstances take their course, and by and by fell into a doze. He continued in a light sleep throughout the meal.

Since Sir Winston was disinclined to make conversation, and I was understandably *hors concours,* the social burden was therefore left to Lord Beaverbrook and Mr Onassis. I have always been at once fascinated and baffled by the conversation of extremely rich people in each other's company. As a rule it treats of matters both financial and technical that are to me so recondite they could as well be conducted in Aramaic or Pushtu. I observed that our host addressed Mr Onassis as 'Harry'; it had never before occurred to me that such was the comradely diminutive of 'Aristotle'. I reflected with some pleasure on that discovery, while the newspaper baron and the millionaire shipowner debated in the mysterious language of money, and the former Prime Minister of Britain slumbered quietly away in his own private dreamland, as remote from the gathering as myself.

It was obvious that I could make no kind of contribution to the financial small talk that would be other than totally fatuous, and since it seemed impolite to join Sir Winston in oblivion, I contented myself with eating my dinner, which was excellent, and consuming as much as I prudently could of my host's wine, which was even better. The whole occasion was invested in a quality of reverie: I was at last in the presence of a statesman renowned for the power of his oratory, on the one evening when it was clear he was unlikely to utter a single word; I was washed over by the table-talk of a couple of immensely rich financiers, whose language I could not even understand.

For one brief moment in the course of this strange party did Sir Winston Churchill suddenly surface from his private considerations and join, albeit momentarily, in the convivial scene. In the middle of some complex discussion about investments Sir Winston suddenly opened his pale blue eyes and said, apropos of nothing whatever: 'Max, did you ever go to Russia?'

Lord Beaverbrook turned to him in surprise and said, with a sort of affectionate acerbity: 'Come now, of course I did; you sent me there yourself; I had the Ministry; you gave me the Mission to Stalin; do you not remember sending me to Moscow?'

'Ah yes,' said Sir Winston in a faraway voice. 'But did you ever *go*?' And with contentment he settled himself at ease, and no more was heard from him that night.

After dinner somebody put a cigar into his mouth and lit it; it seemed a ritual gesture without dignity; the completion of an effigy. Already I had begun to find this a profoundly melancholy occasion. My own admiration of the old gentleman's vigorous and abrasive qualities had always been qualified by opposition to almost every one of his public attitudes; nevertheless he had been a hundred times the person I could ever hope to be, and it was sad to see him, for the first and the last time, diminished into a totem, part of the social image of a rich Greek patron. Of course the old man's achievements had secured him sufficient place in the records of history to transcend the ignominy of a nursery-party at Cap d'Ail. I could have wished, however, not to have been present as the footmen bore the old man out in his chair like a small statue, just still aware enough of his exit to raise his hand in his reflex gesture of the separated fingers.

That was the end of that. I did in fact do the book about 1916, but the papers on which I worked were limited and inadequate, and my enthusiasm soon flagged, and the book in the end was trivial and meaningless. In the intervening period a very curious legend arose, to the effect that somehow or other I had been commissioned by Lord Beaverbrook to write his biography. This myth did not altogether displease me, because its total incredibility seemed rather funny; several people had essayed that rewarding subject and been deflected by Lord Beaverbrook's understandable evasions, and for anyone who knew either of us the notion that Lord Beaverbrook would commission for this task me, of all people, was rewardingly humorous. I did the 1916 book, which profoundly disappointed both him and me, for different reasons, and that was the end of the affair.

Somehow or other we continued to survive, though it became often enough a question of improvisation. The acceptance of a condition of permanent hard-upness was not new to me by any means, never since I could remember had my family had any money at all and I could not imagine a condition where things would be otherwise, nor can I now, nor doubtless ever shall. Elma and I had spent our brief life together on an income that never quite reached ten pounds a week; Elizabeth and I had been in some measure even more beset, since our responsibilities were greater, and practically never was there a week without harassing cares about how to survive the next. I cannot really explain why this should have been so, since there were times when I earned considerable money; we were both improvident, but no more so it seemed than anyone else of our acquaintance, yet while other people owned cars and washing-machines, we seemed incapable of achieving either; I lived in an endemic condition of cashlessness; nor can I say that this has especially changed. Many years later there were intervals when I earned a lot of money; I suppose I was among the better-paid people of my trade; it seemed to make very little difference. I would argue that my extravagances were balanced by my economies: it was true that I drank and smoked far too much, but I was temperamentally incapable of enjoying gambling, and I ate uncommonly little; I owned no car, nor indeed much else, yet I spent the months despairing of raising enough money to pay my income tax. It engendered in me a chronic nervousness of banks; to this day I never enter one if I can avoid it. The perverse aspect of all this was that it bore not the least resemblance to romantic poverty; I was no struggling artist contending with an indifferent or hostile world in the electric despondency of adolescence, I was a middle-aged man with a certain useful if commonplace reputation, frequently earning substantial fees, and I reeled through the management of my life in a state of wondering anxiety. The fact that almost everyone of my acquaintance, even some of great consideration and name, were in much the same boat consoled me in no way. I remember thinking on my fiftieth birthday, with thirty years of work behind me and half a dozen books, that the clear possession of five hundred pounds would have changed my life. It is true that by now a family split so arbitrarily and absurdly all over the place was bound to absorb more than anyone's income; that was bad management too. It was a silly way to live.

Diversion 4: The Lady

By the time I crossed the frontier from Mongolia into Irkutsk the temperature was so low you would have required to get down on your hands and knees to see it. I had not thought it possible for anywhere on the inhabited earth to be so cold. Irkutsk is set, apparently, in the middle of a million miles of snow; it is the kind of place whose citizens might well take their holidays at the Pole.

I was also hungry. It was in those days the custom of the Soviet airlines to sell transportation, and nothing whatever else, certainly no food. All the ancillary services on which the capitalist operators set such store – champagne lunches, cups of tea, cocktails and canapés, sweet smiles and sick-bags and seat-belts: all these the Russians considered decadent and superfluous; it was their contract to deliver you on time, and this they did, when the Siberian blizzards permitted.

At Irkutsk I was peckish, at Novosibirsk I was uneasy, at Omsk I was ravenous, at Sverdlovsk I was rattling like a bongo drum. I finally reached Moscow, and if ever I had felt the need of kindness and consideration it was at that time. Not always did the trans-Siberian traveller find it then, in mid-winter Moscow.

It was one of the few coincidences of fortune in a generally luckless life that it was exactly then that once again I met Amelie, whose name was in fact something quite different. She was the wife of a diplomatist in one of the Western embassies – a splendid place with wine-cellars and Manet prints and new novels and log fires; a bourgeois enclave if ever I saw one and, for one in my condition, after so long among the beguiling but stark austerities of China, nothing went more instantly to the heart. I owe a great deal to many acquaintances all over the world, but to none more than to the friend who long ago and in another place had given me the introduction to Amelie.

During my stay in Moscow Amelie occupied herself with me. She fed me, she mixed me Bloody Marys, she gave me rides in the Chancery car. If my attitude sounds grasping and ignoble, it must be remembered that the rouble rate at the time was punitive, and in any case I was virtually penniless. Without Amelie I would have been in poor case. I was always very vulnerable to kindness. It is possible that this colours the memory.

The trouble with Amelie, however, was her nature, her temperament or her manner, which was so cordial and affectionate, so persuasively absorbed in whoever she had befriended, so subtly responsive, that even the Soviet winter seemed benign and warm. She was both beautiful and attentive; a rare combination. Try as she would, Amelie could not help giving the impression that she had spent every moment of her life until now breathlessly waiting for the arrival of whoever had unexpectedly turned up.

Such was her spirit that one rejoiced. One did? Hundreds had. The diplomatic world was littered with young Second Secretaries, and not a few distinguished Counsellors, who cherished in the secret hearts the illusion it was they alone who had aroused her serious intention, and that somewhere or other Amelie was waiting for their return.

It was all the most tremendous nonsense, of course; Amelie was the most devoted wife in Europe, and furthermore the mother of quite surprising numbers of happy children. It was just that she could not help looking at one in that way.

She took me to the Mrac Theatre, where I sat on a wooden seat through three and a half hours of Gogol of which I understood not one syllable; they passed in a haze of enchantment. She took me to the night-club under the Sovietskaya Hotel; it resembled the third-class [*sic*] waiting room at Crewe Station, and I had never felt anywhere so sympathetic and romantic. She took me to the Gorky Park of Rest and Culture, and if there is one thing that in the ordinary way casts me into an anaesthetic gloom it is a Park of Rest and Culture, but on this occasion it appeared like the Elysian Fields. She took me shopping in the GUM Store, and even that seemed good.

Then one day we were coming away from Saint Basil's Cathedral at the end of the Red Square and passing by the great Kremlin gate beneath the Campanile, when the electric bell at the gate began to shrill, as it does when a high dignitary's car is emerging.

At this the traffic pauses, the police salute, the curious stare and the nervous glance away. As the long black car came through the gate beside us there was a glimpse of a man in a fur hat, who appeared to catch sight of Amelie, and raised his hand in recognition. I glanced at Amelie; she was smiling demurely, her lips parted, her little face warm and alive, her soft eyes glowing with the same sweetness that had caused so much sweet uneasiness to me and to so many others. She said in her gentle voice: 'That is the biggest and most unprincipled shit in Russia. I hope and believe,' said her pretty lips, 'that very soon he will be denounced, demoted, and dead.'

And by and by he was: all three.

You may guess who it was; as I say it was some time ago.

Chapter Twelve

ONE evening I was in Paris watching some yogis demonstrating to Unesco when someone rang me from London and told me to go that weekend to Tibet. Until that moment it had not occurred to me that this would be a good thing to do.

However, with the formal docility engendered by a life almost wholly governed by the caprices of other people, I went back to my room and sketched out, as far as such a thing were possible, a tentative schedule, an itinerary; pondered on the inevitable domestic explanations and apologies. It was late, and the concierge, in the prudent fashion of functionaries in very obscure French hotels, had secured the telephone with a heavy padlock; I had to tramp as far as Saint Germain before I found a café willing to trust me overnight for half a dozen trunk calls. Even at that time it all seemed an excessive amount of endeavour for a somewhat tenuous chance. But that was merely one more hazard of a professional life that has not, after all, been without its preposterous aspects.

All that winter Europe had been fretful and ill at ease, adrift in a half-life in which conjecture and disenchantment had taken substance; casting its eyes intermittently to the East, where one war after another had reached a nadir of both achievement and morality, or so it seemed. One spent one's time trying, with slackening conviction and mounting impatience, to explain what appeared to be realities – no one wanted to know, no one required any more than the reinforcement of this preconception or that; in the midst of argument one saw their eyes cloud with suspicion, or worse, boredom; soon one ceased to insist.

Why should one pretend to know, anyway? The yogis in Paris had been consoling, one watched their contortions with a sense of refreshment: two old gentlemen obsessed with the discipline of each other's viscera. As they dangled or writhed on the floor their isolation communicated itself: minds untroubled with anything more complicated than how to control the pulses of the gut, the divisions of the spine, the throbbing of the heart. There might be something of that sedative influence in the high Himalaya, where, after all, it had all begun.

So now we were off again. I collected Bert Hardy, the photographer, my collaborator in several other such maniac ventures; there was an hour or two of that most satisfying occupation: liberal and fanciful shopping at someone else's expense – tents, sleeping-bags, curiously shaped boots.

It is true that we had reason for wondering what, in fact, was going on in Tibet. For months past most of the Asiatic attention that could be spared from Korea had been fixed spasmodically, on that extravagantly obscure country. General Liu Po Chen, Commander of the Chinese Second Field Army had declared that Chinese forces would shortly move into Tibet 'to drive out the aggressive influence of British and American imperialism' – a familiar enough phrase, though somewhat unreal to the dozens of capitalist-sponsored word-mongers who had failed so often in the past to stick their aggressive noses one imperialistic half-inch into that impossibly obdurate country. Tibet's kingdom's rulers would be allowed regional self-government, he said – referring as he was to a region so exclusive and feudal it were as though he conceded a measure of authority to the Governor of Sing Sing. Tibet's armies would be incorporated into the defence forces of the People's Republic – again a curious requirement from a state whose armies, everyone said, would have difficulty in standing up for ten minutes against the Eastbourne Boy Scouts. It was impossible to know whether this meant anything or nothing. No country except India maintained any overt representation in Tibet; the Chinese Mission had been expelled the previous summer, which possible accounted at least in part for the Chinese petulance. British influence over the years had been confined to a few not very admirable punitive raids and a good deal of diplomatic horse-trading. Tibet had no overseas representation anywhere, their foreign policy having always rigorously been to have none at all, on the irresistibly reasonable principle that no good ever came of getting oneself involved, however academically, with anyone else's affairs.

Then at last, in October, New Delhi confirmed that the Chinese had invaded from the western provinces of Sikang and Chinghai and that the town of Cham-do, capital of Kham province and just three hundred miles from Lhasa, was in Chinese hands.

Then Tibet at last shouted for help. Her appeal to the United Nations was dated from Lhasa 'on the twenty seventh day of the Ninth Month of the year of the Iron Tiger'. It sounded, at the time, like a thin and indistinct voice in the wilderness. In the United Nations it was left, God knows why, to the delegate from San Salvador to call on that body to condemn an 'unprovoked aggression'. It all seemed, on the whole, a proposition of the most academic kind.

Immediately, however, a flock of the most bizarre stories began to emerge from the East. Tibet was a name to encourage flights of fancy; it carried connotations of mystery and glamour that were journalistically most desirable. The public prints of Britain and the United States, already depressed and irritated by the repetitive dismal associations of Korea, seized gladly on inspired accounts of mobilized monks, of underground movements on the roof of the world, of mountain batteries on yak-back led by mystics in exotic costume.

Above all the newspapers were entranced by one especial aspect of the news; the escape of the Dalai Lama. Here was this ineffably sacred figure, of uniquely picturesque glory, of whom not one reliable photograph existed in anyone's files, already in flight over the impregnable passes in a vast caravan loaded with matchless gems and bullion and religious objects (so it was said) carved from solid emeralds; a sensationally attractive picture to those whose thoughts automatically leaped to double-page spreads and the irresistible dateline: *Lhasa, Monday.*

In such circumstances anyone with a reasonable familiarity with the East, who could represent himself, at least in the unchallenging surroundings of Fleet Street, as being able to recognize the difference between a Tibetan and a Bhutani, could profess to be an authority. I made no such claim; nevertheless I had been travelling in Asia long enough to be considered qualified for Tibet at least as much as the Berlin correspondent, or the expert on nuclear fission. In such a fashion, I have observed, are journalistic reputations made: one chance visit to some unlikely neighbourhood gives to the traveller an arbitrary mantle of authority, at least to the editors of influential journals, few of whom can ever afford the time to journey farther afield than the country homes of their proprietors. Thus ordained by the casual encounter, many an earnest writer has been returned repeatedly to the scene of his alleged *expertise*; by virtue of this he eventually becomes willy-nilly the authority he was all the time supposed to be. At that precise moment, by the immutable newspaper tradition, he is then compelled to write about some other place, to which he has never been and of which, more than likely, he has never heard.

That awkward moment I had eluded by spending my time so variously, and in so many incompatible environments, that I was considered to have special knowledge of one thing only: abrupt and violent changes of surroundings. Moreover my inoculations (the prime qualification for a contemporary foreign correspondent) were reasonably in order; my passport was endorsed, it seemed, for every spot on the earth's surface that had accepted the civilizing influence of immigration control. I had a fraying document, forged for me some years before by an obliging colleague in East Africa, certifying that I was free from infectious disease, including omnis t.b. and trypansiniasis, leprosy and venereal infection at a contagious stage, which had been a valuable talisman at many suspicious but uncritical frontiers.

So at last it was once again Calcutta in the soft clammy darkness of two in the morning; the familiar sounds and scents, memory flooding back, renewing the consciousness, reconditioning the senses to half-forgotten attitudes of body and mind. Lurching in the wooden bus from Dum Dum airport through the flaring lamplight of the suburban slums, clamorous and turbulent even at such an hour; staring, still half-anaesthetized with fatigue, at the silent sleeping gutter forms, the glow of naphtha-flame on copper; how could one be even momentarily absorbed at the sight of a place one had hated so much? Calcutta for me had disturbing, buried associations only of the more wretched emotions: fear, compassion, desperation; I had seen it howling with riot and racked with famine; there I had myself sweated out my first terrified battle with malaria; I remembered powerfully the joy with which I had left it, thinking it was for the last time.

Another aeroplane, another country, another conception of gastronomy; the sun had arisen on a Dry Day, with a sombre barman replacing all the bottles with Orange Essence and Quinine

Tonic; and breakfast was high over the Ganges: cold scrambled eggs in a paper bag; in mine I found a blackened cigarette-end.

Only then, only as we drifted down to the barren strip at Baghdogra, as we stepped stiff-legged out on to the parched and brittle grass and the heat leaped off the ground in stunning waves, only then did I feel that the journey had really begun.

At Calcutta we had been told that there would be a bus, or a car, ordered and ready for us at Baghdogra. It would take us up the road to Darjeeling for eleven rupees. Like almost everything else connected with Asian travel, this proved to be an illusion: there was to be no bus, and no car, no eleven rupees – and, as it turned out, no road.

There were, however, three or four vociferous men in crumpled pajama, who ran up to us shouting as we stood aimlessly on the perimeter track. Still labouring under the false impression that some kind of arrangement had in fact been made for our arrival, we discussed the matter of driving to Darjeeling. They made scornful gestures. Hardly, since there had been an earthquake, or a cataclysm of some kind; the road to Darjeeling no longer existed. This we took in good part, as one of the routine stratagems by which Indian drivers at all times seek to enhance both the difficulty of their task and the price they exact for it. They all presented the same story: they would take us to the final point of the road's disappearance, by no means for eleven rupees, but for forty.

It seemed there was a portage over the landslide, with cars waiting at the other side. The forty rupees would include transport in this fashion to the very heart of Darjeeling. So we closed the deal, there being in fact nothing else to do, whereupon the drivers decided that the first expressions of good fellowship and bonhomie had served their purpose, and relapsed into saturnine and meditative silence.

The only other passengers were a party of four Theosophists, two middle-aged couples with quiet determined manners and keen relentless tourists' eyes for notable bridges, unusual shrubs and local curiosities of all kinds. They were Australians, and they had been attending a convention of their society at Adyar in Madras – I remembered it well from three years before: tall palms in the twilight, a soporific heat, willowy spectacled Europeans looking diffident and strange in Indian costume, an atmosphere half-devotional, half-social, a metaphysical garden-party to the tune of teacups and the throbbing *vina*. Now, before they returned to the brisk materialism of New South Wales, they had decided to tour India from north to south, absorbing its vast variety from the Snows to Ceylon in three weeks.

Far away, the hot horizon vanished in an impenetrable heavy steam; higher the steam turned to mist; and somewhere behind that curtain lay the soaring extravagant skyline of the snows: indeed the Lost Horizon itself. As we moved up into the *tarai* it began to get noticeably cooler. Our driver, who by now had sunk into a sour and morose reverie, reached from time to time into the recesses of his seat for a shawl, or a scarf, or a fragment of decaying rugwork, and distributed them about his person with what seemed to be exaggerated gestures of discomfort. He manipulated his car in a fashion characteristic of all Asian drivers for whom the internal combustion engine is an unsympathetic and slightly hostile servant – on reaching a gradient he would permit the engine to grunt and labour until the pinking sounded like the ringing of temple bells; only at that ultimate moment would he change down, vindictively, as though making an irritable concession to some absurd mechanical principle. His face never relaxed its melancholy except once when, passing through some shabby village, he contrived to roar past an old Hindu with a barrow so suddenly and so closely that the ancient man collapsed fainting into a doorway; this brought a fleeting smile of appreciation to the driver's face.

By the afternoon the nose of the car was pointing permanently upwards, the cool had changed to genuine cold, swirls of mist eddied around. The road began to writhe spectacularly round the spurs of invisible mountains, along the edge of vaporous ravines. Then, abruptly, it stopped. We came to a jarring halt behind the tailboard of a gigantic lorry. Our driver turned, with the first evidence of genuine pleasure he had yet shown, and said: 'Getting out now. No further go.'

When at last we saw it, the roadbreak was a vastly impressive sight. Quite suddenly the road had gone – awkward and obscure and difficult as it might have been, it was nevertheless the great highway of North India, the indispensable road from Bengal to Sikkim and Tibet and beyond, in a sense the one major trade-route from the south of the sub-continent to the great hinterland of Central Asia, and without warning it had collapsed, and vanished into the abyss. Weakened by the monsoon rains, it had fallen off its ledge for three quarters of a mile and disintegrated into an avalanche of rocks and gravel far below. Far across the valley was the road again, as it were in another country.

An indistinguishable multitude of passengers, porters, drivers and casual bystanders milled around, appearing and disappearing like phantoms. Everything was being unloaded to the backs of the porters – from sacks of mail to baskets of fruit to the enormous components of vast machines; piled in impossible quantities on the backs of men and women and children who trudged slowly off and disappeared into the fog.

As soon as our car arrived on this confused scene part of the crowd detached itself and surrounded us in what the Theosophists took to be a highly menacing way, shaking bony fists and uttering piercing cries. They were, however, only promoting business in the usual fashion of northern coolies, and very soon every piece of baggage had been removed from the car and had vanished into the impenetrable fog.

They had advised us that the portage entailed three quarters of a mile walk; what they had not said was that it was to be three quarters of a mile almost vertically. A constant stream of porters overtook us, like a procession of upward-moving Atlases. Their meagre bodies seemed capable of bearing phenomenal loads; frail old ladies and gentlemen on stick-like legs flitted past us under incredible mountains of baggage, bearing on their heads and shoulders vast steel trunks, packing-cases, great cast-iron gearwheels for what can only have been the equipment of a powerhouse. The loads of machinery, petrol and rice going north passed the loads of tea and hides going south. Occasionally we came on exhausted coolies balancing their loads on a rock; their breath came in long noisy retching gasps; one of them had a little dribble of scarlet at his lips. I learned later that a coolie was expected to carry up to two-and-a-half maunds – some two hundred pounds – for which at the other end he received eight annas, which was ninepence.

The long file of humanity toiled upwards, winding, gasping, climbing, like a Doré picture of the damned. By and by I was gratified to recognize my own gear proceeding dimly ahead of me in the mist. It was the only luggage visible that had been actually designed to be carried by a climber: a rucksack. Nevertheless the porter had been at some pains to rearrange the harness so that it hung upside-down, in the one possible position in which the steel frame would press painfully on the shoulders and render any kind of movement full of discomfort. I pointed this out to the porter and reversed the load; he nodded breathlessly and hurried on; when I met him again at the far end of the trail the rucksack was once again upside-down.

The scene on the north side of the portage was exactly the same as on the other: trucks, debris, confusion, an apparently immovable congestion. After some casting about we found the car which we had been given to understand was in some sort of loose partnership with our first driver; hours later we walked stiff-legged into the hotel, exactly forty-one and a half hours after leaving Paris.

Like almost everyone who has ever had to move a great deal from place to place, I like to consider myself an authority on hotels. I am prepared to admit to being a hotel-snob in a perverse even perhaps inverted way; I consider that after some five and a half circuits of the globe I am familiar with more wretched and abominable hotels than any other contender of my weight: I have debated this claim with many travellers equally well versed in the global science of bad innkeeping, and I have usually been able to secure the decision on the recollection of some little-known but incontestably terrible place of entertainment, almost invariably named in the English tongue.

Darjeeling in midwinter cold, post-war Darjeeling, the Darjeeling from which the tide of the Raj had long receded, was a place of solitude and desolation. This hotel was probably, at that especial moment, the emptiest in all the world. It was a barren vacancy, an echoing cavernous gelid place from which almost all sign of life had been removed. It had been built to accommodate hundreds of guests; now there were only six. Had it not been for the Theosophists, still querulously with us, there would have been but two. And had no sudden whim struck the controllers of our magazine some days before, no hankering after the unattainable picturesque, there would have been nobody at all.

I bear no grudge at all against this place; I have known many hotels slightly worse. By the standards of Trinidad, say, or Tanganyika, this was not unreasonable. It was merely abandoned; a vast lounge resounding bleakly to every footfall, furlongs of freezing corridors, a deserted and lockfast bar, an untended chill pervading everything.

The hotel had the curious characteristic of being many degrees colder inside than the wintry open air; after a while we acquired the trick of leaving our thick coats in the hallway, to put *on* as we went in, plunging for meals into that deadly interior. When we asked for a fire they said that each bucket of fuel would cost four rupees; a bearer would then spend the evening puffing uselessly at three smoking sticks and a handful of coal.

There are moments in India, and no doubt always have been, when every function of human domestic behaviour appears to be performed with a futility, a hopeless and infuriating lack of the meanest dexterity that drives one almost to mania. At such times it seems past understanding how this ancient and numerous people ever contrived to get their race propagated at all, let alone produce undying work of beauty and scientific permanence. At other times there is the corrective – some unexpected demonstration of extraordinary skill and resource, some extravagant dinner prepared in a tin-can oven; a delicate bauble suddenly moulded from coloured mud. No such surprise made its appearance at Darjeeling; the apparently endless depths of this great gaunt hotel laboured, and produced a dinner of tinned fish in tinned gravy; the bearers struck interminable matches and produced a wreath of smoke and a little pile of ash.

Next morning at dawn I opened my eyes directly on the window, and the shock of that tremendous view nearly bounced me out of bed. It was sensational: a soaring extravagant horizon of enormous peaks, petrified melodrama, the apotheosis of Himalaya, with the highest mountain in the world invisible only because the second-highest mountain in the world was in the way . . . It is customary, and frequently proper, to disparage the better known and generally praised aspects of famous beauty, to profess a sense of disappointment when confronted at last by the Taj Mahal, the Victoria Falls, the Golden Horn. Indeed it may be that too much renown vitiates the final experience. But on this day, this first Himalayan dawn, the impact of Kanchenjunga standing most undeniably monarch and among that staggering barrier, peach-glow against the grey, the momentary rosy irridescence, so far surpassed anything I had foreseen that I stood trembling with cold at the window, staring at that fading achievement of rock and snow, as swiftly the clouds assembled and engulfed it before my eyes.

Almost exactly fifty airmiles away, on a bearing just north-east and over yet another wild grille of mountains, was the objective: the dim and rickety village of Yatung. To that much, now, had the supposed majesty of Lhasa dwindled: a peasant encampment on the frontier. There sat the refugee Court of Tibet, that ineffable coterie of monks and mystics and inscrutable smart operators and anxious businessmen with braided hair – just in Tibet, and no more. That extraordinary country might well see its remoteness disintegrating, some of the canvas scenery might be visible through the cracks; nevertheless Tibet remained Tibet – some get out, few get in.

Between it and us lay Sikkim, and India continued to regard Sikkim as a buffer territory to be controlled with extreme care. The Tibetan situation had sharpened this to an obsessive suspicion.

That morning I had set off on one of those endless paperchases that afflict all enterprises in the East, the game of hunt-the-functionary that frustrates the operations of all travellers in a hurry. Before we could move into Gangtok it was necessary to get from the Deputy Commissioner some sort of formula in writing – no one was very sure what – that would convince the police on both sides of the frontier that we had authority to travel. It seemed a strange necessity in this neighbourhood of unmarked boundaries, of empty hill-tracks, of formidably desolate grandeur.

We were told that we might find the DC in his office, some way down the steep road. Alternatively he might be in his home, a few miles around the rim of the valley. Or indeed he might be 'on tour' – the generic Indian term embracing every kind of journey from an Everest expedition to an afternoon in the country. No one offered any real hope of finding him. The DC, they said, was a Bengali, and everyone knew what Bengalis were. These small high-cheeked mountain people spoke of the Indians almost exactly as the British used to do, with either exasperation or contempt. Indeed, as I grew to know the hill people better I was increasingly struck by their resemblance to the English – they are good-humoured on their own ground and ill at ease away from it, intolerant of strangers, given to laughing abruptly at obscure jokes, greatly admiring physical prowess and somewhat impatient with the reflective qualities; they have a liking for living in inaccessible places and for not being bothered by things; they also tend to assess their fellow-men by the colour of their faces. They had no high opinion of officialdom and the intrusion of Delhi bureaucracy; it was almost embarrassing to find that the word 'babu' held for them exactly the same connotation as it had held for the Sahibs. The DC, they said sourly, was part of the price of Independence.

His office, when I found it, was deserted. A dispirited chaprassi crouching in the passage directed me upstairs. Eventually I wandered through a wooden doorway unexpectedly marked 'laboratory'; this too was utterly deserted; there were a few bottles and jars and a broken umbrella; on a deal table lay the remains of a dog, opened up and skewered flat where some easily-discouraged pathologist had tired of his work and abandoned it. Only the intense cold prevented this situation from being more repellent than it looked.

I hurried back to the hotel and telephoned the DC's house. After a considerable time an infuriated voice replied; when we asked if the DC were in the voice said testily that it would enquire; we heard it breathing heavily while we waited, then abruptly the same voice barked that this was the DC; what did we want? Certainly we might not call; all official business was transacted at the office. No, it was most doubtful if we could arrange an appointment for several days. Under pressure, he conceded that he would see us next day at ten a.m., but not one moment later, as tomorrow was a day of exceptional preoccupation.

That left the rest of the day to kill in Darjeeling, never at any time a place of intense or varied distraction. It wore an air typical now of most hill stations established during the spacious administrative days, of forlorn desuetude, not unlike that of Bognor Regis in November, only here one knew that the season, such as it was, would never return; the paint would continue to peel, the weeds to grow on the gravel, the terraced roads to crumble and fall, with greater and greater frequency and less and less inconvenience, into the valley below. In its heyday it must always have been a reasonably good example of how the world's most sublime natural situations can be chosen for the world's most frightful town planning. This foothill range of the Himalaya, with its incomparable aspect of Kanchenjunga, with Everest itself visible after a short climb, its contours and terraces disposed with splendid grace around the curve of the vast glen – it would have been worthy of some brave and soaring experiment of architecture, something elegant and fine like the treetops, or vast and monumental like the mountains – something, possibly, of the ponderous towering mass the Tibetans devised for their fabulous Potala at Lhasa. Instead, Darjeeling got a scattering of stone villas like those designed for retired Bolton mill-owners, full of tricky gables and castellated ineptitudes; what wasn't opulent was gimcrack; one stared at the mountains over a fringe of red corrugated iron.

Next day I was outside the DC's office some time before ten. The chilly passage was already full of the miscellaneous group of supplicants and henchmen invariably to be found outside every one of the countless Government offices throughout India. They disposed themselves in attitudes of practised endurance, munching nuts or squatting before little braziers that they surprisingly produced, already burning, from the recesses of their garments.

After two hours a clerk appeared from the office, glanced around the group with unconcealed dislike, and said: 'DC not coming.' I protested that I had an appointment. Very well, I could see the DC's D – an extraordinary piece of cognomination that turned out to mean the Deputy Commissioner's Deputy.

He sat in his office doing the *Statesman* crossword; he received us petulantly, his manner combining in the Bengali fashion both servility and insolence, a firm assumption of office and a professional inability to make the most trifling and simple decision on his own authority. A pass for Sikkim? Impossible. I insisted: not impossible; the frontier was controlled, but not closed. Well, for that I must see the DC. How could I gain access to the DC? Only through himself, the DC's D. And for himself, the DC's D, to make such an order would require instructions from the DC, who was unavailable.

So far the negotiations were running to form. I produced several impeccable credentials; I produced also a letter very luckily received just before leaving London in which a high official of the Government of India had written in most friendly and even fulsome terms of an article I had done not long before on Jawaharlal Nehru. This affected the clerk visibly; he asked for

my passport as proof of my identity. For some time he brooded
over this; having opened it the wrong way he chose to concern
himself wholly with the recorded facts that I had at various times
received allocations of francs, dollars, pesos, yen, ticals, lire,
piastres and Lebanese pounds – an interesting study in irrelevant
economics, but no; he decided inevitably against responsibility, I
must wait for the DC. When would he become visible? No one
knew. One must be patient. If one were really anxious, one might
possibly trace the DC to Kalimpong.

By this time I had a car hired and waiting; I left for Kalimpong
angrily, resentfully, full of exasperation; I have never regretted
anything less. Kalimpong, after Darjeeling was heaven.

Our car, in which I was to spend so many curious hours thereafter, was an ancient and deafening German Opel; it must have
been old long before the war, and yet – the perversity of a
country where the rules always break down – it ran superbly,
reliably, valiantly. Its driver was a gentle young Nepali called
Sani, small and superficially feeble, with a profile like an ivory
cameo and a battered Gurkha hat that he kept, when not wearing
it, in a brown paper bag.

From Darjeeling to Kalimpong is perhaps no more than twenty
miles as the eagle might fly; it is so tortuous and erratic a road that
the journey takes several hours; it is also perhaps one of the most
extravagantly beautiful rides in the world. The road mounts,
mounts among the deodars and rhododendron, and dives in a
spiral through groves of nutmeg and pandanus fern, hugging one
side and then another of some gigantic slope, leaning over and in
on itself like an aircraft in a steep gliding turn, towards the great
rivers far below. From time to time it passed through the tea-
garden terraces, with their bushes laid in regular bumpy patterns
over the contours, like knitting. The little Opel ground up and
down and round with a dogged roar; by and by I fell asleep since,
however dominant and superlative the view around me, the back
seat of a moving car is the only place on earth in which I can be
perfectly certain of sleep. I roused myself to find the car stopped,
steaming and gasping; I got out to stand on the verge of a steep
slope overlooking the grandest defile I ever saw. Deep below
wound the channel of the Great Rangit river, just at the point
where it joined the Tista, mightiest stream of the North. The
Great Rangit at that point serves as boundary between Nepal and

Sikkim, the Tista unites the wild desolation of the snows with the remote heat of the Brahmaputra plains. From that eyrie where we stood, Sani and Bert and I, we could see the unlimited receding heights of the mountains, all so similar, yet in five countries. Below us lay Sikkim, behind us India, to the west was Nepal, to the east Bhutan. Dead ahead, a cluster of hills behind more hills, was Tibet. There can be few more embracing views, for men still with their feet on solid earth.

As the sun left us and the road began to shrug itself into shadows, a chill swept down from the heights. From time to time some strange thing would caper momentarily in the headlights; once I recognized the almost unrealistic domestic shape of a great wild cat, with blazing blinded emerald eyes. We churned on. We dived deep into the Tista valley; over it and zigzagged up the other side. At the end of the day we came to Kalimpong.

The discovery of Kalimpong was I fear not mine; the place was not, as I should like to think, revealed insubstantially in an enchanted everglade at the end of some unearthly wandering. It was substantial enough, by all means, and tolerably well known; to previous generations of old India-hands it was a hill-resort of a certain but not remarkable charm, and though that evening it had a vaguely mirage-like quality, it was certainly no Shangri-La. Nevertheless it remains in my mind as one of the three or four oddest places I ever knew, and most endearing.

Kalimpong, hanging on to a hillside in North Bengal, main roadhead for all the caravan traffic from the north, had somehow become a rendezvous for what was probably the most impressive collection of human eccentrics in Asia. Where the trail met the town was now the funnel through which Tibet was filtering what she could of her property; the wool, the hides, the borax, the musk, the furs, and other commodities less easily identifiable. Wealthy refugees and peasant-traders, bumping south down the Chumbi Valley on their mules; curious individuals drifting north to see what was going on – a miscellaneous double stream of irreconciliables had silted up in Kalimpong and turned it into a place where anything might appear round any corner. There among a fluttering forest of prayer-flags, a smell of incense and a rickle of corrugated iron, strange characters moved around in concentric circles, eyeing each other sharply. The district had gradually filled up with a complex variety of remarkable, almost surrealist people; to the ordinary background confusion of Nepali farmers, Indian merchants and Lepcha tribesmen had been added a rich seasoning of wizards and sorcerers, Tibetan aristocrats, angry exiles from China, remote sprigs from the forgotten European nobility, Indian yogi, Bhutani politicians, professional anthropologists, linguists, students, pilgrims, miracle-workers and innocent by-standers, all milling around with curious axes to grind and trying either to get into Tibet, or to get out. There were European Buddhists attempting to convert the Christians, and Christian evangelists retaliating on the Buddhists, and many itinerant abbots of indescribable piety and filth. There was the last remnants of the Tibetan Mission to the United Nations, bewildered and forlorn, dismally spinning their prayer-wheels without the remotest idea of what was going to happen next.

Vaguely in the centre of this pageant of fantastics was the Himalaya Hotel. This is a commonplace name for a most exceptional place. If I keep so persistently harping on hotels it is only that, having spent quite a disproportionate part of my life in them, I have come to classify and record them much as, I believe, accomplished winelovers define clarets, less for their appearance and cost as for their associations and bouquet. The Himalaya was, by those standards, a collector's piece. It was (and I hope still is) the nearest thing to what I imagine the seventeenth century English inn must have been, in its broadminded and casual attitude to the one factor absent from almost all other hotels, hospitality. People came in, and drifted about, and occupied themselves with erratic pursuits, and told incredible stories in several languages, and made abrupt appearances in extravagant clothes, and no one was there an hour before he would find him-self involved and embraced in the inescapable community life of the place. Which was all the odder since the place was full of those most exclusive and (as we always imagined) unclubbable of all peoples, Tibetans.

That night I bathed in a large tin tub and went into what in any other hotel would have been called a lounge, for what anywhere else would have been called a quick drink, before what in most other places would have been dinner. In no single particular was this purpose accomplished; rather, in every aspect did it material-ize some ten times life-size. To call this room a lounge would have been ridiculous; it was a salon, a caravanserai, a large room crowded, as we saw with surprise, with a multitude of striking and picturesque people in richly-coloured costume and exceptional hairdressings; they were occupied not, as one might have thought, in being photographed for the *National Geographic Magazine*, but in a variety of pleasantly domestic occupations such as pouring tots of rum and knitting socks, and discussing questions of mutual interest in an animated and formal way. Most of them were Tibetans; there were also several people who might have been economics lecturers on vacation, refugees from Cheltenham Ladies' College, and at least one who was quite evidently a Benedictine monk in disguise. Before our entry we had considered dubiously whether our appearance – unshaven, khaki-shirted, carpet-slippered – might have been thought indecorous. We need not have worried.

We were received with a courtesy that was almost enthusiastic. The hostess, Mrs Annie Perry said: 'Now do come in and meet some lovely people; I know you won't mind joining us, it just happens we were having a little party tonight.' (It turned out later that one would require to be singularly out of luck to arrive at the Himalaya, at any day of the year, when this was not the case). 'Now sit down somewhere, and what will you have; it so happens there's only rum. You must talk to this dear lady; I know you'll want to meet her; she has come a great distance.'

This was a Tibetan lady of high degree, attired most gaily in a dark blue smock with the traditional apron of vivid horizontal candy-stripes, high felt boots and gold earrings; she made a place beside me on a divan and said, in impeccable English and with a grave interest: 'You come all the way from England!'

Then I realized that values had to be changed.

The character of that evening – unremarkable, simple, possibly commonplace in such surroundings – has ever since been hard to convey; an atmosphere both grotesque and elusive; certainly unforgettable. I have spent many bizarre and curious evenings in almost every recognized quarter of the earth, but that night in Kalimpong remains in my memory as something not to be judged by ordinary standards. On reconsidering it, there was little in it that would have been unacceptable in many a conventional setting; nobody ate pickled mice or executed strange Oriental rites, nobody made dramatic pronouncements nor fell into any mystic excesses. Nevertheless I was on the edge of something remote and unprecedented; I count it still as one of the memorable evenings of my life.

It was a long low wooden room, intricately furnished with great numbers of curious and complex articles of copperware in some way associated with the domestic processes of Tibet; its walls hung with *thangkas* – the great cloth votive paintings of the Lamaist creed, many diverse representations of the Lord Buddha and the Wheel of Life, used to help in meditation on the cause and purpose of the endless chain of existence, bordered with silk and intensely restful to the eye. The room was warmed by the customary North Indian brazier, which those who know it accept as the one really functional and decorative form of interior heating – a large, circular, shallow iron dish on legs, filled with glowing charcoal; it has the inestimable advantage of being portable; one can shift one's fireside to any convenient part of the room; it is admirable for the preparation of popcorn and the boiling of toddy; and furthermore any given number of people can sit around it in a complete circle. It has but one disadvantage; after some time in an enclosed room it produces a gentle, imperceptible miasma that causes those around it to drop one by one into a torpid state that will eventually develop into a fatal coma; fortunately somebody usually remembers to open a window in time.

For a while we sat around and drank rum-and-hot-water, fortunately a serviceable drink for the climate, since there was never anything else. Rounds were called with a punctilious regularity, a bearer would trot around with trays of steaming mugs, somebody would sign a chitty, or perhaps not sign a chitty; from time to time a gentleman in a long silk skirt and braided hair would rise to his feet and bow generously around the room. The ladies hummed and chattered gently. Most of the company were Tibetan exiles – the first swallows of the invasion – wealthy emigres who had observed the happenings at the Chinese border with dismay, also the shrewd eyes of wealthy property owners everywhere, and had got over the edge just before the rush. They were a solid, restful people wearing heavily embroidered garments of such imposing though simple magnificence that I took them to be ceremonial robes, until I was assured that such was the conventional evening wear of persons of quality. One of them, who wore his braided hair in a tight coil around his head, carried in his left ear a long gold earring, and in the right a small stud of turquoise. At the time I pondered the possible social or religious significance of this assymetry; later I was told that it was merely considered more becoming; only a dull man would dangle the same ornament from both sides.

We were, as it turned out, by way of celebrating the onset of the Tibetan New Year, in this case the Year of the Iron Hare, but with none of the extrovert zeal such as one associates, say, with a Scottish Hogmanay. The gentlemen sat around with faces upon which it was impossible to detect any expression whatever, smoking heavily, holding their cigarettes in two hands, like flutes. They had none of the febrile verve of Indians on such occasions, none of the rotund amiability of high class Chinese. They were very evidently a people on their own. They were also very different from any Tibetans I was ever to meet later.

Among them were several young women of what seemed to me then, and increasingly so as the evening extended, considerable charm and beauty. They were introduced collectively by intricate names which I never precisely caught, and individually, a little later, as Dolly, Molly and Polly. They, too, spoke English with varying accuracy but great fluency. Knowing something of the highly insular Tibetan attitude to education, as to everything else, I wondered how they had acquired this grasp of what is to Tibetans (I later learned) a language of extreme grossness and difficulty. The answer was perfectly simple; they had been to school in India. The rigorous conventual laws of their people did not apply to them, as aristocrats. They were among the most widely-travelled of Tibetans; they had been to Darjeeling.

There were also several guests typical of the surrounding population: an Austrian ex-Baron who had been engaged for some time on the work of collating and translating a number of Tibetan sacred volumes; this task he casually said would probably take him another nineteen or twenty years; an American wool-buyer (whose great importance to the economics of the situation soon became clear); a displaced and understandably tetchy Professor from North-West China; two European students from the International College at Benares, young men with long beards who were, it was said, seeking manifestations of the after-life. Very soon we found ourselves discussing the philosophic implications of the works of Mr Graham Greene, as indeed who at that time was not. Then somebody put on a gramophone. It was at this point, I still recall, when all aspects of normality evaporated from the party and fantasy took charge.

Through the heavy air of the room, perched on the edge of the great Himalaya, drifted the thuds and wails of Manhattan dance-music, the remorseless, unidentifiable four-in-a-bar of the Broadway folk music that is, perhaps, the one common background factor for all environments today. The Tibetan gentleman at my side nodded peacefully, his left earring swinging in gentle rhythm. Then the record was changed; there came the click-clack swish-swoshing offbeat energy of something almost as universal; something vaguely Latin-American, perhaps a samba, or a rumba. I ruminated dimly for a while on the curiosity of circumstances that seemed bent on projecting to this remote neighbourhood every kind of inapposite impulse. Then somebody stood beside me; either Molly or Polly; a Tibetan girl in a vivid apron and bright yellow waistcoat.

'We dance,' she said.

I explained in the usual deprecating way that I was an indifferent dancer, and that sambas and congas were as out of my line as I imagined they were out of hers.

'I teach,' she said, resolutely.

There have in my time been many interludes both unexpected and extraordinary; I have involved myself accidentally in incongruities of great variety and rumness over a number of unlikely places, but I do not think that I have ever assisted at a ceremony quite so preposterous as this, that I should receive my first lesson in the rumba in Kalimpong, on the Sikkim border, and that I should have as my tutor a citizen from the final repository of feudal medievalism, a lady from Lhasa. 'Knee wag now,' said the Tibetan lady, holding me in a practised grip like that of a Metropolitan policewoman. 'Round-about going so,' she said. Somewhere in Nicaragua or Forty-Second Street the maraccas chuckled and whirred; united in this monstrous circumstance Tibet and London skipped round a stifling Indian room while the People's Army of the China seeped slowly over the roof of the world and the Dalai Lama crouched bewildered in a hut fifty miles away.

The Tibetan costume evolved for a country of enormous altitude and bitter cold seemed unsuitable for a true ballroom execution; it was somewhat like embracing an agile bolster. Encased in no one could guess how many swathes and layers of homespun and silk and brocade, Dolly remained bland and cool. Then she sang. Fluty and wavering and Oriental still, to a half-heard melody and just-familiar words, the voice of Shangri-la gave a strange sureness to that ancient Western tribal lay: *Buttons and Bows*.

So, I thought, are illusions always thus brutally dispersed – the pearl-divers of Mikimoto discussing baseball scores; the juke-box on the Pacific atoll; the Siamese Princess with the dry martini. This was my first Tibetan night. It could scarcely have been less characteristic; I was not to know that at the time.

I asked: 'Where did you learn to sing that?'

'Hearing on radio,' she said. 'Like this,' and again she sang; her aural memory was photographic, as she sang the meaningless words to the banal tune it was neither just the words nor the tune that she sang; the very inflexion of the recorded vocalist was reproduced; through the high-pitched Asian voice could be detected every one of the crooner's slurs and run-ups. It was a virtuoso performance, and very sad.

At some time we began to eat, in erratic relays, a process that went on spasmodically for the rest of the evening: green peaches and herring, nuts of mutton stewed in gravy, Chinese sweetmeats, peanuts, dried dates and onion, small bowls of curds.

At last we came to the Cups: Tibetan noodles, a sort of vermicelli soup. The moment one cup was finished it was refilled, and again refilled. There is a ritual significance about the number of Cups that must be consumed; the social minimum is four, thereafter five is considered to be an unlucky number and must be increased to six, and to stop at six is considered a discourteous act, whereas seven, being an odd number, cannot be contemplated on a festive occasion, on the other hand eight . . . at every pause the desperate visitor is confronted with some serious and un-challengeable accusation.

It was explained emphatically that this was *not* a Tibetan meal; only an approximation; a reasonable dinner should include Fish with boiled Bacon, Bamboo Roots and Pork with Jam Dumplings, Green Peas in Ricewine, Eel Soup and Onions, Sea Slugs in Stew and Shark's Stomach, Minced Yak and even more cups of noodles.

The brazier in the centre of the room was now an incandescent core of heat.

Four dozing Tibetans were roused and asked to dance a formal Himalayan measure. They behaved exactly like four similar gentlemen at a soirée in Kensington; they smirked and protested and shrugged, and finally took their places in a line across the floor. The gramophone, which could invoke Tin Pan Alley or the Copacabana, had no means of producing Tibetan music. Somebody hummed, a quiet, meandering, pentatonic croon; by and by hands began to clap gently in a broken beat; the dancers moved. The figure of the dance was almost imperceptible: a swaying, a momentary shifting of the weight from one foot to the other; four pairs of tall coloured boots moved below the robes, an inch or two at a time; a half step forward, a pace back. The faces relapsed into immobility, withdrawn, the humming stopped, there was no sound but slip, slip of felt soles on the boards. *Buttons and Bows* fell away; the Rumba shrank back twelve thousand miles and a hundred years and vanished. Somebody called for more rum, but the rum was gone.

Now it was four months since that first confused news that the Chinese had invaded Tibet; even still the world was little better informed. In Kalimpong bazaar talk had now achieved a high pitch of picturesque improbability. The Dalai Lama was expected momentarily, plodding over the ridge at the head of a golden-caparisoned caravan of yaks or soaring over the peaks on a pearly cloud; the Dalai Lama was dead; the Chinese were at this moment at the gates of the Pass; the Chinese had been routed by divine intercession on the Chang Tang plains; the Russians, infuriated at their reverses in Korea, were about to land an airborne army along the Chumbi; the rebellious Tibetan peasantry had risen in Lhasa and were even now storming the walls of the Potala. All these things were recounted solemnly, fearfully, anxiously, sceptically, or with the mercenary zeal that overcomes many good and simple people at the sight of visiting newspaper men.

Tibet, which had by now reached approximately the condition of social progress achieved by Britain in the fourteenth century, knew that the Chinese could have a walkover whenever they chose. Tibet knew that the days of isolation were gone, emergency had at last arrived, and, as is customary in such situations, the big boys tended to be most swiftly off the mark. Many wealthy citizens were outside already; many more were fidgeting on the brink, waiting for the correct moment, and passing the time searching the Scriptures in any of Tibet's three thousand monasteries. The peasantry, having nothing to lose, were waiting to see what showed up – or so one supposed; everything in Tibet was supposition, for nobody knew.

Tibet had of course become legendary, part of the professional travellers' stock lore. The baldest and most simply factual account of the Tibetan methods and manners acquired in the telling a curious unreality, a hint of something rather spurious, as of a place self-consciously untouched by any of the developing conventions of the rest of the world. There is, however, no way of improving on the facts as they are. There was no simple way of explaining the wholly theocratic nature of a State where priestly power and temporal authority were inextricably mixed, where a third of the total male population were monks and where the ruler is God, and technically several centuries old. There was no short-cut definition of a religion which mingles most aspects of the Shamanist culture, Tantric mysticism, devil-worship, pantheism and Indo-Tibetan demonolatry, tinged here and there with the teachings of the Buddha, and involving the largest possible pantheon of gods, saints, demons and canonized evil spirits. The recognition of these was alone a life's work, from the pinnacle of Boddh, Amitabha and Avalokitswara, through the tutelary deities, the familiar Demon Kings, to the countless Brahminical godlings and angels to the rank and file local and country gods; a grotesque series of considerations.

Above it all sat the Fourteenth Dalai Lama, the living incarnation of all before him, free from human error, all-knowing and all-powerful, the man with, without doubt, the most exclusive job on earth. Under the staggering hieratic form of Government still then preserved in Tibet, supreme authority over all the land was wielded by this excessively holy person who was regarded as not only hallowed, messianic, almighty and divine, but secular and administrative too; he was *Gyalpo Rimpoche*, 'the glorious king', ruler and Pope and Almighty; Viceregent of Buddha on Earth.

That is, until the Chinese came.

Of this bizarre and preposterous situation, and indeed of the man himself, I was to write at some length in another book, since years later it was to come about that I eventually met this quaint antediluvian young divinity at – of all places – a cocktail party in Peking. For that mad anecdote you must seek out, with some difficulty, a previous book.

The then incumbent, a boy of fifteen had been enthroned in 1940 and given his names: Jampel Ngawang Lobsang Yishey Tensing Gyatso, which meant 'Tender Glory, Might in Speech, Excellent Intellect, Absolute Wisdom, Holding to the Doctrine, Ocean Wide'. Now he waited, and pondered, and beat his gongs, just over the border in Yatung. Just how much this strange cloistered being was in control of his own behaviour nobody knew. He was surrounded by a close entourage of his Ministers – the Shapes – advisers, courtiers, chaplains, and assorted nobility, all of whom had the best of reasons for staying clear of any possible Chinese flying columns, since the picturesque and romantic character of their medieval satrapy had been matched only by its medieval barbarity. So the Dalai Lama waited, twenty minutes flying time away (had any aircraft chosen to risk those hopeless skyways) and contemplated the future of his country – as, they said in Kalimpong, he had done so often before.

It was that aspect of the Dalai Lama's powers and personality that was primarily so baffling to the Western mind – the accepted continuity that linked him with the past, not just one link in an ancestral or dynastic chain, but personally, as an individual. The Dalai Lama was not the inheritor of his predecessor's functions: he *was* his predecessor, and the predecessor before that, and before that, for thirteen times. He was not merely the contemporary bearer of the Yellow Hat; he was the precise personage for whom it was originally created. It was accepted that he had, in simple fact, lived for six hundred years. It was a fantastic truth that when Mr David Macdonald of the Himalaya Hotel, who had been familiar with the previous Dalai Lama, and was anxious to re-establish contact with his successor in his time of trouble, sent a message over the Pass to Yatung, he wrote in effect: 'Your Holiness will recall our meeting in 1905 . . .' so, to this sacred boy, born fifteen years before, he wrote without affectation of the contacts they had enjoyed forty years before.

(Similarly, one of the more remarkable records in the British diplomatic files is that of the message of congratulation sent by the Governor-General in India, then Warren Hastings, to the new

Lama of 1783 who was then eighteen months old: 'The Governor-General on receiving news of your decease in China was over-whelmed with grief and sorrow, and continued to lament until the cloud was dispelled by your reappearance . . .')

Thus when the Chinese Manchu Emperors invaded Tibet in the eighteenth century, the Dalai Lama was there. When in the early years of this century the Chinese Imperial Government attempted still greater control over the land, it was this Dalai Lama, still thirty-seven years unborn, who fled to India; when the Chinese Revolution overthrew the Manchus in 1911 it was this Dalai Lama who had broken the final ties with China. It was he, too, who had ruled Tibet when the Simla Convention of 1914 had once again recognized nominal Chinese suzerainty over Tibet while forbidding her to interfere internally. It was he who had expelled the Chinese Mission from Lhasa in 1949 ('as we wish to live apart, uncontaminated by the germ of a highly materialistic creed'), and now it was again he who sat beside the State Oracle in the dim village of Yatung, heavy with the weight of sixteen years, con-templating the strange facets of a life that had endured six centuries, stretching as tediously into the past as it unescapably did into the future.

Throughout the vast land-masses of Asia the high wind of revolu-tion had blown, was blowing still, dispersing the fields of estab-lished empires, ventilating the aspirations of half-a-dozen nationalisms from Manchuria to the Middle East, from the Hindu Kush to the Timor Sea. Only here was the process in reverse, the theorists of nationalism now on the defensive; helpless in their ignorance, clinging to a reaction that was both inexcusable and pathetic. What could Divine Enlightenment do against Marxist-Leninist orthodoxy? Revolutionary social-democracy on the march, and against it the barricades were manned with fluttering prayer-flags, and throbbing gongs.

From time to time I was reminded that somehow I should have to do something about this, however superficially. As a corres-pondent I had always been hemmed in with limitations of the most professionally useless kind: the longer I continued at it the more impossible it seemed to make a wholly unqualified judgment on anything.

Here a new problem arose: that of knowing not too much but

too little. Yet already it was hard to consider this new war in the obvious and expected way: the innocent and unhappy mountain community threatened with extinction; the gentle priests and recluses menaced by the totalitarian drive; the Saint attacked by the Dragon, with the odds well on the Dragon. Everyone knew that Tibet was a barbaric country, that the system that maintained it was inequitable and degenerate and corrupt and politically indefensible in every way – the arguments, in fact, so sternly put forward when Britain thought fit to invade Tibet behind the guns of General Younghusband forty-seven years before. Yet no one had ever produced a *satisfactory* justification for the liberalizing of a country by force of arms. The Chinese case was legalistically fair, and their diplomatic methods, particularly vis-à-vis Nehru and India, extremely unhelpful. As with every bitter international situation since the war, two blacks failed to make a white, and the resulting grey was not something to be convincingly analysed in a brisk thousand words.

The prayer-flags stood in spinneys like the masts of delicate and invisible ships, sails half-furled, slender bamboos with fifteen feet of striplike sail, restless and swaying. The message and the invocations were faded or invisible; not that it mattered; every flutter a prayer, every stirring in the breeze a propitiation and a duty fulfilled. Some were tattered, half the flag long since vanished: would that be then only half a prayer, or a prayer half-heartedly said? You heard them above your head, purring. They stretched thinly up the road and over the slopes; here and there a sudden dense cluster of them, like palms at an oasis or sudden corn on a fertile patch, their topmost shreds leaning together in whispered breathless conversation. Below the densest plantations then would be a *mani*, a little wall painted with the Dragon-Horse, sacred symbols, deities, and those famous words in the angular Tibetan characters one came at last to recognize: *Om ma-ni pad-mi Humh* – magic and meaningless syllables, the most recondite in the language, which some people say represent: Hail to the Jewel in the Lotus Flower. To utter the words is ritual; even to look at the characters is to be in a state of grace; they are the first words framed by the child and the last mumbled by the dying: *Om ma-ni pad-mi Humh* – thus is favour sought from the gods; efficiently, without excessive pain or effort; a shorthand worship.

Somewhere along the trail India changed into Sikkim and imperceptibly into Tibet. This was power-politics now, with the world seeping in, yet it was only a lifetime ago that Lhasa was established geographically, its latitude and longitude calculated – for the first time – and even then by a stratagem. Then Nain Singh, the exploring pioneer, made his way into the uplands disguised as a trader from Ladakh, surveyed the country – fantastically – with a prayer-wheel and a rosary. He was seen here and there, deep in his devotions on the hillsides – and inside his prayer-wheel was no scriptural scroll, but long notes of measurements and compass-bearings; and the beads of his rosary were not the sacred number of a hundred and eight, but one hundred: an abacus for his distances; one bead for one hundred paces. And that was only in 1874.

Meanwhile, here in Kalimpong was the roadhead, the mouth of the funnel. Over in Yatung the Dalai Lama could wait, but business could not. This was the other face of Tibet, not the plaintative Tibet of the fumbling literary phrases in the diplomatic note, 'living a cloistered life in her mountain fastness', but the Tibet of shrewd traders and dealers in material things, the people for whom invasion was not so much a matter of 'maintaining her separate existence', but of the emergency sales and the quick deal.

All through the hours of daylight the thin air echoed with the steady donging of the mule-bells, distant and near; the long caravans wound over the single trail.

The place was crawling with wool, and hides, and sacks of borax, and the tails of yaks.

Kalimpong strayed up and down along the hill road, neat and trim here; vague and sprawling there. A hundred and fifty years is no time at all in the history of India, yet it is everything; in a century and a half no place escaped the subtle mark of the Raj, not Kalimpong itself. Here was the final transition, the ultimate fining-out of Imperial suburbia into the frontier wastes.

Now the Raj had gone, the villas remained; like the rest of the remnants in a state of incipient decay. Down the gritty road, by the mouldering statue of Queen Victoria and the sign that said: 'Galloping Strictly Prohibited', the bazaar shelved the ridge: a tumble-down impermanency that had endured for generations, lined with the gimcrack wooden caverns of the grain-sellers, the cloth-merchants, the bhunja squatting before his brazier in a nutty haze of maize and gram parching in a bowl; the sweetstuff man frying his curds and sugar into squares of luddu and jellabis; baskets heaped with ochres and turmeric, crimson Holi powder and indigo, aconite, Dream Compellers, glauber salts. A drift of people wandered through, Nepalis and Lepchas, a few Bengali Hindus.

Here and there on the walls were posters that said, in Tibetan and English:

ALL TIBETANS PASSING BY TOWN
MUST REGISTER BEFORE FEB. 26
AT FOREIGNERS' REGISTRATION
OFFICE, AT
KALIMPONG HAPPY VILLA

Kalimpong resembled a town that had been subdued and occupied by the troops of Genghis Khan. The drovers and the muleteers were extraordinary individuals to a man, quite extravagant swash-buckling figures in their embroidered fur hats, their kilted togas, their brooches and reliquaries, their tall boots, their matted hair, their gorgeous broadswords. Mostly they wore a heavy knee-length tunic of such vast dimensions that when tucked up and around under a belt it formed a great capacious pouch or pocket into which all manner of goods, purchases, daily needs and travelling equipment was stuffed, to disappear without trace. I saw one of them put his mule's harness there. This robe was worn in a peculiar, casual, studiously degagé way, thrown over the shoulders with the left arm sleeved but the right sleeve empty; in some way reminiscent of a fashionable officer in the Hapsburg empire. It gave a smart, doggish look even to the most debased and filthy driver. The custom served the purpose of keeping the right arm free for heavy work; it marked out the labouring Tibetan from the upper classes. (These, as I had observed at the rum-party, had an equally indicative fashion: the rich man's *ichhu-pa* gown was made with sleeves that extend a good six or nine inches below the length of the fingertips; in the tradition that made the old Cantonese mandarin grow his finger-nail to grotes-que length, this is to emphasize the social level, of the idle rich, who do not have to use their hands.

The muleteers were heavy and powerful men: they moved

around with the confident air of big men in a country of small people. Some of them indeed had an air of almost contrived rakishness, like musical-comedy brigands, deliberately pictures-que; one would have said they were almost consciously playing Tibetans, with their great jangling display of amulets and charm-boxes and phylacteries, their swinging necklets of turquoise and coral, their cutlasses hanging with ostentatious negligence at their belt. They gave the impression of being a potentially merry people among themselves, though here they moved around the market place with a rather saturnine wariness, as of tough men who knew they were going to be deceived sooner or later. I have no doubt they were, perpetually; they showed almost a tourist's interest in the trinkets and knick-knacks of the bazaar, fingering and fondling with powerful stubby fingers, black with wool-grease, while the Mahwari shopkeepers lurked around them, insinuating the more trumpery gadgets to the front.

They had one truly striking trick. It is the Tibetan custom to show respectful greeting by sticking out the tongue; it can be a disconcerting gesture. Like almost everything else Tibetan it has its roots in obscure mythology – in this case, from the time when the old Nyngmapa red-hat sect held power in the country, and who owned the power of the *mantras*, the mystic spell or invoca-tion. When their religious competitors, the yellow-hat Gelukpas, overcame them, it was necessary to examine everyone for the power of the *mantra*, which was evident by a black mark on the tongue. The tongue was therefore exhibited as far as it will go at any meeting deserving of respect, as a European would doff his hat. It makes for startling encounters.

It was incidentally also against Tibetan social usage, at least among the proletariat, to wash at any time between birth and death, a decision readily understandable in a people who live in conditions of such climatic acerbity, but one which nevertheless tended to make their company oppressive.

I went back to the hotel and found the Baron at work among his books. If that suggests a scholarly picture of a firelit room and rows of darkly glowing morocco bindings, then it is misleading; Tibetan books are not like that. Their pages, to begin with, are loose, and of a curious shape – perhaps two feet wide and six inches deep, secured between two carved wooden boards of the same shape, wrapped in damask and tied with decorative cords.

The workmanship of the printing is almost unbelievably intricate and beautiful, when one considers the tremendous technical difficulties involved – they were printed not from type (there was until recently no common or standard faces for the Tibetan characters) but from wooden blocks, the size of the total page, in which the *entire* text of that page has been carved, like a fabulously complex woodcut; the material chiselled and excised away, leaving the angles and serifs and curlicues and inflective marks of the letters in relief. There could obviously be no re-setting of a Tibetan printed passage; a slip of the knife and the block, and the page would be ruined.

These volumes – many of them of great age and value – contained only works of theology and philosophic dissertation, Buddhist history and Tibetan liturgy, poetry, astrology, and the lives of the saints; there is no such thing as a popular literature of Tibet. The holy scriptures of the *Kangyur* and *Tengyur*, the teachings of the Lord Buddha, come in many volumes; there are The Hundred Thousand Songs of the Venerable Milaraspa, the work of an ascetic of the seventh century. For each book the paper has to be made, the blocks cut, every word proof-read by the lamas for dogma and accuracy.

Down the road, not far from the Himalaya, lived Prince Peter of Greece. From time to time he clattered up the drive to the hotel on his horse, a vigorous and sociable figure in enormous leather cowboy chaps. Odd though it may seem, among the many notable, picturesque, curious or dedicated people in this congested neighbourhood, he was the only one who provided a factual link between Kalimpong and the rest of the world; our paths, as they say, had crossed before, in Cairo, in the mad end-of-the-war days; in Afghanistan, pursuing his life's study, anthropology.

Now he was leading a wing of the Third Danish Expedition into Central Asia. He had driven up from South India in what must have been the biggest, broadest, most opulent and intricate motor caravan in Asia. It stood in the grounds of his house on the hillside – a vast and specially built Dodge, bigger than many a cottage; inside it was something between a laboratory and a gentleman's country residence of the better sort, fitted with air-conditioning, electric generators, refrigerator, and photographic darkroom, not to speak of such conveniences as beds and lounges, and even a running-water bathroom. On the whole it was probably the most civilized and comfortable residence in North Bengal.

How this gigantic affair had ever been manoeuvred over those terrifying hill roads was beyond me. Nevertheless a year ago Prince Peter had done it, edging his ponderous craft round the bends, over the shoulders, along the rim of those precipitous drops, with outriders clearing the road for several miles ahead. It must have been a gripping experience. And then, before he could regroup himself for the next stage of the journey – he was to rendezvous with the expedition's other parties somewhere in Central Asia – the political situation had flared up in Tibet and he, like us, could go no further. To complicate the situation still further, no sooner had he passed on his northward trip than one of the Tista bridges – demoralized, no doubt, by his rumbling passage – had collapsed behind him, and now there was no retreat.

Prince Peter had with him among his effects an efficient tape-recorder on which he had managed to record on tape part of what might be considered a Buddhist service.

It is conceivable that from that day on the hallowed course of lamaist procedure took a slight deviation; a new rubric was born. For centuries, lamaist prayer has operated on what can only be called a simple system of technology: the prayer-wheel, the prayer-flag, the prayer-drum – all simple mechanical devices built on the labour-saving plan, whereby one inconsiderable ritual action can accomplish what would otherwise occupy many hours of serious praying. A whirl of the wheel, a flutter of the flag, and the gods are taken care of with the minimum of effort.

But even with this system *something* had to be done. I visualized the reactions of this monkish company as Prince Peter played them back their record – the narrowed eyes, the shaven heads thoughtfully nodding, the shrewd looks suddenly exchanged: here, now, was the ultimate refinement of their own principle. Just somebody to go through the chant and invocation, just once – and the little machine would do the rest, indefinitely. Here, at last, was the Prayer-Wheel of the Twentieth Century.

For days we made increasingly hopeless attempts to regularize our journey north, to establish contact with the DC, to assure him of our blameless intentions, to secure some sort of authority to move through Sikkim into the Pass.

I have often observed that there are few of the procedures of daily life that do not take about nine times longer in India than anywhere else. It is woven into the character of the land that the most commonplace encounter which involves the changing hands of money becomes a consideration of long and complicated intrigue, drawing the worst out of both sides. The despatch of a telegram is such an operation. The Indian post-office clerk is of a deliberate and timeless temperament that makes the British Civil Servant seem in comparison to be a crazily impulsive opportunist. Only under the most insistent compulsion will he withdraw himself from his other preoccupations and accept the message. He will read it seven or eight times, both forwards and backwards, study and analyse it, object on principle to such words as he does not understand or approve, and finally put the message aside while he leaves the office for some time on his own personal occasions. Often the telegram goes; sometimes it arrives. The *longueurs* of this transaction, in Kalimpong, were accentuated by the fact that the pigeon-holes through which one conducted one's affairs were placed in a most extraordinary position: about three feet above the ground. For anyone taller than a dwarf Nepali, there was no way of communicating through these little windows for any length of time but by kneeling on the ground, as it were at some sort of a confessional. I could come to no other conclusion than that this was the most direct means of impressing on the customer his lowly and degraded position vis-à-vis the postal clerk. I can still recall the expression on Bert Hardy's face when, after awaiting my return for some three-quarters of an hour, he found me genuflecting on the post-office floor, shouting entreaties through a little hole, like Alice in Wonderland in the house of Bill the Lizard.

Doubtful of what lay ahead, uncertain of our destination, by no means assured of our reception en route, and above all conscious of our inability to express the most elementary matters in Tibetan, we had organized the services of a Tibetan-speaking guide. This had not been easy, but after we had been passed round town a number of times, we found a friend of a friend who undertook to provide what we were seeking; he would be powerful, and fluent in Tibetan, and rich in the wiles of shikar and field-craft, not only an interpreter and guide but a counsellor.

He was waiting at the hotel next morning; he was broad and

sturdy and without any exception the most reticent person I ever met in my life. As we emerged into the freezing dawn he greeted us monosyllabically; from that moment on he refused to say a word. He climbed into the front of the car beside the driver Sani, and stared resolutely ahead of him. From time to time we made remarks of strained good cheer, or commented on the weather; he would smile grimly and reply nothing. He gave us immense confidence; no man could be so silent and not be strong.

The plan was to drive north along the trail from Kalimpong until we had to stop. We knew that would be very soon, since the moment the car left town it would be breasting the Himalaya.

Before we left there were two calls to pay: to the bazaar and to the Newspaper Office. I had long coveted the Tibetans' fur hats; they seemed to me – though I heard they were very low class – to be as decorative as they were practical; their shape and embellishment recalled the photographs in old Edwardian travel-books: stiff rows of robed figures staring impassively, among them a pair of knickerbockers and a moustache: 'The Author among Nobles from Tsang Province'. I discovered the one shop in the bazaar where such a hat could be bought.

Disillusion again: outside the hat was all glamour and Tibet; turn it over and it was all camouflage and fake, an Army surplus khaki Ghurka felt hat, the brim cut into flaps and edged with bear-fur, encrusted with gold thread and braid, most elaborately done. Here was the Orient again: the hours of delicate craftsmanship and manual tradition wasted on unworthy material; skill and patience and beauty, and something spurious always there to ruin it. One thought of the lovely Kashmiri boxes of carven wood, and the rubbishy tin hinge that always breaks; the superbly-considered and chosen mounting of gems in brooches, made to fall out of a trashy setting in a month.

Now *that*, I thought, was pedantry and snobbishness; there was in fact no reason why a Tibetan hat should not be built on the foundation of an old Army felt. The basic material was probably better and more enduring than they could have manufactured, it was equally functional; anyhow in the end it was the fur and the gold braid that meant anything. But I put my hat into my pack with a certain disappointment; in any case I did not dare wear it in front of the Tibetans.

The Newspaper Office stood on the edge of the town: up an

ancient wooden ladder into a little room full of dust and antiquity, with windows giving over the valley. This was the home of *Yulchog Sosoi Sargyur Melong*, The Tibetan Newspaper – *The* Tibetan Newspaper; there is no other, and even this one was not made in Tibet. It was a beautiful paper, small pages within a border of scrolls and swastikas enclosing two wide columns of Tibetan script, 'edited, Printed & published by Tharchin, at Kalimpong'; in an English imprint.

Of all the world's newspaper appointments his was possibly the least exacting. 'We have a circulation – perhaps three hundred, sometimes. A weekly? Ah, no. We emerge – say, from time to time.' He gave me the latest issue, dated two and a half months before. There was only one passage I could read: half way down a column of Tibetan the English words:

1. A muleteer coming from Phari to Kalimpong in charge of wool must bear with him copy of this Challan issued by the Phari branch of Tibet Traders Association, Kalimpong.
2. On arrival if a muleteer or any person (Tibetan or India) cannot produce such Challan, the wool in his charge will be deemed to be stolen property and person concerned will be liable for immediate legal action.
3. Holder is not authorized to part with any portion of goods covered by this Challan. Any one dealing shall do so at his own risk.

They had not been able to get halftone blocks, so they had stuck prints of the photographs into the paper. Downstairs an ancient flatbed machine went flip-crash-flop; an old gentleman stood at a case putting strange types into a stick; the last printshop between there and the Arctic Circle.

As we drove north it began suddenly to grow deathly cold. It stretched imagination to recall that this bleak place was somewhere on the latitude of the Bahamas. The road went up and up; on one side a slope with the rhododendrons petering out, every mile fewer shrubs and wider patches of rock; on the other side the valley; somewhere down in that eight-hundred-foot channel of fog and dampness was the Tista, born miles and miles away somewhere in the Zemu Glacier in the chilly arms of Kanchenjunga, heading for another world in the broad heat of the Bengal plains. Accompanying it, that curious anachronism: the telephone wire, tenuous link between countries.

The road grew worse and worse; suddenly it disappeared – it did not fade away into a track; one moment there was a road and the next there was nothing at all but a trench filled with stones, a bend round the mountainside, an end and a beginning.

We got out of the car and said au revoir to Sani; we shrugged ourselves into our rucksacks and began to walk. It must have been a pathetic and rather futile sight, neither dramatic nor adventurous; a couple of sanguine and slightly inadequate men plodding into something of which they knew nothing without any serious chance of ever finding out, and with them a silent and taciturn guide who, even then, had not the slightest idea what it was all about, and who did not seem to consider it worth while to ask.

It is time to explain the mystery of this interpreter. He had been assigned to us for two reasons: his familiarity with the Tibetan language and his knowledge of campcraft. In both respects he failed us more completely than anyone could have foreseen, though for neither could he have been held at fault. The truth was – and it was around this point that we discovered it – that they had not lied, he did in fact speak fluent Tibetan; moreover he spoke fluent Nepali; the one and insuperable snag to his usefulness to us was that he did not speak a word of English. We had asked for a Tibetan interpreter; we had got one. It had not occurred to anyone that Tibetan translated into Nepali was as valuable as it would have been into Serbo-Croat. Hence, it became clear, his solemn silence hitherto; the poor fellow had possibly been in his nature a man of garrulous and even convivial turn of mind; he had kept his mouth shut because there was nothing he could say. I began to feel that probably his disappointment and sense of injustice was greater than ours.

Anyhow, there we were, at the lonely and desolate gate of Sikkim, accompanied by a worthy man with whom we had no means of communication. I did not see what could conceivably be done about it. We trudged on. Very soon it began to rain.

One of the things that surprised me, and that any meteorologist could doubtless explain in a moment, was the absence of snow in the Himalaya. Here on this road it was petrifyingly cold, it was also extremely high; furthermore it was in the depths of winter. Anywhere in Europe, in similar circumstances, we would have

been above the snowline, even in the Scottish Cairngorms I have
climbed corries at a far lower altitude that were snowfilled in
March. Here the snow, when one saw it, was celestially remote; it
clothed the highest peaks in glowing splendour, but nothing
seemed to bring it lower than fourteen or fifteen thousand feet.
Here on the knees of the Himachal, the Mountains of Snow, we
had no snow, but drifting mist and a breeze like a razor and, now,
a steady, bitter rain.

You could hear the caravans coming miles away. The copper bells
gave out a thin, mountainish clonking; sometimes it was twenty
full minutes after the first sounds were born on the wind that the
head of the caravan appeared round a bend of the trail. First there
would be a dog, and a donkey or two, caparisonned with red fur
and swinging below their chins those yaks' tails that would
escape being made into Santa Claus beards. The column of beasts
would become denser, and here and there a few men, Elizabethan-
looking figures with amulets, the empty sleeve, the fur hat. (There
was a mode, too, of wearing the hat; at least one of the fur flaps
to be tucked inside, another of the engaging dandyish tricks of the
Tibetan, who seemed to cultivate the same sort of mannered
insouciance of costume as the Chelsea art-student.)

The caravan might be three-quarters of a mile long, and at the
very end would be the muleteer chief, astride a yak or a heavy
hill pony; he was not infrequently fast asleep. Sometimes an
India-bound convoy would meet a returning caravan homeward
bound for Tibet; for ten minutes or so there would be utter
confusion and mingling, full of shouts and imprecations; then
gradually the opposing masses of dogs and mules and men would
extricate themselves and filter through each other along their
respective course – the wool and the hides jangling south; the
cases of tea and kerosene and cloth clattering north.

As one of the northbound caravans passed us we attached ourselves to its tail. The tough Tibetan keeping the rear on his pony
looked at us in some surprise, and made a hoarse observation to a
colleague at his side. I smiled and made comradely gestures;
surprisingly he grinned broadly back. The so-called Interpreter
had gone far ahead; there was no remark we could usefully make,
so I trotted along beside the pony feeling like one of those little
boys who used to follow milk-carts in England.

It was not as easy as one would have thought; from a distance the caravan appeared to be creeping along the track, but at close quarters it was doing a good steady, unrelenting six miles an hour. Every so often, in order to keep up, I had to break into a shambling run; at such an altitude this became increasingly painful and exacting. As I hastened along at the flank of the muleteer's pony I became oppressed by a sense of injustice: here was a Tibetan, born to and adjusted by environment to great physical effort at enormous heights, and he was riding; here was I, who could be called a plainsman only by courtesy – a denizen of the pavements and the saloon bar – and I was walking. Moreover it looked as though I should have to walk for ever.

After a while the effort became too much; I tried to think of a reasonable excuse for packing up. After so long it seemed a discourteous gesture suddenly to stop; though we had no common language I felt some word of farewell was called for. Happily at that moment a small noisy landfall ahead caused a kind of panic among the animals of the caravan. They shied and jumped about, and one small donkey suddenly leaped without warning clean over the cliff. I was aghast at this, until I realized that at that point the precipice was no more than a very steep slope leading down from the trail through woods and shrubs into the mist, and presumably, a thousand feet below, to the river.

One of the foot muleteers immediately swore, and jumped down after the donkey. For a long time afterwards we could hear the pursuit, invisibly; a diminishing tinkling of bells and a string of Tibetan oaths and entreaties, gradually fading away through the vaporous ravine.

In the confusion I slipped behind, and leaned for a full fifteen minutes recovering against a streaming rock.

It was a long time before we finally reached the hill village of Algarah: a cluster of small stone houses, a tiny bazaar that was no more than a line of half-empty stalls, a group of Nepali tradesmen, smiling heartlessly. There was also a policeman. We saw him from some distance off, standing in the road with his navy-blue puttees and his little militia cap. As we reached him, trudging heavily, he stopped us.

He did not say anything, he merely stopped us, and after a while a young man in civilian clothes came hurrying along and asked politely for our passports. He kept them for some time, copying every piece of information they contained into a small exercise book with an indelible pencil. He asked how far we were going. We said: Just up the road. He looked at our monumental packs, our load of gear, and he shook his head in a way that was either sad or reproving. Then he wished us good day, and on we went.

It became increasingly difficult. If a competition had been held throughout the land to design a surface that was at the same time intricate of construction and impossible of simple navigation, this would have won the prize. Long ago it had been made of thousands of heavy cylindrical stones, about five inches in diameter, set upwards about half-a-foot apart, with the spaces between the stones filled with earth and rubble; it must have been a very serviceable trail. But the years had worn all the soluble matter from between the stones, leaving the cylinders themselves projecting half-a-foot apart – not quite big enough to stand on, not quite far enough apart to stand between, too wrongly disposed to bestride. To make any progress necessitated a series of little mincing steps, with the eyes constantly seeking a new foothold; the moment you ceased to concentrate you risked a broken ankle. It went on for mile after mile.

All the time the rain beat down unremittingly; it slid off my waterproof jacket in streams down my neck; it soaked my woollen Nepali cap until it began to shrink and bind my brow into a persistent ache. This was somehow not what I had expected; I had been ready for snow and ice and cutting footsteps in glaciers and sub-zero camps over crevasses; I have done enough mountaineering to find that exhilarating; but this, except for the intense cold, was like hill-walking in Inverness-shire.

My pack began to get intolerably heavy. It held the usual mess of camping gear and, over and above, the stores we had bought, very hurriedly and inefficiently in Kalimpong, a few tins of meat and sweets and biscuits, two bottles of rather dubious local brandy called Best Glory. We had also remembered at the last moment that although we had a tiny petrol stove we had forgotten the frying-pan; a last minute scramble through the bazaar had produced nothing but an enormous native-made cast-iron utensil, big enough for a boarding-school.

We made the speechless Interpreter carry it; he might as well, we thought, do something. He plodded ahead with the frying-pan on his back like an instrument for some sort of game; it gave me a perverse satisfaction to see that he, too, found these monstrous cobbles hard to negotiate.

The rain sogged down, as though for ever.

The *gompa* was on a little ridge some way off the road – a lamaist monastery of, we had heard, great antiquity and local fame. It was detectable from a distance by the copse of prayer-flags, the little painted *mani* wall; the rest was hidden until you reached the crest.

At first sight disappointment: low roofs of corrugated iron, a tin chimney, a pathway littered with orange peel, more galvanized iron – could this be *anything* of antiquity, let alone a seat of inspired knowledge and inner revelation? It was a thoughtless reaction – why should not an ancient roof be mended with corrugated iron and still give shelter to the eternal spiritual rhythms? A litter of physical refuse could imply a philosophical disregard of material surroundings. Yet I came to the gate doubtfully.

A large square courtyard was bounded on three sides by low single-storey sheds; on the fourth by the temple itself, a surprisingly attractive and elaborate structure of dark wood; vast doors at the top of three low steps. The quadrangle seemed deserted. From inside the temple came a dim confused clamour of gongs and drums.

After a while a monk appeared, a young man with shaven head – or rather, if it can be so described, a head with two or three days' growth on it – and a garnet robe that was little more than a great multitude of adhering rags. He looked blank and said nothing. Introductions became immediately more difficult than we had foreseen; the Interpreter had not accompanied us inside the monastery, for reasons that were either militantly anti-clerical or excessively devout, we never discovered which, nor would it have made much difference if we had.

There was little to do but bow respectfully and make sympathetic noises; the monk clearly knew no English and my smattering of Hindustani merely made him look the blanker. Then he hurried off towards the temple, and came back in no time at all with half a dozen more monks of varying ages but identical raggedness and grime; they stood around us in a group, nudging one another. One by one more lamas appeared, several of them very aged and decrepit and hobbling on sticks, others – who could scarcely have been more than ten years old – hopping and darting about like chickens. Soon we were surrounded by large numbers of the brothers, murmuring and whispering and giggling. Inside the temple the gongs and drums fell silent.

There was not the slightest sign of resentment or hostility; on the contrary the holy men appeared full of the liveliest curiosity. From time to time one or another of them would approach with what seemed to be a long and friendly question; when we shrugged and made courteously hopeless gestures they would shake their heads and laugh in a fluting way, rapidly telling their beads – 108, the sacred number. When we walked about that courtyard, peering nosily into the dark shadows of the living quarters nobody made any objections; frequently one of the baby monks would tumble over himself to open a door so that we might the better see inside – gloom, barrenness, a mud floor and a squalid pile of rags on a wooden bench.

I did not know how one approached the subject of gaining entrance to the temple room. There was no way of asking, and to stroll casually through those great doors might be a solecism of the worst kind, all the more embarrassing because the lamas were so evidently well-meaning and hospitable. On arrival at the steps we stopped, indicated the doors, made exaggerated gestures of enquiry. There was no delay at all; half a dozen of the holy men popped up the steps and pushed open the heavy, groaning door, and in we went.

It was a great and lofty room without windows; the flickering light from rows of butter-lamps made vast and fearful shadows leap from wall to wall. Tremendous pillars of wood rose into the blackness of the ceiling, from which hung enormous *thangkas* of the Lord Buddha and the Wheel of Life; wall paintings of the Four Directions and the Wheel of Poetry, which must say the same things whichever way it is read, pigeonholes for the sacred books; a dusty row of little cakes, dried and old, offerings to the altar. Over everything the endless burning of the butter-lamps had cast a thick film of grease. Much of the wall painting and the *thangka* design was indecipherable. The rest of it was tense, dramatic, turbulent, grotesque.

Lamaist art is a matter incomprehensible by western purists, since it is based wholly on philosophical principles derived from religious technicality. It is only one of the infinite manifestations

of the spirit and therefore can base itself only on accepted truth,
can be inspired solely from the unique source. It is utterly symbolic; the artist will contrive in his design the Eight Lucky Signs –
the umbrella, the shell of victory, the vase, the lotus, the golden
fish, the lucky diagram, the banner, and the wheel. Or, alternatively, the Glorious Offerings – the white turnip, the mirror,
the intestinal concretions, the dharwa grass, the curds, the Bilva
fruit – or the Seven Personal Gems, the Five Sensuous Delights;
with everything bearing in mind the significance of conventional
form and the traditional meaning of colour. There can be no
improvising. Here and there emerges a formalized parallel to the
tormented erotic writhings of Hindu temple carvings with their
vast and elaborate phalli, their apotheosis of the mystical lust –
the canonised Tibetan fiends, portrayed in violent copulation
with their deified consorts and decorated with skulls, conveying
the transitory nature of human existence and the momentary
passions of the senses – the duality of externalized nature, reveal-
ing at once the hideous and the sublime. Everything is symbolic
of one stage in the passage of human consciousness through its
earthly evolution. Life has only one force but many manifestations; enormous study makes it possible for the initiate to direct
this force and release the latent power in man, that the labyrinth-
ine process of transmigration may be fulfilled. In a word, it was
an incomprehensible mess.

It seemed difficult to reconcile our hosts, the ragged odorous
old men and the capering shaven children, with these profound
considerations. They were a group of rather simple-minded
recluses, chattering and chuckling away like schoolboys; they had
none of the serene impassive dignity of the monks of Burma or
Siam, none of the macabre dedication of the yogi; they differed
from the peasants on the trail below only by their shaven skulls
and their garnet capes and their surroundings. They were lamas,
one reflected, because Tibet has three thousand monasteries and
because almost every family in the land sends them at least one
son. The little monkish children running around the courtyard
were the *Ge-nyen*, the novices; the rest were the fully ordained, the
Ge-long. They were the priesthood and the government, the word
of God and the word of the administration, *imperium in imperio*;
they had two hundred and fifty three vows to observe, and one
wondered what the hell they were.

By and by one ran away and returned with the Abbot, a genial lama with a robe rather more decrepit and grease-stained than the others; he came across the courtyard to us cracking melon-seeds, and spitting copiously on the ground between his bare feet. After some consultation, the lamas then led us up a narrow stair to the place of special worship.

There, in a gallery just half-lit through a slit of window behind a woven screen, were the monks whom we had heard from the courtyard. They sat in a row in the gloom, before each a little drum, a gong, a cymbal; at the end was a lama with a thin reed instrument like a chanter.

We had obviously arrived at an intermission; the monks had put down their drumsticks and were about to fall to a number of bowls of rice that had at that moment been brought by a novice. It must have been an astonishing experience for them, the unexpected visitation of two bizarre Europeans with scrubby beards into what was probably the sanctum sanctorum of the monastery. However, they clearly saw no reason why this should interfere with their dinner; after glancing at one another dubiously they started to devour their rice.

This appeared to offend the conducting lama, who reprimanded them sternly. The lamas put down their rice-bowls with a sigh and once again picked up their instruments. The chanter began a reedy note, wavering through a scale full of semitones, the others picked up an undetectable rhythm with a steady donging, broken with strange pauses and accelerations. In the shadows beyond could just be seen the shape of the demon, carrying in each of his sixteen hands an instrument of violence, demonstrating thereby the many opportunities man is offered for destruction. Behind the tortured imagery was much of the same spiritual masochism that animates the Hindu symbolism I had worked for years to understand, the pattern of sanctions and formulae grouped always round the image of violence. Mind, the lamas argued, is for man equally an instrument for his inner expression and for his own destruction; until he has sifted through his senses a knowledge of his own disabilities – by rote, by endless repetition, by interminable meditation on that fact – he has no access to his own subconscious, which alone puts him in touch with the possibility of revelation.

Quite suddenly the nearest lama thumped his drum loudly

twice, and the music stopped. It seemed a hint for us to go. We bowed to the monks and left the gallery; even as we turned away the hands stretched swiftly out for the bowls.

Downstairs the Abbot was waiting for me with the Visitors' Book, a school exercise book with ruled pages, the back cover printed with multiplication tables. I signed with diffidence; there were no other names in it at all.

I looked around enquiringly; there was surely some method of making a contribution to the monastery. The Abbot divined my purpose in a flash; he led me quickly to the porch where stood an immense wooden coffer, brass-bound and locked. The hole in the top revealed it as an offertory box; it was big enough to hold a fortune in gold – who could ever fill it, since no names appeared in the book? I put a five-rupee note through the hole in the top – an immense contribution. As soon as I had done so the Abbot unlocked the coffer with an enormous brass key, removed the note and slipped it swiftly into the recesses of his clothing. He then locked the box up again with much ceremony and bade us farewell.

We saluted the lamas, by now out in strength, and were escorted from the precincts by a squadron of dancing little deacons. It was necessary to circumnavigate the building round a long verandah lined on its inner side by wooden prayer-cylinders, the size of oildrums, carved with sacred phrases; this route had to be followed in a clockwise way, spinning the prayers in a like direction; it is sacriligious and invalidating to pass a holy place on the left side. The novices scampered merrily ahead, thwacking the cylinders till they buzzed round like tops, precisely like London gamins playing tag on the railings – *Om ma-ni pad-mi Humh*; the entreaties and invocations to the gods went revving giddily to heaven with a terrific clatter.

They saw us out through the gate, waving; when we turned a little way down the hill they were gone, and the heavy door was closed.

Over the hill and there it was – the highest, bleakest, coldest, remotest, most inhospitable country in the world; a great soaring place fifteen times the size of England, where the depths of the valleys were higher than the summits of the Alps, a country where you were either a slave or a demigod; the final stronghold of the dead days of Asia.

By now the difficulties bore down on us like the unrelenting rain; the thin and rarified air made each step a developing penance. Ahead lay the only entrance to Tibet, the road over the Jelep-la – if you could call a thing a road that climbed to nearly sixteen thousand feet between the thighs of the world's loftiest and bitterest mountains; a little more than setting a course over the peak of Mont Blanc.

One way or another it was journey's end, with nothing accomplished, nothing to show to the Year of the Iron Hare.

The Tibetans calculate their dates from what was the Christian year AD 1027, when astrology was introduced into the country. Time is divided into cycles of sixty years, each composed of the five Elements – Earth, Iron, Water, Wood and Fire – and conjoined to the twelve Animals – Dog, Mouse, Frog, Dragon, Ox, Tiger, Hare, Serpent, Sheep, Horse, Monkey and Bird. Moreover each Element comes twice, first as a male, then as a female. As I plodded in deadly slow discomfort along the trail I tried vaguely and irritably to compute the sequence of Tibetan reckoning, but the altitude had made me stupid; I gave up trying.

What forced the decision was nightfall. We made up our minds too late; it was now too dark to select a proper camp.

The Interpreter, so singularly useless at that function, turned out to be ill-adjusted even to his role as campmaster. We stood about, trembling with cold, waiting for him to decide on a propitious place for our tents; he merely stood silently beside us, awaiting instructions. When we tentatively indicated a place at random he made no argument but set to work with the dripping strings and flaps; when we discovered that he was arranging the tents across a bed of jagged flints and suggested an alternative he accepted the proposition without demur and began to establish us on a quaking stretch of bog.

When we pointed these difficulties out to him he would stand stock-still, a rope dangling from his hand, and wait for another idea to be presented. Soon we were shuddering with cold and it was too dark to see where we were; we put the tents up anyhow.

It was the same with the fire. Any tenderfoot Boy Scout from the asphalt of Edmonton could have given the Interpreter lessons in woodcraft. He was eager, but somehow utterly without reasoning power; he would plod off into the dripping undergrowth and return with a handful of saturated brushwood; he tried to set fire to the dank mass, muttering words of frustration and concern.

There were only two things we could do; sit and freeze in the downpour, or go to bed.

Our efforts had been inept and amateur, our provisioning insufficient and careless, our objective clearly beyond us materially, politically, and physically; in short our performance throughout had revealed a sequence of deplorable shortcomings; but in one respect we had shown thoughtfulness and foresight: we still had the two bottles of Best Glory brandy.

We were a very long way from our starting-point, but we were a very great deal longer away from our destination, wherever that might be – Yatung? Gyantse? Phari? We thought resentfully of the remote, busy people in London who had initiated this absurd assignment.

Reporter's lore is full of such things: correspondents' archives are full of cables instructing them to take taxis from Khartoum to Johannesburg; demanding weekend coverage from Patagonia of the man in Trinidad. It was my own speciality; for years I had laboured at the whims of a charming and travelled executive whose official conception of the world, nevertheless, was the terrestrial globe he kept on his desk, a thing the size of a grape-fruit; from this he was able to demonstrate incontrovertibly that there was no place on the earth's surface that was more than five inches from any other. This godlike attitude caused his principal minions to dart madly from country to country, from continent to continent, indeed from hemisphere to hemisphere, spinning through the airways, burning up the roads, queueing up for visas, wiring home in greater and greater desperation for more varieties of currency with which to pay for their fares, their ham sandwiches, their bottles of whisky. And always, as they stumbled exhausted from the place in Bangkok, the cable announcing that their destination was Hong Kong; the arrival in Cairo for the inevitable re-routing to Damascus; the brooding knowledge as they touched down in Durban that they would be told the story was in Algiers.

The state of affairs, which had seemed monstrous and inhuman an hour before, now appeared increasingly droll. Over the hill in Yatung stood the exile court of God Reincarnate, under canopies of cloth-of-gold, a stockade of sacred objects, bursting sacks of gems, and the bejewelled teams of yaks browsing on the hillside –

we knew very well what *that* would be: a line of leather shanties
and lean-tos, smouldering dung-fires, a crowd of seedy lamas
drinking buttered tea. It wasn't worth it. It would be against the
law, and a spell in Gangtok jail at this time of year would kill us.
And we were not Dalai Lamas; when we died we stayed dead.

When I awoke it was light, and my ears were full of a sound like
church-bells – a caravan, the biggest yet, clattering down the trail.
My head was bursting and I was racked with thirst. The mule-
bells seemed only an extension of what was going on inside my
own skull.

We began the dreadful job of breaking camp, staggered about
untying knots, rolling things up, moving in a laborious creaking
way, like old machinery. There was nothing for breakfast but
sardines. As the light grew over the eastwards mountains we
harnessed ourselves without debate or argument – straps cutting
into yesterday's weals, the loose buckle renewing the same old
bruise – rejoined the trail and followed in the steps of the caravan,
headed back for India and the south, one step nearer home.

As it turned out, the Dalai Lama *had* intended to leave Tibet. Even
while I was shivering and despairing on the hillside the Living
God was packing his ten thousand effects on the other side of the
mountain and making ready for the journey down the Jelep-la.

In Kalimpong his mother waited, the Gya-Yum-Chembo,
Victorious Mother of Glory; her daughter the Yapshi Semo; the
eight-year-old Incarnate Buddha Ngari Tulku, her youngest son.
But His Holiness never came. When at last he did return to his
capital, a Chinese General went with him.

His older brother, the Taktser Rimpoche, managed otherwise.
It seemed his rheumatism was troubling him. He crossed into
India to see the doctors. When he reached Calcutta there was the
Chinese Communist Ambassador, full of concern for his well-
being, solicitously recommending – indeed insisting – that the
Taktser Rimpoche hasten back to Tibet where they, the Chinese,
would undertake his treatment, and not to stay a day longer in
India. Thoughtfully the Taktser consented; that very night he
took an aeroplane to America, where he had prudently made
arrangements in Virginia, and from which he equally prudently
never returned.

And so the Chinese won the war at last, without difficulty or bloodshed, without special endeavour; there was in the end neither a bang nor a whimper.

The new chapter began without delay. The circumstances may have been strange and in their way unprecedented, but the pattern was the same the world had seen many times before. The nominal quisling was not hard to find; the pretender Panchen Lama, who received his accolade and his orders in Peking in what must have been a ceremony of some originality, probably the first man to be confirmed in supernatural and divine authority under Marxist principles. The days of the Mountain Fastnesses were gone. The Chinese told the Personification of the God Incarnate what to do and when to do it, and that was the end of Shangri-la.

It was many years later that the Dalai Lama *did* finally emigrate and take refuge over the Assam border, and I was there to see that also. By that time it seemed pitifully unimportant.

All the way back to Silfiguri, down through the rhododendrons and bamboo, down through the thickening air and the growing warmth, back at last to the dust and the grit of the plains.

Then it was Karachi, and Cairo, and Rome; brown earth growing green, the toy subdivisions of human occupation; suburbia below: a pattern of chimney-pots and little gardens.

Down through the concrete outskirts into London, a Victorian chapel decaying away among the cinema queues, the rows of brick and the television aerials. 'For the Gautama laid it down: Everything corporeal is material and therefore fleeting, it carries within itself the seeds of dissolution; nothing is eternal but the law of cause and effect.'

There must be a book to be written about these matters, I thought as the taxi jerked and crawled through Pimlico; but by then it was too late, and tomorrow one would have to start work again.

Diversion 5: Big Deal

WHEN first I went to China under its new management, which was some time before it opened up to enterprising MPs, travelling salesmen, and political pussyfooters of all varieties, I was warned of the disappointments that lay ahead. You will only see what they want you to see, I was told: a familiar forecast. It suggests that the Chinese, in the Oriental duplicity, seek to make a good impression. It implies that visitors to our free Anglo-Saxon lands, instead of being guided to the Houses of Parliament, Grant's Tomb, Westminster Abbey, and Lincoln Centre, are instantly conducted instead to Dartmoor Prison, Stepney Green, and Harlem.

In Peking, I was told, I should naturally see nothing of significance, and certainly no one of standing. As for observing Mao Tse-Tung, or Chou En-Lai, the proposition was absurd; there were 500 million Chinese who had never clapped eyes on them. Perhaps they did not even exist – as, in his latter days, the invisible Stalin was said to be a legend.

When I reached Peking at last, in a haze of fatigue, I expected little, having no ambition but sleep. At the airfield was waiting Shen Chen-T'u, whom I had known in Geneva – a Foreign Office functionary of no great elevation, but one of the many unrecorded men who have had my true affection.

'So you came at last,' he said, with a hint of friendly reproach that seemed somehow unjust, since I knew that he knew that I had been unremittingly asking and pleading for my visa for three solid years. 'And now you are here, would you care to come along to a party this evening?'

I sighed and thanked him wearily; I said I would be happy to do so when I had washed my hands and changed my shirt, rested awhile. He said, with the diffidence that in China brooks no argument: 'It might be better if we went straight to the party; it will have begun.'

I drove with him through the City Gates, through the grey *hut'ungs* and alleys of old Peking, through the walls of the once-Forbidden City, to the once-Imperial Chamber known as the Palace of Purple Light – myself dirty, weary, in the same suit in which, five days before, I had set off from Victoria.

The party had already begun; it was of a tremendous size. Lest it be thought that the resources of the Inner Palace had been mobilized to welcome me, it has to be said that I appeared to be one of some two thousand guests; it was a party of some extravagance. It was not hard to believe, on the threshold of this vast, swarming room, that I was in the heartland of the world's most numerous people. But what riveted the eye, what gave themoment the character of fantasy, was the line of hosts.

Not for the first time had the wiseacres at home proved wrong. There, greeting the guests with quiet nods and smiles and orientally-folded hands, was Mao Tse-Tung, Chairman of the People's Republic of China. And not only Chairman Mao, but his Deputy, Chu-Teh, Head of the Army. And not only him but Prime Minister Chou En-Lai, *and* the Party leader Liu Shao-Chi, *and*, as a surprising bonus, Mr Khrushchev and Mr Bulganin from Moscow *and* Mr Shvernik and Mr Mikoyan, *and* Mr Beirut from Poland and Kim Il Sung from North Korea, and indeed all the leaders of every People's Democracy known to the Cominform. It was in fact the entire top crust of the Communist world, gathered for my very first hour in Peking.

It is true that this luminous galaxy was not assembled to greet the arrival of a solitary Western writer; this chanced to be the eve of the Fifth Anniversary of the Communist establishment and a high day of sensational importance. Yet the fact remained: I, who would have counted it lucky to have met two Deputy Under-Secretaries in a month, found myself, within an hour of setting foot in Peking, hobnobbing – if that be the word – with the most concentrated essence of revolutionary talent since Lenin murmured to his mates round the green plush table.

But of them all the only one who mattered to me was Shen Chen-T'u. For many weeks he was my companion, and my friend. He would talk about anything. He loved to argue, to eat and drink; above all he loved to laugh; no one had a greater capacity for humour.

'You must believe me, I am a devoted Marxist,' he would say, 'but really, some things are so funny. For example . . .'

His wife had just had a baby boy. 'I shall call him Shen Ka Mah-Lon, after you,' he said, 'though it will be hard on him. Do you know what your name means in Mandarin? It means "Face of a Treacherous Horse". We shall have to change the tonal values.'

When at last I left Peking he got up at five a.m. to see me off. 'Naturally,' he said with a smile, 'only to make sure you go. We'll meet again.'

Next year the day came when we set off for the Bandung Conference, from opposite ends of the earth, he from Peking, I from London. But we did not meet again. Shen Chen-T'u and his official party left Hong Kong in an Air India chartered Constellation called the *Kashmir Princess*. While it refuelled, a Formosa government agent slipped a pencil bomb in the starboard tank, and an hour and a half later the plane blew up off Borneo, killing everyone on board.

Shen Chen-T'u lies today at the bottom of the China Sea; he is with his ancestors, and his little boy, after all, was spared the name of the Treacherous Horse.

Chapter Thirteen

In my time, over all those post-war years, I was obliged to attend as camp-follower great numbers of international conferences and confrontations of greater or less moment, according to the dramatic quality of the contemporary crisis and the eminence of the delegates involved. One after another the encounters came, stalled, and dispersed; argument, casuistry, stalemate and shadowboxing, with the recurrent shadow of the late Mr John Foster Dulles gumshoeing across the world like the Inspector of Blind Alleys, a diplomatic bird of prey smelling out from afar the corpses of dead ideals. 'The talks took place in a cordial atmosphere . . . an exchange of views . . . agreement on broad points . . . some progress was made, though outstanding problems remain . . .' Thud, thud, and drip, drip; the anodyne phrases, the sterile handouts, the evasive, meaningless, circumlocutory, halfhearted and empty forms of words, signifying that Premier X had met Minister Y; for what argument and how resolved? Language itself became a currency debased and corrupt; token sentences rubbed clear of message, like worn coins.

Thus did we trot and bark behind the caravan: Geneva, New York, Ankara, Belgrade; each producing its new aspect of unreality, another crop of paradoxes and non-sequiturs. Once upon a time there had been Secret Diplomacy; one knew little about it and could therefore not complain when it misfired. Then there were Open Agreements Openly Arrived At, supposedly to put an end to the horse-trading. This was succeeded by Secret Agreements Openly Arrived At – the day of the leak, the bypass, the calculated revelation. The leaders continued on their way as fruitlessly as ever. Most of the occasions have disappeared into limbo; I find it difficult to remember which was which. One, however, was memorable, and truly to be counted as a milestone on the doomsday trail.

Early in 1960 the world was unusually exercised by doubts and apprehensions, and with reason; a high-altitude U-2 espionage aircraft of the United States Air Force had been shot down over the Soviet Union, in circumstances not wholly explained even today; much of the equipment, including the pilot, Garry Powers, had been captured and placed on display in Moscow. The luckless President Eisenhower was trapped into one of the biggest political *bêtises* of the century, since having initially disowned all knowledge of this extravagantly provocative enterprise was shortly obliged to make the gruesomely humiliating admission that what the Russians angrily claimed to be an American spy-mission was in fact an American spy-mission, and one not only clumsy but also unsuccessful. It was impossible to recall when any head of state, even one as outstandingly naïve and inane as President Eisenhower, had ever been placed in a position simultaneously so ridiculous and so perilous. In this atmosphere was convened the celebrated Summit Conference of Paris, to be attended by Khrushchev, Eisenhower, Macmillan and de Gaulle. No diplomatic correspondent in attendance – and never in my life had I seen such a raft of them, clambering over each other in the Crillon – could imagine any circumstances less propitious, and many foresaw dire disaster. They were right.

The day that was to finish so ill began with a singular beauty, as was proper in Paris in May. Only in the diplomatic ranges did stormclouds start to assemble, like rumours of betrayal. But the sun was bright and the girls were gay, and I wrote a frivolous article to match the mood. It was not the one I was to write that night nor, as for a time it seemed, ever again.

Those who were at the Elysée Palace that morning saw the four cars drive up, from four different directions, at exactly twenty-second intervals, and wondered at the organization of such precision. They might well have done so; that unanimity was the last. At one minute past eleven the four leaders went into the conference-room in the west wing and faced each other, separated by five yards of circular table and an abyss of bitterness.

At eight minutes past two it was all over; 187 minutes; three hours that could genuinely if platitudinously be said to have shaken the world. Just twice during that time did Mr Khrush-

chev's new-found space-engine, the Sputnik, spin unseen overhead; it should have been able to cast its shadow across that table
like an omen.

In the Maison de la Presse, that permanently gimcrack edifice
confronting the Eiffel Tower, some three thousand of the newspaper battalions awaited. This was, beyond any doubt, the most
populous and almost certainly the most significant Press Conference the world had ever known. It is perhaps questionable
whether Press Conferences of any nature achieve the importance
that one attributes to them; nevertheless, making every allowance
for the tremendously heightened sense of occasion that informed
us then, this day could not do otherwise than represent a diplomatic watershed of some kind.

Yet to return once again to that gaunt old campus of the Palais
de Chaillot was again to get a lowering sense of the *déjà vu*. How
often had we plodded the hardboard lobbies of that political gym-
nasium for one more diplomatic exercise in destiny? That day, to
be sure, it seemed improbable that we would ever do so again.

Suddenly, at five minutes to three, Mr Khrushchev arrived,
and walked into this huge lobby populated, it seemed, by prop-
agandists; by now every newspaperman affected to represent an
attitude; Khrushchev was greeted by applause, catcalls, howls of
abuse. I had never before seen a Press conference so openly
turned into a political meeting. Under the punitive glare of the
television lights Mr Khrushchev beamed and sweated, waved and
gesticulated. Far down in the recesses of this immense auditorium
journalists contended, swore, wrangled.

Unexpectedly Mr Khrushchev opened with oddly edged com-
pliments to, of all people, Mr Macmillan and President de Gaulle,
'whose zeal had attempted to make this Conference possible'. All,
alas – said Mr Khrushchev, in vain. 'Had these statesmen taken a
position of objectively evaluating the facts, had they not surrendered for the sake of their alliances, had they shown more
will power, the American leaders might have been obliged to
condemn their own aggressive actions, and a Summit could have
been held for the benefit of the world.'

It was already clear that this was not to come about. Beside Mr
Khrushchev sat Marshal Malinovsky, the monumental Soviet
Minister of Defence, rectangular in grey and red uniform, of all
men in the world the one of whom it could be said that he was at

least he was as broad as he was tall. Beside him Mr Gromyko, with his serious bank-manager's face. On everyone's countenance lay the cast of doom, except on that of Mr Khrushchev, restless and alert, taking each sip of mineral-water as a toast to his vast audience.

In our airless congestion the crowd waited for whatever form the Russians would use to administer their *coup de grâce*. Bleakly, crisply, brutally, uncompromisingly, trilingually the words dropped into the steaming hall like small sharp stones, and it is possible that none of the experienced chroniclers of an antic world had ever before heard one leader of a great nation address the leader of another great nation words of such abrasive and calculated bitterness and challenge. It is likely that such words had never publicly been thrown into the face of a President before, otherwise than on the absolute edge of war. President Eisenhower, the pitiable figure compelled to stand before the world as the uninformed leader of a nation of blunderers, had asked for it, and he got it. No man in the world that day could have possibly been regretting anything as Mr Eisenhower was regretting that mean and absurd U-2.

'It is necessary that the United States admits that the provocative policy it declared is condemned, that it rejects it and admits that it has committed aggression, and admits that it regrets it.' Mr Khrushchev offered the sheet of penitence to Mr Eisenhower with the ultimatum that we would settle for nothing short of the abject. He formally demanded that Mr Eisenhower should punish those guilty of initiating the provocation, with the implication that since the President was the President, and thus Commander-in-Chief, there remained technically nothing for Mr Eisenhower to do but leap personally and publicly into the Seine.

These conditions were obviously unacceptable to anyone other than in a state of unconditional surrender, or lost to any political pride, and Mr Khrushchev knew they were unacceptable; the Summit was therefore condemned to death.

Tremendous howls broke out on all sides. It was a humiliating expression of the principle of a Press Conference, but by now the occasion had taken on itself the character of a public meeting. From corners of the hall came cries of 'Hungary!' The monolithic Marshal Malinovsky permitted his granite face to hint at a smile. Mr Khrushchev called back: 'At least I am gratified to see such a disturbance among the lackeys of imperialism.'

There was an imminent danger of this terrible occasion turning into farce. The whole thing was suddenly tracked back into reality by what to this day I consider the most extraordinary statement ever made even by that master of the impulsive. Somebody – nobody ever discovered who – called out to Mr Khrushchev, requiring to know why he had not challenged President Eisenhower about the U-2 flights when he was his guest in America, since he had known all the time.

'I intended to bring it up at Camp David,' said Mr Khrushchev. 'Of course I knew. I should have done. But the atmosphere was so friendly. It was warm. I was almost persuaded. Mr Eisenhower called me "friend", in Russian; then he asked me to call him "friend" in English. I thought he was my friend. Then I knew there was something fishy about my friend. I had caught him red-handed. Now he says: "I am not a thief; I just have a thieving policy."'

Suddenly and absurdly, all the lights in the hall went out, the microphones died. 'One more capitalist stratagem to keep me quiet!' roared Mr Khrushchev. When the lights returned he was paradoxically convulsed with laughter.

It was a poignant and perilous moment, and I remember feeling extremely emotional about it, though I was obliged to argue that it seemed to me that this Soviet body-blow was in the circumstances the least that could have been expected. I had a strong impulse to return to London and make dispositions for the care of my family.

Instead, the formal minuet of the journalistic performance required that we surged across to a neighbouring room to hear how Mr Hagerty would cope with this clearly incurable situation. Mr James Hagerty was a great phenomenon of those troubled times. He was the official Presidential Spokesman and mouthpiece of the United States; wherever the President went he technically carried the White House with him, and Mr Hagerty with his stocky, rocky frame and his glinting spectacles was integrally a part of the White House machinery. I cannot remember in how many places I had encountered Mr Hagerty as at one moment the revealed word of the American establishment and the next as the oracular source of almost incredibly meaningless material for the gossip-columns, defining in one breath foreign policy and the issues of peace or war, and in the next detailing the exact ingredients of the President's luncheon and the rhythm of his bowel-movements and the texture of his underwear. Nothing was too momentous nor too trivial for the consideration of Mr Hagerty, so long as his flock of American reporters with their insatiable hunger for inanity demanded factual information, even though it concerned nothing more diplomatically important than the President's choice of breakfast food. After several years of practising his craft Mr Hagerty had perfected a technique of granite-faced badinage, holding court wherever it might be, even the temporary axis of the world, ad-libbing his way through conferences that had to be read to be believed. For, not content with the briefing itself, the Americans later would issue a transcribed record of this inspirational nonsense, which many of us believed at the time was then wrapped up and sent to the Marx Brothers.

'Jim, when you say cold gin, do you mean cold or chilled?' 'Otherwise, Jim, would you say the President's bladder is in good order?' 'You say the President got up at 8.04 hours; how would that be Washington time?' 'What did the President pray for this morning, Jim?'

Now, however, Mr Hagerty had no choice but to handle in some way the President's own tormented efforts to escape from his fatal spy-plane trap. Deprived of the gritty invective of Mr Khrushchev, he could reply to the Russians' accusations of 'torpedoing' the Summit by saying that Mr Khrushchev had 'sabotaged' it. Never in his serene career had Mr Hagerty looked or sounded less like Lucky Jim; it was a sad climax to all the years of dedication to a President now bound to play out his last months in office in such inglorious confusion.

It seemed that there was now little to be said that could add to the atmosphere of horrid fantasy in which we all floundered. Both Khrushchev and Eisenhower had now proclaimed attitudes that in any earlier society would certainly have meant war. There could be no meaning to such words other than that each side was somehow conscious that the other side did not mean what it said; thus East and West were formally debasing the currency of language as they had both debased that of international usage.

However disastrous the party and however bitter the leave-taking, there always still remains the glass to sweep away and the dust and ashes to collect. Next day the ghosts walked in Paris: the sour memories of hopes stillborn, of consciences paraded where one side brayed its outrage and the other fitfully protested its honour. President Eisenhower went to Portugal, where that rueful man could at least be sure of temporary sanctuary from political controversy. Mr Khrushchev went to East Berlin, where similar conditions obtained for different reasons. Only we remained.

If Mr Khrushchev thought to make an impression he amply succeeded; his coming and going left a crater in the public mood. Yet this mood was, in the end, sentimental; for most of those who the previous week had felt every sympathy for Mr Khrushchev's case against the Americans, now sought for the helpless Eisenhower every excuse.

That afternoon's *Le Monde* said: 'Perhaps the cost of war is indeed too high for any victor, yet the world must now abandon most of its simpler hopes. We shall now live in insecurity, hatred, lies and concealment. Above all we see, through all the philosophical and social pretensions, that the thing that dominates international relations is pride. The one sincere factor in Mr Khrushchev's eloquence was the immense pride of a man who has conquered space and is still astonished that there are people on earth who refuse the happiness for which he alone has the infallible recipe.'

An American paper put it laconically: 'At least our relations with the Reds are back to normal.'

Surprisingly, life went on.

Diversion 6: The Agent

IT is my misfortune that, born as I was with an urge and, I believe, an aptitude for complicated sin, I was forever slipping back into the paths of tiresome righteousness. Either from lack of opportunity, or perhaps initiative, I blundered through the years almost never seducing a Countess, selling a State secret, or becoming involved in any picturesque scandal. Even the couple of times I was in jail were basically through misunderstanding.

This is almost certainly the reason why I was never approached by casually mysterious men from MI5 and invited to become an Agent. These people – Agents' agents, I suppose – could always detect the political rabbit in me. Only once was I involved in the diplomatic underworld.

In Delhi, around the great days of the Indian transfer of power, there came an event of quite considerable international importance – the Pan-Asian Conference: the first general gathering of the Eastern nations. It was, in a sense, the precursor of the Bandung Conference of several years later, and it was more significant than is remembered now.

For a week the city was filled with the most intricate variety of people, strange in costume and countenance – brocades from South-East Asia, bell-bottoms from the Eastern Soviet Republics, braided hair and quilted robes from Tibet, smelling dreadfully, dozens of curious languages and poly-syllabic titles. One way and another, as we kept reminding one another, this multitude represented nearly half the population of the world. The meeting itself took place in an enormous marquee set in the ruins of the fourteenth century Moghul fort called the Purana Qila. The members were diverting to look at, but their deliberations were unintelligible, even to each other.

By and by, however, it was put about that among the delegates was a man of particularly secret and mysterious nature, whose mission in Delhi was far from purely cultural. Nobody had seen him; nobody even knew who he was. It was said that he had travelled in the most clandestine manner conceivable from somewhere among the southern Armies of Viet Minh, holding the most tremendous aide-memoire from Ho Chi-Minh, then as indeed now a charismatic figure in the developing Asian scene. Many years later I was to meet him; at that epoch he was a legend.

It appeared that his man had been smuggled through the French lines in circumstances of incredible skill and hazard, disguised as a respectable opium-salesman, with documents of sensational importance concealed in the most improbable and inconvenient parts of his person. A hundred men had lost their lives to secure his passage, and now that he was here no one had the slightest idea where to find him. He carried with him, they said, the secrets of a wholly new Asian alignment, and in the queer circumstances of those days this could well have been the case.

One day it was murmured to me in a most devious manner that it might be made possible for me to make contact with this elusive and shadowy individual. The utmost discretion would be imperative; the man was excruciatingly unapproachable. On no account might I mention the subjects of Russia, China, or Indonesia, nor could I make public that I had even seen him, for three and a half weeks, exactly. For the purposes of this encounter it would be necessary for me to be on the verandah of Maiden's Hotel at a certain hour precisely, wearing a certain kind of suit, and reading page two of the *Statesman*, I would thereafter be further informed.

I followed the instructions minutely. Then, at the appointed time, the hall-bearer loudly paged my name, and there entered the verandah a small Annamese-looking man in a seersucker jacket with a bulging briefcase. He walked swiftly up, and withdrew from his wallet the most truly enormous visiting card I ever saw in my life. On it was printed, in clear and heavy type, the words:

Mr San Do Lau

SECRET AGENT

And that was that. We did not mention the subjects of Russia, China, or Indonesia. Indeed for twenty minutes we discussed nothing except how, somehow, it might be that Mr San Do Lau could lay his hands on four thousand rupees cash for a practically new second-hand Chrysler, presently for sale at the Kashmiri Gate.

I could suggest nothing. But, as we now know, the French were driven from Viet Nam. It cannot be said that I was never in on *anything*.

Chapter Fourteen

FOR years, long before the explosion of rancour between the Albanian republic and the Soviet Union split the Eastern world and made this small Communist enclave the political phenomenon of the times, I had nourished an erratic ambition to get into Albania. The impulse, I readily admit, was not wholly academic; there must have been involved a sort of collector's curiosity. I had worked in, or at least been to, almost every country in the world; but although I had moved through all the Communist states, including China, Albania was the one that seemed impenetrable. From time to time I made representations at Albanian missions and consulates in Paris, Rome, Ankara, Sofia – remote legations in obscure streets. Invariably I encountered either a total refusal to discuss the matter or, more frequently, the blank wooden face of some closed door with a dusty card explaining that the official was out for lunch. In any case, I had long ago written off Albania. And then suddenly, in 1963, I was there.

Some months before, an advertisement for a travel agency in Cologne appeared in a West German paper announcing an eighteen-day tour-group through Albania. There was nothing in it to suggest that it was addressed only to Communists. Consequently, on the principle of trying anything once, I sent in an application to join this tour, in the virtual certainty that it would be rejected or, more probably, ignored. To my great surprise it was promptly acknowledged, with a batch of forms to be filled in, a demand for a deposit of one hundred pounds, and the odd request that my passport be sent to Germany to be duly fitted out with an Albanian visa. This would presumably take place in East Berlin.

I felt in no way persuaded to send my passport, on which I depend for the pursuit of my living, into some unspecified German limbo. These matters are, however, more manageable now than they used to be. A short consultation in the right quarters produced another passport, which was then sent on its way.

For weeks thereafter nothing happened. I put the matter out of my mind. Then, with the kind of maniac suddenness that seems to characterize most things that happen to me, an urgent message arrived: the tour was on after all, the group was ready. Would I, said the agency, make my way at once to Munich, where the tourist group would rendezvous at the airport and where I would collect my passport and my Albanian visa.

It seemed to me that there must be something either very naïve or very devious about an agency that could cheerfully propose that a man travel from one country to another to *collect* his passport. However, I obeyed; if they were not disposed to ask questions, nor was I. Thus I came to Munich, and there it was that the pantomime began.

I admit that it had crossed my mind that, while my stratagem for infiltrating Albania as part of a tourist group had been ingenious, it was not necessarily exclusive. I was prepared to find that some other writer, journalist, or kindred tradesman had latched on to this body of innocent visitors. I welcomed the possibility of a colleague, and I prepared to detect him if I could.

What I had not expected to find at our Munich rendezvous was this: among the seventeen of us was not so much as one who could claim to be, in any sense, a tourist. This discovery required no great talent since, so far from dissembling their purposes, the entire party except myself were most palpably laden with technical gear, 35-millimetre cameras, tripods, sound equipment, lights and lenses, wires and cables, and television machinery of great weight and complexity, and were standing around with the wearily watchful demeanour of those who live with such affairs.

Thus, when our tourist group eventually touched down in Tirana some hours later, it resembled not so much the wide-eyed arrival of those on pleasure bent as the annual outing of some wild and capricious Press Club.

This manifestly took the Albanians somewhat aback, though with great composure they refrained from comment. You are, they said, as the passports vanished one by one into a black leather bag, tourists? Everyone nodded urgently, fiddling with exposure meters. Very well, said the official in level tones, Welcome, and we climbed out of the aircraft into Albania.

I do not know what I had expected. Most airports of Eastern republics are, in my experience, much the same. They have a common quality of charmless austerity, are always at the end of long straight roads, and are ceaselessly preoccupied with the reception of fraternal delegations. Tirana proposed every kind of difference. Here in the evening light was a scene of haunting loveliness: a backcloth of erratically sculptured mountains, a purple frieze against the darkening blue, a long broad valley between the climbing olive slopes, a block of low buildings that could only by courtesy be called an airport, yet bordered and embowered in a profusion of roses. On the far side of the perimeter I could see what appeared to be about two squadrons of early Migs; between them and the runway an old man in a loose turban tended a flock of sheep.

The frontier examination was conducted with impassive civility, but most surprisingly interrupted by a shirt-sleeved waiter with a tray of minute brandies. The woman customs inspector accepted all the television technology calmly enough, and the owners, on whom there had settled a kind of depressed embarrassment, began minimally to cheer up. As it turned out, this was premature. The Albanians had not the slightest intention of allowing the cameras to be used; on the contrary, they had devised an inspirational technique of discipline. Instead of impounding the equipment, they sealed it and insisted on its owners taking it with them, tottering around under the weight of gadgetry that served no purpose whatever but to remind them, if this were ever necessary, who was boss.

My own condition was very different, and my attitude tended, with fatuous optimism, to smugness. Alone among this bogus company, it seemed, I had gone to some lengths to resemble a tourist, at least in having nothing in particular with me – no typewriter, not even a notebook. Yet it was my ostentatiously innocent valise that most absorbed the customs lady, because, as it happened, it contained half a dozen paperback editions of assorted books – a novel or two, a book of essays, and *Tristam Shandy*, which I have been dragging around the world for years and years against the day when I should be driven to such desperation of idleness that I would actually read it. The customs lady had them out on the counter and studied them with the resentful doubt of a scoutmistress uncertain if she had been landed with Henry Miller in a Bulgarian translation. By and by she took them into a back room, where she was joined by two more officials, and for a while I saw their heads together in baffled disapproval. When the customs lady returned and closed my valise, the books were not in it, nor did I ever see them again.

We climbed into a bus and drove into Tirana through the gathering twilight. All around us the physical grandeur of the country faded into the dusk, and the creaking of the cicadas was dying in the trees. Along the potholed road we passed one group after another of soldiers; youngsters in the shabby secondhand Soviet Army uniforms that were part of Russia's aid – ungenerous, it seemed to me – in the days when the two countries were talking to each other. On that first evening it seemed that Albania was wholly populated by young crop-headed soldiers in grey smocks and soft high boots. That impression was soon to change; nevertheless, this little nation was manifestly the most over-armied I think I have ever seen.

There was nothing surprising in this; all Albania's recorded past has been one of almost uninterrupted tumult and violence, a history of conquests and tyrannies, oppressions and insurrection, occupations and liberations, bitter exploitation and recurrent revolution. Here was a country steeped in the tribal memories of endless war; add to that fact – since the population of Albania is still largely Muslim – the exclusivity and withdrawal of Islam; superimpose the new suspicions and disciplines of twentieth-century Communism: no wonder I felt, as the dim lights of Tirana drew nearer, that Albania is a tough place in which to feel at home.

The Albanians are among the most ancient peoples of Europe, the Illyrian tribesmen who somehow maintained their identity under the Greeks for six centuries, who contrived to survive five hundred years of Roman occupation and another five hundred under the Byzantines, who chose these impossible highlands as their battlefield against the kingdom of Bulgaria. Albania was the bridgehead for the repeated eastward incursion of Europe – the Normans in the eleventh century, the Venetians in the thirteenth.

Even after the great Turkish conquest in 1478, the Albanians refused to settle down as good colonials and continued to be the biggest nuisance in the Ottoman Empire for four hundred and fifty years more.

After the Austro-Hungarians, the French, and the Italians had fought themselves to a standstill over Albania in the First World War, there came the curious interlude of the tribal chieftain Zog, who declared himself first President, then King, in the 1920s, and who vanished with the wind in Mussolini's Italian invasion at Easter, 1939.

In the inevitable progression of the times, the First World War produced Fascism, the Second produced Communism. Licking the terrible wounds of the years of guerrilla fighting and counting their losses – 28,000 dead, 43,000 deportees in the concentration camps, 60,000 homes destroyed – the partisans of the Albanian hills proclaimed their People's Republic in 1946, under the protective arm of the Soviet Union. So went the honeymoon for sixteen years. And then had come the great divorce. Once again the featherweight nation with the massive and furious pride was on its own.

The hotel in Tirana stood off the main boulevard behind a belt of evergreens. It was unexpectedly grand. Like almost everything else of any pretension in town, it had clearly been built by the Italians in an expansive mood, but it had long ago acquired the colourless antiseptic cheerlessness of all Popular Democratic hotels. This is very difficult to define; it has something to do with a dim economy of underpowered electric bulbs, an immobility of elevators, a dusty emptiness of show-cases, a greyness of table linen, an absence of servants, and a superfluity of unidentifiable shadowy functionaries who are clearly neither staff nor guests. These characteristics are, in my experience, shared by all hotels in the Communist economy, and are explicable in the simple fact that, as befits their function in societies where people circulate only on specific instructions, they have long since changed from hotels to institutions.

However, the Daiti Hotel in Tirana put on as fair a show of hospitality as was permitted by its manifest lack of practice. To deny by implication the travellers' tales that Albania is a country of unexampled filthiness, the place reeked of floor polish and germicide. I was given a large, dispiriting, but spotless room with a most elaborate bathroom, complete with bidet, most certainly a memento of the Italian occupation. The profusion of taps and faucets emitted a series of hollow clanks and groans, but no water. Of the set of five wall switches, one alone was operational, producing a thin subaqueous light.

It was unfair to blame Albania, of all places, for an inadequacy with tourists – even tourists as spurious as we. And yet the peculiar fact was that Albania really did affect to believe that it *was* a tourist centre. The bleak lobby of the hotel was littered with leaflets and brochures extolling the virtues of its *richesses archéologiques*, its *culture artistique*, its *vie sociale*, its *traditions etynographiques*. Some of them looked as though they had been there for centuries. They were printed in several languages – German, French, Russian, Italian. To produce an English version was presumably pointless. Americans are neither sought nor, indeed, permitted, and there have been no relations whatever with Britain since 1946, when Albania inconsiderately mined a couple of British destroyers in the Corfu Channel.

What was the purpose of canvassing for visitors while simultaneously making it virtually impossible for anyone to get into the country? For now, of course, there were not even any Russians. The great schism between Albania and the Soviet Union may have been one of the weirder phenomena of recent times, expressing as it did doctrinal differences of an importance far transcending Tirana, but there was no mistaking its visible effect on Albania. Albania was a tributary dammed from its river, and most evidently drying up.

The quarrel between Nikita Khrushchev and the Albanian boss, General Enver Hoxha, had been brewing slowly since 1959 and came to a head in the summer of 1961. Whether, in fact, the whole row was a development of the growing rift between Russia and China, with Albania playing the role of a political shuttlecock, is still a matter for some speculation, but not in Albania, which suddenly found itself upholding the banner of pure Marxist-Leninism against the corrupting tide of Soviet Revisionism and Tito Imperialism. It is said that the row began when Khrushchev, on his official visit to Enver Hoxha, became aware for the first time of Albania's singular and, indeed, striking backwardness, even by Balkan standards, and thereupon advised General Hoxha in a paternal way to abandon his wild and ambitious plans for industrialization. Albania is an incurably peasant community, Khrushchev is said to have observed; let it stick to growing tomatoes and olives, and never mind the steel mills and fertilizer factories. One can readily imagine Khrushchev saying this; it is also understandable that his celebrated homely nudges and rustic aphorisms cut no ice with the furious General Hoxha.

Anyhow, the storm broke; Khrushchev denounced Albania at the Twentieth Party Congress, stopped all Soviet aid, withdrew all credits, recalled all technicians, and cut Albania dead. The large and opulent new Soviet embassy in Tirana was stopped half-way up, and remained to that day exactly as the workmen left it, without a roof. Not a Soviet diplomat remained, not even a caretaker.

The blow to Albania's economy, such as it is, was of course appalling, but far worse was the jolt to its pride. Having no economic cards whatever up its own sleeve with which to counter-attack, Albania could take its revenge only in a manner that still seems somewhat comical: it recanonized Stalin. In Moscow and Prague and Sofia and Bucharest the statues of Stalin were carted away; in Tirana, on the contrary, the massive concrete images of the great man were not only rooted to the ground but garlanded with flowers. It was the perfect, the textbook case of human bloody-mindedness adopted as a national principle. There was something almost admirable about its senseless arrogance.

However, all this left Albania without a friend in the world – except the Chinese. The new diplomatic togetherness between China and Albania had deeply perplexed everyone, since it would be hardly possible to envisage two nations for whom an exclusive alliance could be more improbable temperamentally and more difficult physically. The largest nation on earth and one of the smallest; a vast Oriental country of 650 million and a Balkan province of 1.6 million, separated not just by seven thousand miles but by every conceivable human, traditional, racial, and linguistic difference – how did they even communicate? Accepting that the relationship was, in fact, a political cover-story, that Albania existed to be denounced by Russia and exalted by China; nevertheless, the Chinese must do something about it, and if so, what? The Chinese had, it seemed, produced a credit of 140 million dollars. But what about the *présence Chinoise* in Albania – where were they all?

It was hardly to be expected that the streets of Tirana would now echo to the cries of rickshaw boys and Mandarin-speaking cadres in blue boiler suits. Yet I had just heard that two new plane-loads of Chinese technicians had recently been flown into the country – to do what? Could Chinese advise Albanians on the harvesting of olives?

The fact was that several hundred Chinese in Albania were behaving there just as the Russians used to behave in China eight years ago; strictly keeping their heads down and remaining out of sight. Only once, on my second day in Tirana, did I blunder by chance into the wrong section of the restaurant, and there they were, some two dozen Chinese, dining in discreet segregation. They looked up in a very startled way, and I backed out in embarrassment.

For two days, then, before I made my irremediable gaffe, I had the freedom of Tirana, and a beguiling town it was. This was due more to the old than the new. The new was banal indeed: a pattern of broad, even stately avenues, lined with Party buildings in the Italianate style, with a carriageway wide enough to take several lines of traffic that was, for eighty per cent of the day, totally empty.

The desolation of the streets was eerie. At each intersection stood a smart white-uniformed traffic policeman, rigidly poised to direct a press of vehicles that never came. Once every five minutes, perhaps, an old green truck would appear clanking and grunting up the street, the traffic cop would spring to attention as it appeared on the horizon and wave it on with great panache, against no opposition whatever. At even rarer intervals would appear a dark Zim saloon, heavily curtained, on some mysterious official errand. In all Albania today there existed, I was formally told, not one single private automobile.

Down past New Albania Boulevard, down past Skanderberg Square, where the vast statue of Stalin brooded over the spinney of banners demanding long life for the workers' state, Tirana petered out gently into a tangle of wayward little streets and lanes of unmistakable poverty and increasing charm. There, where the tinsmiths beat out their gimcrack plates and jugs, there strolled the sort of Albanians one would not have thought ever to see outside a *fête folklorique*. Half the people wore the drab serge of a normal urban proletariat, but the other half, without any kind of self-consciousness at all, swaggered around in the white Macedonian tarboosh, the embroidered *xhublete*, and the enormous baggy pantaloons of the Muslim highlander. Albania must be one of the few countries left where what is known as peasant costume is in fact worn by peasants. It gave the back streets of Tirana a wonderfully rakish air.

These splendid wild men had one unexpectedly charming custom: that of carrying flowers in their mouths, as other people wear *boutonnieres*. Scores of times one would come across some swarthy brigand of most ferocious mien, darkly mustachioed, from whose scornful lips drooped a rose or a spray of honeysuckle. It gave an odd suggestion of Ferdinand the Bull. Even the drab and tattered soldiers redeemed their surliness with this insouciant habit. Once, outside Tirana, I saw a morose sentry at some wired stockade or other who had even thrust a nosegay of field flowers into the barrel of his carbine.

The first and very serious problem I ran into was that of communication. The Albanians speak a language of, it seemed to me, insuperable difficulty; a sort of tormented Turkish with heavy Slavic complications, by no means to be picked up overnight. It has, for one thing, an alphabet of thirty-six letters, with seven vowels and twenty-nine consonants. The words for Yes and No are *po* and *yo*, but that should lead no one to underestimate its intricacy. I very soon discovered, for example, that Albania does not, in its own tongue, call itself Albania at all, but 'Shqiperi', which somehow struck me as unreasonable.

Baffling though Albanian may be, few people appeared to speak much else. Since our tourist group had originated in Germany (and was, for that matter, largely German), the interpreter provided spoke German, which was unhelpful to me, as my German is none too good. I met nobody who spoke a word of English. When my own contretemps came to pass, involving some rather fierce and complicated discussion, it was translated in committee – from Albanian to Russian, from Russian to German, and from German into French.

A little local difficulty completely changed the character of an already somewhat shapeless expedition. I could see that the Albanian authorities (which, in effect, means everyone with whom we came in contact) had been dismayed by the transparently professional nature of our tourist group, though it seemed to me that their reactions had been unexpectedly civil, in the circumstances. On the day after our arrival, therefore, I sent a very short telegram to a newspaper in London. I sent it in the ordinary way, through the hotel desk, and while its main purpose was simply to give my address, I thought it could do no special harm if it were couched in terms of which the People's Republic could not disapprove. There was, after all, a certain news value in the arrival of Western foreigners in Albania, and this was my starting point. 'This small, proud, isolated Republic, which has gallantly challenged both east and west,' I wrote, 'has opened its doors, etc., etc.' If I had any doubts about the phrasing, it was that it was conciliatory to the point of being fulsome; it might well earn the derision of any Albanian censor with sensitive tastes.

What I had not foreseen was the extraordinary reaction. By and by, I was sought out by a small group of very tight-lipped functionaries, clearly in a hostile frame of mind. After a great deal of bamboozling multilingual sparring, I was given to understand that my telegram had been considered unpleasant, unfriendly, contemptuous, that it had fascist undertones and was an intolerable breach of my status as a visitor, let alone a tourist.

I found this so astonishing that I deduced some incomprehensible misunderstanding. What, exactly, did they object to? The terms describing the Republic of Albania, of course; the offensive adjectives. But, I protested, the words I used were not generally held to be hostile – 'gallant', 'small', 'proud', 'isolated . . .' That's it, they cried. 'Isolated!' Who but a Western lackey would use a word so bitter, so inaccurate! I protested that 'isolated' was not a term of reproach. Why, I said, not so many years ago, during the early days of the war, we in Britain used to brag about being isolated. Right, they shouted, and so you were; so you probably still are, but Albania isn't! The term was held to be atrocious.

By this time the conversation was verging on the preposterous. All right, I said crossly, so I take it you've stopped the message. Not at all, replied the committee; all that happened was that the postal workers who read the telegram found their loyalty so outraged by its tenor that they refused to transmit it. Moreover, they had put an exit visa in my passport and they did not care how soon I used it.

At this point, however, there arose what from their point of view was a very awkward snag. It is all very well to make the big gesture, fling open the front door, and say Begone, but the climax loses something of its drama when it turns out that there is nowhere to be gone to. Tirana was far from being the traffic crossroads of Eastern Europe. Its airport dispatched about two planes every fifteen days. The frontier roads were cut, and the railroad did not work. Short of flinging me over the end of the pier, there was no practical way of getting rid of me for at least ten days. The officials seemed to appreciate this, and, after some cold and courteous handshaking all around, departed to consider the situation.

Thus I was left alone for another day while the People's Republic reflected on the next step. I found my situation far from irksome. I asked if our tourist group could look around the University of Tirana, and this was agreed with surprising readiness. The university was by far the most imposing building in town and was described with some pride as a monument to the new Popular Democracy, though actually, like most substantial real estate in Tirana, a monument to the reverse, having been built some twenty years ago by Mussolini as the Casa Fascista of the occupation forces. The students were a robust and likeable crowd; they drifted and sidled among us with a sort of watchful curiosity; to me it was like being in Moscow fifteen years ago. Indeed, there was much of Albania that was like the Russia of the immediate post-war years; it was like China had been seven years before, when I found in the schools and universities communities of youth consumed with the impulse to communicate, yet totally inexperienced in the technique of doing so.

The main problem in these circumstances – apart from the language, the permanent presence of interpreters – was that the only questions that came to mind were the awkward ones. In a kind of Franco-German lingua franca I tried to break through. Why do you personally feel this revulsion toward the Soviet government? It seemed that Khrushchev had somehow promised the Greeks to support their claim for the northern Epirus, which to them was south Albania. He had deceitfully agreed to sustain Tito, and everyone knew what *he* was. When Khrushchev had visited Albania in 1959 he had been insufferably patronizing and called Albania a 'market garden'. Further than that, no one

seemed able to go. As for now being virtually alone in the world
– by no means; were they not indissolubly allied to the greatest
nation on earth, the Chinese?

But, I asked, while the Chinese were a great and potent people,
were they not inconveniently far away? No, they were not. Was it
not possible, then, in the somewhat larger and more complicated
differences between Moscow and Peking that Albania was being
used as a marionette? No, it was not. Was it not inevitable that
sooner or later this indomitable little nation would have to come
to terms with someone, if only to survive? No, it was not. The
debate was without much give and take, and soon it flagged.

The next day they put us all in a bus, drove us down to the
seaport of Durres, and left us there. I was not to see Tirana any-
more.

Durres, the Durazzo of Italian days, is one of the really ancient
places of Europe. It was the Epidamnus of the Greeks, the
Dyrrachium of the Romans. It had been the capital of the Illyrian
dynasty of the Talantines; it had been the very landfall from
which the Romans colonized Eastern Europe, the gateway to the
Balkans. Almost every kind of foreign hand had seized Durres,
developed, sacked it, left it – the Bulgars, the Serbs, the Ostro-
goths, the Spaniards, the Venetians, the Turks, the Italians. Now
it looked as though nobody had ever wanted to be bothered with it.

As it turned out, I was to see little of Durres. For an hour or
two we paused on the way through and drank a raki in a curbside
café and strolled to the massive overgrown walls of the old
Byzantine fortress. A long crocodile of tiny girls trotted up the
street on the way to school, all identically dressed in rose-pink
smocks, each child firmly holding the hem of the one ahead. The
shops were inexpressibly dreary, offering for sale little but
Leninist pamphlets and dusty flyblown sweetmeats. Almost all
food seemed to be sold in the MAPO, the Albanian equivalent of
the Russian chain store Gastronom; it seemed to consist of little
but fruit and canned fish.

Only two things were surprising. As the conductor urged us
back into the bus I heard a faint airborne wail, a chant like that of
a muezzin, and when I looked up, it *was* a muezzin, high on the
minaret of the big mosque of Durres he was calling the faithful to
prayer in the seven names of God. It was clear that here, at least,

as in the Muslim Soviet Republics, Communism had come to terms with Islam. (I discovered later that both in Durres and Tirana the Orthodox and the Roman Catholic churches remain open and collect fair congregations, and the *papas* and the priests are tolerated, if not encouraged.)

The other momentary shock was to glance in a dark and sombre shop window and see, by chance, there among the postal cards of Hoxha and Lenin and Stalin and all the other minor members of the Eastern pantheon, the familiar sulky face, the only too well-known tumbled hair of what was needlessly labelled Brixhid Bardo.

About five miles outside Durres stood the new beach hotel called the Adriatika. It was one of several hotels that faced the sea in various conditions of half-completion. They had all clearly been erected by the Russians for their use as a resort, and when the rift came they had been abandoned, exactly as the embassy had been abandoned. Only the Adriatika was operational, and of its three hundred rooms the only ones in occupation were ours.

It had been designed in what might be called the Soviet Black Sea taste – that is to say, the layout was of an elaboration and grandeur that could only be justified by its fulfilment in costly and sumptuous materials. It had, however, been run up in a hurry and on a shoestring; instead of fine timbers and rich marbles there was plasterboard and gritty cement; in the spacious hall the evergreen plants grew out of oil drums painted green. In my bedroom the divan was so placed that in order to go to bed one had to move the wardrobe, and to open the wardrobe it was necessary to move the bed. The overall effect was exasperating, and lowering.

Below the terrace of the hotel was the beach, and by the standards of beaches anywhere the Durres strand was beautiful, stretching wide arms north and south along the tranquil Adriatic. It was deserted. No gay umbrellas broke that flat expanse of ochre, no girls in bikinis lounged on the searing hot steel chairs of the terrace. The one waiter spent much of his time hiding in the shadowy interior, emerging only after emissaries had been sent to pry him from his meditations. For miles and miles, it seemed, there was no one to be seen but the occasional policeman, plodding moodily along the sand.

For anyone with no greater ambition than the acquisition of a suntan and a sea-numbed brain, there was, I suppose, little wrong with the beach at Durres, but for anyone who asked however little more from the Albanian experience, it was anaesthetically dull. On each side of our hotel stretched smaller hotels, villas, rest homes, vacation bases for the syndicates and government departments, every one of them totally empty. New as they were – some, indeed, were barely completed, with unglazed windows and unplastered walls – somehow they had already acquired a mournful air of neglect and rejection. Every day in the Adriatika the waiters philosophically set the restaurant tables for three hundred diners; every day they served the same seventeen customers.

The food was almost indescribably terrible. I am no gastronome at the best, moreover, I have, over the years, eaten in so many unpropitious circumstances and from so many truly awful kitchens that I have come to consider myself almost as much a connoisseur of bad food as other men are of good. But here in Durres was something that transcended anything I can remember. It is very hard to define its nature, other than to say that it was Balkan food taken to its final and desperate conclusion: pasta that had been cooked, or apparently so, many days before, then passed through some compressing process: vague and improbable cuts of antique meat subjected to brief and inadequate heat; hollow tomatoes filled with a kind of herbal sawdust. It puzzled me that there should be no fish at all, until the explanation dawned: there were no fishermen. There were no fishermen because there were no boats. With Italy only fifty miles away across the Adriatic, who would let a fisherman over the horizon, since he would most assuredly never come back?

So, for my stay in Durres I lived almost exclusively on bread, which was less awful than might have been supposed, and apricots, which were capital, and *konjak*, which was better than nothing. One crushing disappointment clouded the week: here was the first place in the whole world where I found one totally undrinkable wine – which is not said lightly, since I had always been of the impression that I could drink almost anything.

During all our activities, if that is the word, we were attended by, and conscious of, numbers of what in such societies as this are inaccurately called 'secret police'. They sat around in corners, they brooded in pairs at the ends of bars, they lurked about the lobbies in a fashion almost ostentatiously furtive. They were always to be found grouped around tables in those inhospitable and draughty parts of hotel foyers where no normal guest ever lingers, and whenever one caught their eyes, which happened extremely rarely, they dropped their gaze. They were by any standards the most conspicuous secret policemen I have ever observed in a fairly long experience of their craft. They were dressed always in shirts and suits only marginally less worn and frayed than everyone else's, and they were only just detectably better shaved. The one thing they had in common was their footwear – leather shoes presumably of government issue, so constructed that they gave out a harsh and penetrating creak with every step.

These individuals had several names; they were called 'Sigurini', or sometimes 'spooks'. All societies conducted on this system invent euphemisms for their watchdogs; for some reason, in Albania they had come to be called 'Historians'. It was not a bad name, combining respect, distaste, and a loose kind of accuracy.

The Historians rarely ventured into the dazzling light of the seashore, preferring to sit together in their silent communion indoors. I therefore spent most of the time in the sea or on the beach. In one direction lay a small jetty; in the other direction a couple of hundred yards brought one to the soldiers. They lounged around a concrete blockhouse, cradling their machine guns and spitting cherrystones. Beyond that point we might not go. 'Because,' I was told, 'we have not yet cleared up the minefields from the war.' It seemed a curious reason. After dusk a battery of floodlights broke out from a cliffside across the sea. Somewhere along that coast had been the location of the submarine pens built years ago by the Soviet Navy. The Russians had pulled out months ago, but, according to legend, not before the Albanians had managed to sequester two of the subs. But that was miles away to the south. A couple of hundred yards was the limit of my investigations, and being in disgrace already, I was not disposed to push my luck.

By now I was aware of the disability I had been subconsciously dreading since the hour of my arrival in Tirana: I had nothing whatever to read. This was not, as so often happens, bad management; by confiscating my books at the Customs, Albania had deprived me of all my resources. There was nothing to read in the hotel. I might have filled in an hour or so by trying to worry a word here and there out of the local newspaper, the *Zeri i Popullit*, but, mad as it sounds, I was not allowed to have one. Carrying incredibility even further, when I asked our guide-cicerone to translate one or two of the headlines for me, he said that this, too, was not possible. I took to gnawing my nails for want of something to read. What would I not have given even for *Tristram Shandy*.

Therefore, I was immeasurably relieved when the authorities suddenly told us that we could go on an expedition. They would take us to Kruja, a hill township of great historical importance, some twenty miles up in the Central Mountains. After several days marooned on the Durres beach, it seemed like. liberation.

We were all packed into a very old Ikarus bus that seemed rather less than usually decrepit (it had two new tyres, I noticed, a Barum from Czechoslovakia and a New China) but would nevertheless, I am sure, have passed no test known to the Western world. I observed with some alarm that the play on the steering wheel was so immense that the driver appeared to steer the bus as if it were an ocean liner, whirling the wheel around and around on every curve. For the first time I was able to see that the country road behind the hotel was arched across every hundred yards or so with banners, calling down blessings on the several objects of official approval. The Albanian word for Vive or Long Live is 'Rroshte!', and very onomatopoeic it looked with those two golden r's on the scarlet cloth. 'Rroshte Partija e Punes Shqibereje' the banners said, 'Long live the Albanian Party of Labour' (which the Party might well do, there being no other), and 'Roshte Markisisem-Leninizmit!' and 'Rroshte Choka Enver Hoxha!' (Another oddity of the Albanian tongue is this word *Choka*, meaning 'Comrade'; it was pronounced 'Shocker' and gave an extremely fanciful sound to every greeting: 'Good morning, Shocker.' 'In the words of our great leader, Shocker Hoxha . . .').

The drive to Kruja was the most electric experience I had known for some time. The road, which was rugged, and covered with loose stones, wound in hairpin bends upward through scenery of breathtaking loveliness, which could be appreciated by nobody, so riveted with anxiety was everyone's gaze on the fearsome precipices around which we slithered. Something of our dread must have communicated itself to the driver, a wild-eyed mountaineer of unbounded gaiety and confidence, as he wrenched the creaking bus around the bends he would sing: '*Hup-la!*

Hup-la!' and at moments of acute and petrifying peril he would turn around to the passengers with a demoniac grin of reassurance. I was genuinely glad when we soared up through the last terraces of olive trees and acacias and pulled up with a screech in the main square of Kruja.

Kruja was indeed impressive, a strange and wandering little town clinging to the slopes of a majestic mountain, all red tiles and whitewash, rosebushes and open drains, streets of enormous cobbles, and at the summit the remains of a most looming and dramatic fifteenth-century castle. Kruja had a special place in the Albanian memories of historical pride, because it was for years the home and fortress and headquarters of the incomparable national hero, Skanderbeg. The great Skanderbeg made the Kruja fastness the enduring centre of Albanian resistance against the Ottomans in the 1450s. He had been one of the Sultan's most celebrated generals, until he abruptly rejoined his own people against his old master. For thirty-five years then, his 'eagle's nest', as it was called, in Kruja held out against the Turks, defied four sieges by 120,000 of the Sultan's men. In the end it was conquered only by famine, and after Skanderbeg's death.

Even now, five centuries later, the place looked impregnable. From every corner of the township the view extended across miles of savage mountains – ridges like saws, valleys like scars.

We were given an hour to kill. It was so hot, and the opportunities for any conceivable sort of mischief-making so slight, that the Historians gathered in the shade of a tree and smoked. I walked up and down the precipitous main street of the town and wondered at the extravagant numbers of barber-shops, always full.

By and by I came to a place like a café. It was marked in large letters outside: 'Klub'. Reckoning that the conditions of membership were unlikely to be onerous, I went in and asked the neat little waitress for an ouzo, not because I particularly dote on Albanian ouzo (which, unlike the Greek kind, turns with water into a threatening shade of green) but because I found it the least ambiguous thing to order, and because it cost just eight leks – about sixpence.

The Klub was full of silent whiskery men, also drinking ouzo and grouped about in attitudes of studied abandon suggesting that at any moment they might rise and sing some operatic

Robbers' Chorus. There was the reaction to which I had become accustomed: every eye in the room swivelled simultaneously to fasten on me for one long reflective stare; then swivelled back and never returned.

It seemed remarkable, in this land of Labour Above All, what an immensity of time the citizens appeared to have for the simple occupation of sitting around. Every little coffee-house, at almost any hour of the day, had its half-dozen baggy-trousered workers dozing over a minute drink. When, one wondered, did they fulfil their norms – or were norms in Albanian society pitched at a level that allowed for unlimited leisure? Or was it, as I came to feel, that at least a proportion of every group anywhere were Historians?

At this point I found that I had run out of matches, and I pantomimed my neighbour at the next table to beg a light. He produced a box, which with the friendliest of smiles he urged me to keep. He could have given me nothing to divert me more. Up to this time I had seen but one variety of matches, a brand called Jumbo, made in Poland, but whose label announced itself most mysteriously as coming from an Indian firm of distributors in, of all places on earth, Mauritius. This had seemed rum enough, but my new variety was even more extraordinary, since it was called (also in English) the 'Channel Island Match', and its label bore an unmistakable map of Jersey and Guernsey, the most improbable sources of matches in the world.

As I pondered this, a uniformed policeman walked into the Klub, his top boots creaking like rusty gates, and sat down at a table. At once the silence became in some curious way more silent. Without anything perceptible having taken place, one was aware of a different kind of immobility. Moreover, in some manner impossible to explain, it became instantly clear just which of the customers in the Klub at that moment were Historians and which were not.

The policeman ordered nothing, and very soon he walked out, and within a few minutes I heard the bus in the square klaxoning for our return.

Back on the beach at Durres life returned to normal with one excitement: on that Saturday we had visitors. Albania, it seemed, had *un weekend* too, and for an hour or two our desolate playground took on a small but encouraging semblance of controlled festivity. Up and down the strand there were little parties of Albanians with the day off, drinking in the sun, feeding their babies, knocking rubber balls around. On our exclusive hotel terrace appeared the VIPs – a party of bronzed and confident Czechs who produced a hamper of food and ordered a round of *limonados*. Then there arrived a party of a dozen or so Chinese who established themselves at the extreme end of the terrace in a tight enclave, which the hotel staff isolated even more by removing the intervening chairs. And – most unexpectedly – a quiet and civil man in a bathrobe said with a smile: 'J'ai le plaisir de vous dire bonjour.'

In the People's Republic of Albania only three Western missions existed: the French, the Italian, and the Turkish. They were the vestigial diplomatic corps, the Robinson Crusoes of foreign affairs. Their establishments – a trio of small villas in Tirana – were exiguous, their movements strictly restricted, their house-keeping problems fearsome. One of them was our visitor on the Durres beach. He heard of our presence; he had had the consummate and almost Christlike consideration, for which I pray one day he will be rewarded with the highest possible preferment, to bring down a bottle of diplomatic whisky.

Before he left, the lonely diplomatist sighed a little and said, 'Life could be worse for the three of us, but it would be untruthful to conceal that it is dull. Indeed, deadly. There is no possibility of an American recognition. One wonders if the British might make some accommodation, someday. I am not passionately exercized over the politics. But it would be wonderful to have, at last, a fourth for bridge.'

The next day the authorities came for me in their bus to take me to Tirana. At last there was a plane – for Bari, and on to Rome.

One final argument remained. Since my return ticket to Amsterdam was useless now, it was necessary to pay for a new one, and, said they, in a tone at the same time somehow tense and careless, in United States dollars. In *dollars*? I said crossly. It is the custom, they replied: fifty dollars and sixty cents.

Now, it so happened that I had in my possession the precise sum, to a penny. At this they demurred; they were not, they said, allowed to accept coins. How, then, I asked, do I produce fifty dollars and sixty cents without the use of coins? You give us, said they, the next piece of paper money.

My only remaining piece of United States paper money was a five-dollar bill. From this, I asked, do I get change? Certainly, they answered. In what? Why, they said, beginning to lose patience, in leks. I have to give you five dollars, so I get four dollars, forty cents worth of leks? And what do I do with those leks? Well, they replied testily, there is this difficulty that you are not permitted to export leks. So, said I, you propose to confiscate my change and chisel me out of four and a half dollars; I'll be damned on that for a deal. It is the rules, they shouted – but already the bus was hooting, the Historians were making urgent signals, we were late. They snatched my fifty dollars and crossly gave me my ticket. but they stuck to their point: they didn't take coins. Albania owes Great Britain three million pounds for those mined destroyers; I owe Albania sixty US cents.

I was taken back through Durres, through the outskirts of Tirana, past the plodding lines of the people I had never known, the people who looked and acted like their fathers had looked under Mussolini, under Zog, under the endless succession of sultans and kings and doges who had ruled and exploited them; all the dominations they have overthrown, to fall into yet another. They may never have been free men, but they looked like free men. They had the highest birthrate in all Europe, and their children were clearly loved. There they lived, perhaps, obsessed with the curiosities of inter-Marxist schism. When I smiled, they momentarily smiled back.

When I reached the airport the plane was waiting. A Historian took me swiftly aside – the first I had spoken to. He said in bad French, 'I should have offered you a *konjak*. I am sorry about the books.'

Diversion 7: Brigitte

The news some years ago that Madame Jacques Charrier was soon to become a mother had an especial piquancy for all students of foreign affairs, and I for one heard the announcement with a warm appreciation. I had been a student of the career of Madame Charrier, as she was then, for some time, ever since she had been a fresh, eager, public-spirited young woman called Brigitte Bardot, and walked into my life across the Okhotny Riad in Moscow, many long trips ago.

It is not generally known, except to those of my acquaintances who have now heard the event described so often that they flinch at my approach, that Brigitte (or Miss Bardot, as I came to think of her) was once a Fraternal Delegate to a Moscow Conference. The word Fraternal is not one I would have used myself. She was, in a sense, an envoy. Nowadays, to be sure, there can be few people who have not found themselves a delegate of some sort to the Soviet Union; even so there tends to be a lack of glamour in the occupation. Certainly in those days Union business was rarely in the hands of small blondes with square mouths; indeed very much to the contrary.

I had been despatched during the winter of 1954 on some undertaking or other which involved much plodding around places like Kharkov and Stalingrad and Rostov-on-Don, not on the whole centres of much bohemian delight. Nor did I await any more rich diversion back in Moscow, a city where I have usually found it only too easy to be well-behaved.

I was of course not established in Moscow, and consequently I lived not in one of the matchbox apartments in the Katelnicheskaya Building, but in the Nationale Hotel. After even a day or two among the old Edwardian plush and fustian of the Nationale life tended to form a simple enough pattern: putting in a few

hours a day in the restaurant waiting for food; filling up the afternoon window-shopping among the plaster hams and stone-age
suits of Gorki Street; slipping in for a quiet retreat in the Mausoleum with the late V. I. Lenin. One by one the old urges and im-
pulses faded into the subconscious.

I had a neighbour who was new to this monastic approach to
the socialist formula; he was still at the bromide and cold water
stage. He represented a London newspaper, and lived a few doors
down the corridor from me. We developed the habit of calling
formally on each other from time to time, cultivating the illusion
that we were thus in fact visiting a different establishment, though
indeed the rooms were fundamentally indistinguishable in their
ponderously comfortless way – the same red velvet curtains with
bobbles, the same faded carpet of a once electric blue, a wardrobe
like a sarcophagus, a writing-table like a shrine. I had an inkstand
shaped like a bear; my friend's was in the likeness of the Summer
Palace at Tsarske Seloe. Neither of them held ink. Both rooms
had a similarly vast table lamp of brass and marble lit with a
25-watt bulb; so massive was its velvet shade that it was sometimes difficult to know whether the light was on or off. Both
rooms tended to be littered with a curious miscellany of food-
stuffs and groceries. The Soviet Government had a concession
that new arrivals in the capital were permitted to import their
requirements duty free from a firm in Scandinavia that specialized
in this trade; it was an invaluable privilege, though it resulted in
everyone's bedroom looking like tuck-in-the-dorm. The newspapers which maintained correspondents at such expense in
inflated roubles would have been astonished to see the costly
opulent squalor in which they lived.

Nevertheless the boredom of life became increasingly oppressive, and the limited circle of one's acquaintance seemed to shrink
around one's head like an iron band.

There was little distraction except the Bolshoi. I could never
be defined as an eager balletomane but, as it seemed to me,
it was better to spend an evening at *Giselle* watching the Wilis than
sit at home in the Nationale getting them.

I had some kind friends at the French Embassy, and such social
life as there was tended to accrete around them. On the evening in
question they rang up unexpectedly and asked my friend and me
out to the theatre and to a party afterwards, and we were down-

stairs and through the swing-doors before the guardian could say *Pazhalst*.

It seemed to me quite early on that there was something odd, or at any rate unusual, about the Bolshoi that night, with rather more big black Zims and Zises than normal rolling up to the portico. It was an Ulanova night; she was dancing Prokoviev's *Cinderella*, and I concluded that must be the reason.

At the curtain the huge theatre thundered with clapping. Galina Ulanova came through the drapes taking, as it seemed, call after call with her usual wan and deprecating grace. Then the house lights went up, and what did they reveal but an unheard-of scene, with at least half the audience standing with its back to the stage, applauding a spotlit box peopled, it appeared, with beings from another world. It took me some time to realize that the box was inhabited not as usual by visiting Director-Generals of the Uzhbek Fertilizer Control or the Vice-Commissar for Kazakstan Culture, but by film stars, and moreover by French film stars. I cannot now remember who they all were, except that there were Gerard Philippe and his wife, and René Clair, and I believe Arletty and Martine Carole, and certainly Danielle Darrieux, and there at the back, because she was a pretty small potato then, was the future Mrs Charrier, and Mrs Vadim, to name but a few; at the time still Brigitte Bardot.

I turned to draw my friend's attention to this phenomenon, but there was little need; the man was staring at these sparkling creatures with a rapt, almost dotty, expression on his face; he was as though entranced. What had happened was that Moscow was at that moment presenting a French Film Week for the first time (those were the early euphoric days of the Geneva Spirit) and in its honour the cinema producers of Paris had despatched an export sample of its major decorative talent. They had well fulfilled their norm.

I have had to assist at many an international conference and observed the demeanour of many a delegation, but this had marked aesthetic advantages over any I had ever seen before. For Moscow, where one got indeed few enough assaults on the old Adam, they were outstanding. They had style. They wore genuine clothes. They were built unmistakably in the shape of women, and not hewn from the living rock. In contrast to the honest craggy ladies of the Bolshoi audience they, and Miss Bardot above all, seemed to belong to some hitherto unknown sex.

'All I ask,' my friend was murmuring about the tumult, 'is that you pinch me. This cannot last.'

By now the Bolshoi appeared to have gone a little mad; the audience was crowding round the box and hopping up and down, applauding, letting down their programmes on strings from the balconies for autographs, and uttering hoarse cries of appreciation. What I never did discover was how the Russians knew who these ladies were, since Moscow had not exhibited a French film for many years; there had never been any publicity for alien cinema personalities; and the normal variety of Bardot photograph was not generally to be found on the back page of *Pravda*. Perhaps they did not know, after all; perhaps they were just happy to see some pretty people. Certainly my friend and I were by now like men under a light anaesthetic.

The great point of the evening was that we were all invited on to a rather splendid dinner-party after the theatre at the Sovietskaya Hotel; we were to accompany the ladies to a *soirée française*. As a non-established visitor to Moscow I was, it seemed deputed to escort the junior and least-known of the film delegates, Miss Bardot. By the time we assembled in the lobby I, for one, had put the Report of the Twentieth Party Congress out of my mind. By this time I was in an avuncular relationship with Miss Bardot which, short lived though it may have been, was not to be taken lightly.

What awaited around the corner, then, was for this reason little short of tragedy. We drove across town in a haze of perfume and kindling excitement, with the tense air of buffaloes who, after long days in the desert, scent the water-hole at last.

Then, as we trotted through the doors of the Sovietskaya in the wake of all this fragrant material I was stopped by an enormous female policeman, if one can use the word female in this context, and told to go away.

'This hotel,' she said, 'is not for foreign guests.'

I knew this to be in principle the case, but the party now heedlessly sweeping towards the *salles privées* had obviously been permitted to break the rules; nobody could have mistaken them for commissars.

'What about them?' I cried as the doors began to close. 'Are they not foreigners?'

'Ah,' said the wardress, kindly, 'they are *French* foreigners. Good night to you.'

So I went back to the Nationale and watched a television film about the development of light industries in the Ukraine. Much as I normally enjoy that sort of thing, it wasn't quite the same. For the first time I began to understand the Cold War.

Chapter Fifteen

Iт was often thought that I was among the many hands who went down in the wreck of the *News Chronicle*. This is not so; I had taken to the boats just before the end. No one had to mourn for me. When that sad scuttling of a decent newspaper came to pass I was already on my personal raft, itself none too seaworthy, but at least alone.

Some years earlier I had been delighted and touched to be offered a job on the *News Chronicle* – an unexpected cable caught me in South Africa (those were the days when I could in fact enter that melancholy country) from Tom Baistow, the Foreign Editor, then as now an immeasurably sturdy and reliable comrade. It began a relationship with a paper happier than any I had known. Like everyone else I had endless criticism of the *News Chronicle*, but it was the criticism of those who felt free to point out short-comings in a friend. I liked the *News Chronicle*. I had been brought up by my father to respect its precursor, the old *Daily News*, which was said by those supposed to know to be truthful and brave and on the side of reformation. In my day it seemed to me that its descendant was at least the most worthy among the papers of the day, standing out in a fairly shoddy company as representative of a sort of non-competitive sanity. Under the successive editorships of Tom Clarke, Aylmer Vallance, and Gerald Barry it had maintained a position of dignity, even of honour. By joining it I would be in the company of friends and respectable men; I would be labouring in the same vineyard, or cocoa-plantation, with admirable fellow-bondsmen like Tom Baistow and William Forrest and Vicky – poor comical tormented Vicky, then the most considerable political cartoonist possibly in the world, who was to become my dearest and most valued friend; who took the growing wretchedness and suffering of the world so seriously and personally that in the end he could take it no longer. In the spring of 1966 Vicky, feeling himself irremediably betrayed by a Labour Government that had exchanged principle for power, killed himself; at this very moment in time I am dividing the writing of these memories with the writing of his obituary book, in which more must be said of Vicky than can be said here.

The line of independent and courageous editors of the *News Chronicle* had slowed down and come to rest with Robin Cruickshank, a kindly and intellectual man whose growing ill-health had sapped his vigour and debilitated his resolution; there came the day when he rejected Vicky cartoons out of apprehension or insecurity. So Vicky left, and thus disappeared the first rivet in the old hull of an independent radical paper, and prepared the way for its inevitable doom. One by one more plates were started below the waterline. More editors came, and did what they could, and went; each one was less of a pilot than a salvage engineer. Had we only known it, mysterious influences below decks had for long been at work, preparing the opening of the sea-cocks for the demise. The whole sad and squalid story has been told at length and in detail by George Glenton and William Pattinson in their book *The Last Chronicle of Bouverie Street*, perhaps the only example of two newspaper men making a labour of love of writing their own livelihood's epitaph.

Long before this, however, I had returned to my occupation of travelling; for the *News Chronicle* I moved around the world again. Ironically the first article I ever filed for the *News Chronicle* was from the city into which, thirteen years later, I managed with such difficulty to return: Hanoi. Then it was the capital of Tonkin, in the north of French Indo-China; my accreditation was with the Foreign Legion, and we were waiting there among the magnolia-flowers and the cartridge-cases for the ultimate punctuation-mark – had we only known it – at an unheard of mountain township called Dien Bien Phu. When I returned, in 1965, it was as an uneasy and diffident Western stranger to a country cast into bitterness and destruction by an atrocious and meaningless war. Of the imbecile and brutal business of Viet Nam I have already written enough millions of useless words; there is now no point in saying more.

All that was to come. Meanwhile I roamed around for the *News Chronicle* – Asia, Europe, Africa, America. At no single time was there a point of difference or question, but the shadows were closing in.

Three months before the debacle I had felt the shades of night drawing over us, and me; I had been quite positively happy on that newspaper and among the friends with whom I worked, but already I knew its light had gone out. At the time I did not know why. All I knew was that the energy had diminished, the impulse and dynamism had gone; the thing was now governed by bores. I continued to write my column touched by neither praise nor blame; towards the end I could have copied out my required nine hundred words from the telephone directory and it would have been surely adequate. This was a melancholy state of affairs for a considerable journal that had pursued its course under a succession of distinguished men for a hundred and fourteen vigorous years, that had challenged governments and illumined principles and in my opinion greatly decorated the trade of newspapers. Now, suddenly, it was dead. I have always been given to feeling uneasy without evident cause, and at the time I could not rationalize my need to abandon what was in all conscience the cushiest job in Fleet Street. I believe it must have been that I was extremely fond of the *News Chronicle* and did not want to be part of its wake.

On 28 June 1960, then, I wrote my final column, the last article I ever wrote or ever shall write as the staff writer of a newspaper. For that reason I have a sentimental reason for recalling it.

'I believe there was a time when it was customary among Grub Street's men of letters to address their customers in the fulsome vocative: Dear Reader.

'As a means of propitiating the market it seemed bogus enough in all conscience, but I can see that it had its uses. In a way I could use it now.

'Since this is the last time I shall be writing this column it might be in order for once to vary the act, to give the old stalking-horses a rest, and to take leave as simply as may be. It has been, when you come to think of it (as I must do) a long time. As far as we are concerned it began, I think, up in the paddy-fields of Indo-China, with the echo of Korea just behind, and the shadow of Dien Bien Phu just ahead. We have all lived a while since then; not many things now seem as simple of definition, as easy of explanation. There is bound to be some kind of a wrench in put-

ting an end to anything, however trivial; even a small craft like
journalism has its bonds and pangs if you have been in it, as I have,
almost all your life.

'My own country appears to me to be governed by a group,
tactically efficient, wholly without moral imagination, which
works on the simple theory that goods equal good. They are
opposed, if that is the word, by another group whose current
activities seem aimed at making socialism impossible in our time.

'My own political attitude, never sound, is now riddled with
heresies. I happened to be in at the start of the nuclear-disarma-
ment campaign; if I have any political ethos I suppose that is it.
This newspaper does not share my views, but it never for a
moment discouraged me from expressing them as vigorously as I
could. It is perhaps nevertheless one reason why I am no longer
a very valid analyst of foreign policies and diplomatic conflict,
since they seem to me now rooted in a fallacy so fundamental that
the detail exasperates me as irrelevant, and leads me to conclusions either hopeless or cynical – in either case a bore for well-
adjusted points of view.

'My closest relative and dearest friend was, I now realize, a
crypto-socialist liberal with deep Tory overtones; a poverty-
stricken capitalist whose wild ambition was to build a Marxist
schism in the Primrose League. He achieved his ambition as
completely as I mine, in the contented recognition of utter
frustration. . . .'

And so it went on, sliding I fear into the banal, though it was
none the less poignant for me. From that time on I preferred, in
Malcolm Muggeridge's deathless phrase, the hazards of street-
walking to the security, such as it is, of being attached to one of
the licensed houses.

Then in October 1960 the roof fell in for the loyal surviving
crew of the *News Chronicle* and the *Star*. My friend Norman Clark,
the Foreign Editor, rang me at five in the evening to say the paper
was dead. In all the history of an industry hardly noted for
probity, this was an outstanding deal.

To professional newspapermen the destruction of the *News
Chronicle*, so startling and dramatic at the time, has now receded
into the arcane and ominous mythology of the trade; to the public
the occasion is forgotten. It was intensely meaningful at the time,
since in its own way it symbolized the melancholy condition of

the British Press, in which a simple and secret financial deal between two proprietors, Lawrence Cadbury and Lord Rothermere, could bring about literally overnight the elimination of something on which a million and a quarter people had come to rely. That evening the *News Chronicle* was swallowed by the *Daily Mail* and the *Star* by the *Evening News*. Mr Cadbury, latest of a long line of Quaker philanthropists, made a statement to the effect that in his view the *News Chronicle* and the *Daily Mail* 'had so much in common in the integrity of their reporting and honesty of outlook'. Thus was blessed the absorption of a liberal and radical paper which had taken issue against Franco and Hitler and Suez by a paper which had reconciled the Nazis and sustained every cause the old guard of the *News Chronicle* had opposed. The whole performance was so lamentable and wretched that even Fleet Street wept its own variety of acid tears, since at last the whole business of newspapers was exposed for the cynical and mercenary thing it was, and is.

The night of the announcement of the *News Chronicle*'s death was for me extraordinary; it seemed that every other newspaper in the country was ringing me up to describe the obsequies. Most of them knew that over the years I had become identified with the *News Chronicle* to a degree I had never been with any other newspaper, that I had represented it almost everywhere in the world and had come to appreciate the respect in which the poor old thing had been held all over the world where fairly well-meaning principles were valued. I had been proud to work for the *News Chronicle*, and I was damned if I was going to be paid by its rich competitors to write a wreath for its funeral.

At the same time I felt I had something to say about it; not necessarily of much significance to anyone but myself and my friends. I lived in Chelsea, and my local paper was the *West London Press*. It had nothing to gain nor lose by the situation. I turned down the national newspapers and wrote my piece for the *West London Press*.

'When the endless rumours solidified at last and it became known that the *News Chronicle* was to die, several of the major newspapers asked me to write its valedictory. In such a way would they have asked any prodigal son to comment on the suicide of his favourite stepfather – if possible, the previous day.

'I had written so many obituaries in the *News Chronicle*; I

flinched from brooding publicly on its wasted remains. I am sad
and with reason. What I could not do for the big dailies I readily
do for my local paper. At this moment the ghouls walk less
plaintively in the King's Road than in Fleet Street.

'The death of the *News Chronicle* is the biggest journalistic
tragedy for many years – I think it is the most meaningful collapse the newspaper business has seen this generation. For the
vestiges of independence in Fleet Street the writing on the wall is
up to 72-point. If the *News Chronicle* could not survive, with its
extraordinary advantages of tradition, and loyalty, and talent, who
can, outside the great chain-stores of the trade?

'It is not a matter of indifference that an old-established and
honourable journal should disappear, or be absorbed by another
organ financially stronger or with heavier backing, as the *News
Chronicle* has been digested by the *Daily Mail*. Not only has a
vehicle of public opinion been removed, and a quality of views
that may not find any other means of expression, but by its
removal the things for which it tried to stand are undermined.
Here is the most insoluble problem of what we rather fulsomely
call the 'Free Press': how is it possible to equate the commercial
success that is indispensable to a liberated paper with the business
interests that will always encroach upon that liberty?

'As far as the *News Chronicle* is concerned it couldn't be done.
It should have been done, and there are many who will say that
with a little guts and intelligence at the top it might well have been
done. The newspaper with the most admirable free-thinking
radical traditions withered on the bough precisely at the moment
when the nation was ripe to appreciate these liberal qualities. Its
greatest opportunities opened out before it, and it surrendered,
because there was nothing at the top but timidity, conventionality
and emptiness. In its closing days, the *New Chronicle* was a
potential warhorse ridden by grocers. And thus it died, and great
numbers of the most gifted, loyal, frustrated, trained, perceptive
and heartbroken men and women are now without a job, while
the grocers survive.

'The great betrayal of the *News Chronicle* began some years ago
and was a baffling phenomenon even to those who knew it well.
It is proper to say that perhaps no other newspaper had a reader-
ship quite so faithful, or which felt such a peculiar, almost
touching relationship with the tuppence-halfpennyworth. This is

a very elusive matter, but unmistakable, and its value incalculable. All this has now gone forever. The 'merger' with the *Daily Mail* is a polite and momentary form of words; the *News Chronicle* has been abolished.

'The *News Chronicle* towards the end may have been uncertain, insecure, compromising and sometimes downright ham, but in its own restless way it groped for some sort of genuine values. Those million odd readers who used to chide us for our failures and applaud our small triumphs – where do they go now? The creeping block-ownership of the industry still leaves them some choice – but not much, and not for long.

'The *News Chronicle* was founded by considerable and dedicated men; its function was defined and its patronage identifiable. Latterly it drifted by default into the hands of lesser people, who thought greatly about commerce and casually about journalism; who permitted its affairs to be run by mediocrities on one floor and sharpshooters on another; who felt that the way to compensate for thoughtfulness in one column was by banality in the next; and who, when both things failed together, were brave enough to tell their staff on Monday that there would be no paper on Tuesday.

'The trouble was the people they so summarily wrote off were the only ones who cared. Them, and us.'

There is no point in recapitulating the obsequies of the *News Chronicle*; its executioners treated them as they had treated most serious and sinister themes – by flinching from them, by avoiding the implications, by equivocating with the facts. The last act in Bouverie Street, when the management stealthily sacked a staff that was even then producing the last forlorn edition, set the pattern for the Fleet Street decline. The paper had in fact died long before; what we saw was merely the laying of the pennies on the eyes. The basic cause of death – I said then, in a phrase groping for irony, was a simple thrombosis, defined as when an active circulation is impeded by clots. There were considerations for the immediate mourners – of which I was by chance not one – but there were others, of which the chief was that this was a body-blow from a proprietorial system that thought of a national newspaper as something rather more expendable than a nut-milk bar. We mourned not what the *News Chronicle* was but what it might have been. Perhaps after all blood and tears might have been a better proposition than cocoa and water.

The *News Chronicle* staff had no agreement to invoke. There had been no contributory pensions scheme, though for years the staff had urged the establishment of one. Whatever this deal meant to the Cadburys and Rothermeres it was disastrous to many men and women of long service, who in many cases had remained with the paper in spite of far better offers elsewhere. And this was without one agreeable word, without sympathy, without a formal gesture of farewell, and with the prospect of long litigation before they would touch even what compensation was offered. I cannot elaborate on this dubious and miserable incident; I was not even there to share the obsequies. The Glenton–Pattinson book has done it all. When the *News Chronicle* died this cheapjack death I determined to attach myself to no more newspapers. It was not always easy, but one can breathe.

Chapter Sixteen

THE day will doubtless come for some fairly dispassionate historian to produce the definitive chronicle of that unprecedented, inspirational and fugitive phenomenon of the '50s and early '60s that was, and indeed still is, known as CND – the Campaign for Nuclear Disarmament. I could not do it myself; on this matter as on too many others I am far from dispassionate; on the contrary I was willingly and earnestly involved from the start, and my thinking about the Campaign is still most subjective and informed by a multitude of conflicts. In a work called *The Disarmers* Christopher Driver has written a study of the movement from, as it were, the public stands; much of it was thoughtful and a good deal of it inaccurate. Canon John Collins, the Campaign's first Chairman, has dealt with the matter also in his *Faith Under Fire*; he, like myself, had perhaps too intimate an involvement completely to interpret its growth and fall.

I still believe that this sudden and spontaneous development of civic activity was the most potentially meaningful demonstration of public protest our generation has seen. It was undermined and finally enfeebled by the very pressures and tensions it had called into being, but for several years it was potent and glowing and it was a decent generation that produced it. I am proud to have been among its founding fathers, and I continue to believe in what it was created to say. In so far as it went wrong, it was because we who made it went wrong. Nor is it yet wholly dead; we shall see.

Towards the end of 1957 the political climate of the world seemed to have reached a kind of climax of blundering and perilous imbecility, inspired here and there by fear and here and there by malice; a condition that I cannot say the years have done much to improve, numbed though we have become to an acceptance of preposterous and endemic crisis. Over all international discourse hung the slip-witted curtain of political double-think whereby armament and disarmament were matters to be debated with indistinguishably urgent enthusiasm. A thousand examples of this crooked folly could be adduced, over the years, when official threats of Overkill – the resoundingly manic word of our century – sanctified all our fatuous denial of its human implications.

I do seriously believe that what future generations are permitted to exist – my own Desmond and Elma and Fergus, and their children Emma and Andrew, and I hope a multitude more – will read back on my era's behaviour in frank amazement at its trifling and bitter argument over terrible technicalities, none of which had in fact any relevance to the fundamental problems which assailed us, in those groping days when I thought that even I might have something to say, and said it without any visible effect whatever. There arose, to be sure, what came to be mocked as the 'stage army of the good', moving from one bleak suburban hall to another, printing our jeremiads where we could, our numbers shifting and alternating under the banner of this protest group or that. We postulated the impossible: a final principle of understanding, and even trust. Nevertheless, the numbers grew.

In those days the public anaesthesia on the subject of the bomb, that was later to blanket protest in a protective boredom, had not yet come about. When a Nobel prizewinner announced that the world was swiftly approaching the point where statesmen 'could know they could utterly destroy an enemy in the course of half an hour, and that their own country would certainly suffer the same fate immediately afterwards', it was heard not as a commonplace, but with dismay. When Parliament was told: 'Major war of the future will differ from anything known in the past in this significant respect, that each side at the outset will suffer what it dreads the most: the loss of everything it has ever known', the warning was none the less real because it was given by Sir Winston Churchill. The Federation of American Scientists reported 'that future H-bomb test programmes by several atomic powers will reach a level that is a serious threat to the genetic safety of all the people in the world'. At the time these things seemed very meaningful. It was argued that to fight a war with nuclear weapons was inevitably to lose everything the war was supposed to win, and that to continue to prepare for such a war was to make the earth's atmosphere possibly inimical to life. It was not an exhilarating prospect, but it had the advantage of being fairly unambiguous.

In those days the word Hiroshima retained its peculiarly awful symbolism. In fact, it was not much of a town – nor indeed was it much of a bomb, by the monstrous standards of the present. It was an interesting consideration, when the anointed ostriches of Defence were speaking of the 'tactical weapon' as though it had the discrimination of a stiletto, that this 'tactical weapon' was precisely the atomic bomb of 1945 that we had equated with the wrath of God, that abruptly ended the life of 80,000 people one August morning. Between that and CND were fourteen years of acceptance, of adjustment, of cynicism, of 'deterrence', of creeping manic depression, of forgetfulness.

There were some of us then whose main, if not only, engagement in politics took the form of this obsessive pre-occupation with the bomb. Some of us had been to Hiroshima, as I had been, deliberately choosing an examination of the most spectacular, destructive, and almost certainly wickedest man-made catastrophe ever known. The ferocious paradoxes of the place were symptoms partly of the baffling character of the Japanese, partly of the traumatic reaction of a community well aware that it had been made the guinea-pig of the most cold-blooded and terrible physical experiment in history (since the Japanese were as aware as everyone else that they were atom-bombed *after* their attempts to sue for peace). We had found the awesome sight of a Hiroshima that was now even bigger than it had been before the bomb, far richer and more prosperous, the chilling fact that the bomb had become Hiroshima's incontestable asset, exploited with a terrifying kind of business-like hysteria by a people whose minds, among the survivors, had been scarred into a compulsion to disguise, distort, forget.

It is a fact that in the years after the bomb everyone behaved in the most extraordinary way, on both sides. For five years the American censorship forbade almost any public discussion of the thing, even Japanese research into its physical effects was stifled; it was as though already a great load of guilt was settling over everyone which could be exorcized only by repression – the Americans by bans and censorships, the Japanese by wild reversions to normality. Even before the occupation troops arrived in Hiroshima the Government was subsidizing the restoration of the

Iansho, the brothels known as Houses of Consolation, with girls brought in by the police. Even among the tormented ashes of the ruined city the *Eta*, the unclean caste, found themselves ostracized. It was as though the most significant aspects of each national character had been fused in the fire-storm to a wild and awful extreme.

It seemed to me that not much good could come out of that. As the years went by and the whole imbecile situation became formalized and established, a few people continued to argue that it might, in fact, be wrong.

One incident of 1957 remains beaten into my mind. It was at the Labour Party Conference in Brighton; in the back room of a restaurant several people met for dinner, including Aneurin Bevan, then the shadow Foreign Minister, my best and closest friend Vicky, the cartoonist, and myself. The occasion had much in it of poignancy, because on the following day Nye Bevan had to make his major speech to Conference on foreign affairs, and in spite of almost desperate pleas and arguments from many of his friends on the Party's Left, he felt obliged to reject their motion that would disarm Britain of the Bomb. It would – in his subsequently momentous phrase – send any British Foreign Minister 'naked into the conference chamber'.

It was a melancholy night. We debated and wrangled all evening, and for hours Aneurin Bevan and Vicky and I paced the dark and draughty esplanade, for the first time in irreconcilable division. It was indeed hard for Nye Bevan too, since inevitably he shared the emotional resistance of Vicky and myself to the attitude to which he was committed; he could not denounce us, his friends, as he could his political opponents, yet he could not change his mind. I think we all went to bed in the early hours in a state of anguish rarely engendered by the normally bleak and formal differences of Labour Party debate.

The next day he made his speech: he could not accept a disarmament policy which might oblige a Labour Foreign Minister to go naked into the conference chamber. I could understand its tactical usefulness, even perhaps its political necessity. I wrote my Brighton article in a mood of deep depression. Vicky's comment was a drawing that made no reference to Nye Bevan nor to the Conference nor to the bomb: he drew a picture of Gandhi, and the caption was: '*I* went naked into the conference chamber.'

As far as I know Nye Bevan never spoke to either of us again. Soon afterwards he was dead, and by and by Vicky too was dead, by his own hand; long after the Bevan age the political betrayals of the British Left were too much for the little emigre artist who had staked too much on the prospects of socialism, and who arrived at despair in the equivocations of a Labour Government groping through 1966 in a capitulation to the bleakest of Tory values. Among all my friends of those days Vicky most uncompromisingly meant what he said. Him I could least afford to lose, and even now it sometimes comes to me to wonder how I shall do without him.

All this, however, was to come. In late 1957 a movement was manifestly growing that denounced the nuclear weapon as the symbol of contemporary folly or, some said, evil. It took many forms, coalescing for a while in the organization with the jaw-breaking title of the National Campaign Against Nuclear Weapons Tests, whose chairman was the Quaker, Arthur Goss. The NCANWT did what it could to publicize the growing danger of radioactive fallout from atmospheric nuclear explosions. Already, however, it was clear that to campaign against testing the bomb, and not against possessing it, was illogical.

Then at the beginning of 1958 there took place a meeting at the Amen Court home of John Collins, Canon of St Paul's, which I believe may one day be accounted a punctuation-mark in the democratic record, because on that evening was born the Campaign for Nuclear Disarmament. A great number of people was present, every one in some way representative of thought and achievement. I seem to recall Bertrand Russell, J. B. Priestley, Jacquetta Hawkes, Ritchie Calder, Kingsley Martin, Michael Foot, A. J. P. Taylor, Commander Stephen King-Hall, John Horner, Arthur Goss and Peggy Duff, who was later to carry the organizational burden of a vast campaign. It was an imposing company. I am unsure why I was there, having neither academic nor political credentials, except that I was of all the group (perhaps of any group that could have been mustered in the country at that time) the only one who had actually seen three atom-bombs in action. Their effect upon me was something I had made very clear over the years. This kind of obsession has always greatly bothered my work; as eight years later I came to be overwhelmed with Viet Nam, so was I then inextricably enmeshed with the bomb. In those days there seemed to me nothing of comparable importance. Looking back, I see no reason to change my mind.

So CND came into being, under the presidency of Lord Russell and the chairmanship of John Collins. I was elected to a place on the national executive committee. It was the first committee I had ever been on; I expect it will turn out to have been the last.

Our first task was to let the country know of our existence. The campaign took over the Central Hall, Westminster, for an inaugural meeting on 17 February. It was an extraordinary success, transcending anything any of us had believed possible. More than two thousand people jammed the hall, four overflow halls were packed. The audience caught the spirit of the occasion with an enthusiasm I can compare with nothing else I have ever seen. We raised more than two thousand pounds.

The Press gave it a few lines. *The Times* ignored it altogether. (This meanness in the British newspapers was to continue. Even as the movement grew into a serious factor of the social scene, the Press boycott endured. All over the country large and crowded CND meetings were held, but rarely reported, and then derisively.)

Peggy Duff and her staff settled down in a small headquarters office in Fleet Street, and we were in business.

From the beginning the argument of the Campaign for Nuclear Disarmament was transcendentally simple. It asked no partisan allegiances; it exacted no local loyalties; it demanded no surrenders. The movement began as a theory, became a cause, and for a while constituted a major factor in the political scene of the country. The initials CND went into the language, and its rather stark badge became a symbol. It was not a political party, and never had any intention of becoming one. It had no affiliations with any political party. It derived its support from individual men and women of all parties and of none, from every variety of religious, social, and industrial groupings, from every walk of life. It had no formal membership, but its administration was democratic and elective. It was organized in regional, professional, and technical groups, and for a while it penetrated the entire nation.

It grew from a handful of anxious and dedicated optimists to a

movement that inspired hundreds of thousands of people everywhere, but predominantly in Britain for whose especially urgent
needs it was created.

In its impact on thinking people it was really not comparable to
any citizens' movement in history. The politics of the Campaign
were not, as was so often said, emotional, though indeed they
were rooted in the elementary emotions of humanity. CND
reasoned that the existence of the nuclear bomb, being a situation
unprecedented in the experience of mankind, demanded a human
reaction equally unprecedented.

The Bomb was a fact; we did not try to un-invent it. But we
argued that it was useless to meet a unique condition of threat
with the old and empty responses of Balance of Power, of Spread
the Risk, of Diplomatic Arrangement. Each day we saw how
every conventional approach and attitude could be distorted by
either side into polemics and propaganda. We had seen how Disarmament Conference after Disarmament Conference had stalled
and foundered on diplomatic technicalities.

The movement for unilateral nuclear disarmament believed,
fiercely and fundamentally, in Multilateral Disarmament. A preposterous notion got about that in some extraordinary way the
CND did not campaign for the universal rejection of nuclear
weapons. The proposition was absurd. The CND people, like all
rational human beings, saw total international nuclear disarmament as the principal chance for any final salvation of the species.
We maintained that we saw a way of bringing it about.

Only one thing, we argued, could break the logjam of fruitless
words, and suspicion, and mutual misunderstanding, and accumu-
lating fear, and that was an *act* that was totally unequivocal,
incapable of misunderstanding. Such an act – in our view the only
one practicable – was the formal renunciation of nuclear war and
the threatened use of weapons of mass-destruction from the
policies of the one nation that was in the supreme position to do
it: Britain.

We believed that all Britain's pretensions to a nuclear policy
were economically unsound, militarily a fallacy, and morally an
abomination.

The Campaign published what seemed to us every finite answer
to every question, provided by a mass of expert evidence. In the
Campaign were men and women of the greatest authority and

eminence in every field of science, politics, and the humanities; it was in their name that the Campaign insisted that there was no value, nor advantage, nor honour, nor hope, in proposing to defend life by destroying life, and that the proposition of preserving peace by the reduction of a very agreeable planet to ashes was worse than wrong: it was imbecile.

It was, we reasoned, not a negative attitude. On the contrary, it proclaimed the one positive argument in the dilemma. The Campaign did not ask the country to opt out of the international imbroglio, to abdicate into impotence – it asked it to opt in. As a semi-nuclear power – as a nation committed to the posture of threat, while holding less than three per cent of the West's potential threat – we were strategically meaningless in the considerations of both Russia and the United States. Our situation as a forward post of the US defence system invited our own personal destruction, while offering nothing to avert the destruction of others.

This was in practice the greatest but philosophically the least of our arguments. We were not in the CND to save our skins. Neither did the Campaign denigrate the value and authority of Britain, but strove to increase it. A Britain, we said, that publicly told a world still aware of her history that she was siding at last with the forces of sense, and reason, and right, would rally behind her at least a thousand million people of the non-Communist, non-American world who had no Bomb, to whom the Bomb was anathema, and who had waited for fifteen years for the moral Great Power lead that could promote logic and decency into the councils of the world.

All this makes as much sense now as it did then.

From the beginning small eddies and undercurrents agitated the leadership of the movement, later to grow into divisive waves. There was complete unity in the aims and ends of the campaign; differences grew in the matters of methods and strategy. The exact character of the campaign was hard to formulate, and in fact never was satisfactorily formulated; as the movement grew strength and achieved a wholly unexpected vigour and momentum many conflicts were resolved in compromise, and subterranean tensions developed, observable only at close quarters. But not for years was this subtle state of affairs to have any effect on the astonishing growth of the campaign.

Easter of 1958 saw the first Aldermaston March. For six years thereafter this came to be for me the one unbreakable Easter(engagement. It was an uncommonly disagreeable experience in the physical sense – a four-day trudge of 50 miles from the Atomic Weapons Research Establishment in Berkshire to London – but it was for me the one emotionally stimulating experience of the year. To begin with this annual ritual naturally attracted the derision of the Press, which concentrated its ridicule on the outstanding eccentrics who were always prominent in the march, the bearded and tousled nonconformists with the guitars, ignoring the long and patient tramping columns of wholly normal and unremarkable housewives and workers and shopkeepers and clerks whose endurance and enthusiasm over this long and fatiguing weekend was for me the great phenomenon of the time. I remember the climax on Easter 1960, arriving in Trafalgar Square among many thousands of single-minded people, with my daughter beside me, as something inexpressibly moving and significant.

By now the Aldermaston Marches had established themselves as something a great deal more than the freakish exhibitions the Press had originally assumed them to be. Their very size had made their management a matter of intricate logistics and organization. Peggy Duff would have qualified for General's rank in any army. The problem of keeping a fluctuating contingent of anything up to 20,000 human beings on a disciplined route-march from Aldermaston to London would have been daunting even to a military command, for never at any time was there anything random or improvised. Sleeping places had to be arranged, police consulted, canteen vans and mobile latrines provided; the whole enormous cavalcade was followed by sanitary squads who cleared the litter from behind the column – so efficiently that it was said that the Berkshire and Middlesex roads were cleaner after the passage of the marchers than they had been before. It was an extraordinary feat, and an exhilarating experience.

Until 1960 the Campaign grew and prospered. All over the country new groups arose; meetings sprang up everywhere; young people all over Britain found in CND something unprovided by either politics or the Church, which was a *rationale* for hope and sanity. The big unions began voting for CND policy; many politicians who had ignored or ridiculed the Campaign in its early days realized that it was something to be taken seriously. The climax came at the Scarborough conference of the Labour Party, when unilateralist resolutions from the AEU and the TGWU were passed: the Campaign's greatest victory.

If the Party had committed itself, however, the leader had not. That day Hugh Gaitskell made the most dramatic and impassioned speech of his life, declaring that he would 'Fight, fight, and fight again' to get that policy vote reversed. The Labour right wing settled down to help him in that fight, with the Party machinery and virtually all the British Press on their side.

And just at that moment of potential triumph the Campaign began to destroy itself, and to fall to bits under the pressures of its own internal divisions.

The struggle for power that had always been lurking within the hierarchy of the Campaign began to assert itself; it was immensely distressing, and perhaps inevitable in an organisation with a democratic machinery so loose and improvised. From the beginning there had of course been the schism between those who believed in direct action, who favoured the techniques of civil disobedience, and those who believed, as I did, that so long as we were existing within the liberal framework of a democratic state we should operate on those principles. This fundamental difference of attitude was finally to destroy the unity of CND altogether.

The major split was initiated by Lord Russell, who sent out a number of circular letters jointly signed by the Rev. Michael Scott, inviting a number of people to join a Committee of 100 to organize civil disobedience on a mass scale. Later Lord Russell was to explain that this was only a tentative and discreet feeler to determine what support such a movement might expect. However, a clanger of some dimensions was dropped when the Russell organization made the imbecile mistake of accidentally addressing one of their letters to Mr John Connell, a journalist of markedly right-wing humour whose detestation of the CND and all it stood for was renowned. He broke the story in the *Evening Standard*, and the cat was out of the bag in a very big way.

The ensuing feud between Lord Russell, President of CND, and its Chairman, Canon John Collins, has long gone into the folk-lore of the protest movement. It is of little importance now to anyone else, but for the fact that its repercussions eddied through the Campaign and stirred up even more dispute and controversy, and the solid and universalist foundation of CND began to crumble. Both Lord Russell and John Collins subsequently resigned their offices, and six members left the Executive: Anthony Greenwood, Michael Foot, Jacquetta Hawkes, Antoinette Pirie, Arthur Goss, and myself.

The Aldermaston march of 1963 was marked by another development which could have been hilarious in any other context. The direct action group, whose industry and whose intelligence service were both beyond praise, however impulsive their judgment, caused an immense sensation by discovering at Wargrave in Berkshire, almost on the line of the march, one of the RSGs – the Regional Seats of Government, which were said to be the allegedly bomb-proof shelters distributed around the country to house local administrations in the event of atomic war. The fact that this information was apparently protected by the Official Secrets Act did not prevent it being revealed in detail in a pamphlet freely distributed to all comers on the road from Aldermaston to London, and of course equally to the Press.

I got my review copy of the famous Official Secret about half a mile along the Reading road from Aldermaston. It was almost comical that one was forbidden to talk of Regional Seats of Government, since only several thousands of the pamphlet were drifting around like supermarket handouts, and being distributed by the Royal Mail.

A gimmick like the pamphlet was a godsend for opponents to hang round the neck of CND, even though CND knew as much of its origins as did the Royal College of Heralds.

In any case the revelations could surely have astonished few people. Given a policy that envisaged nuclear war, any Government would presumably have been mad not to make provision for their cadres. One could deplore a system without considering it wholly crazy.

Since the bunkers existed, it interested me in no way where they were and only mildly who was in them, since I knew it would not be me.

This 'Peace Spies' debacle nevertheless brought nearer the moment of truth for a campaign that was doing its best to express the undirected anxieties of hundreds of thousands of reasonable people, whose politics were simple enough, but whose methods were perhaps a bit uncomplicated for a hostile world. Since those notions were my own I could hardly complain; for seven years I considered they might, with luck, prevail. One or two did.

The CND, being an assembly of infinitely varied people, associated under no Party banner, governed by no Constitution, was by definition bound to dispose of many heresies. It came about that the objectives were fragmented; there was a diffusion of the exact and manageable aim of Nuclear Disarmament into fringe protests which were distractions from a greater need. The Campaign had not been created with so much effort and dedication to be the repository of all miscellaneous resentments. Its purpose was to Ban the Bomb; when that was forgotten it was easy to lose heart.

By 1963 it was possible to say that one phase of the Campaign for Nuclear Disarmament was over; that the first stage of its historical purpose was complete. It had been, after all, unique. It had done more than teach people to think about the Bomb; it had taught them how to think. Great numbers of people in peculiar clothes made themselves uncomfortable, to some perhaps ridiculous, and suffered in prison for demanding a Test Ban – and by and by there was a Test Ban.

The CND was one of the good things in a discouraging world; it earned its place in the records, and with honour.

Diversion 8: A Matter of Taste

DURING many years after the war it fell to my lot to travel a great deal in Africa. I believe that of all the new multitude of sovereign African states, all politically reborn with names increasingly hard to remember, there are in fact none which I have not known in other and probably less desirable days. Unlike so many of my specialist friends, I have little intuitive or spontaneous love for Africa. I am obliged to say that while I came to know this enormous continent passing well, and while I was fortunate in finding in its various corners many friends and lovers of almost every hue and humour, there is no part of this great land-mass in which I could willingly contemplate passing the evening of my days. This is somewhat curious, since I spent much of those earlier years arguing and agitating for its liberation from the colonial yoke, as the term used to go. Each time this or- that territory, most arbitrarily defined by the random frontiers so casually imposed by the European mapmakers of the nineteenth and twentieth century, was ceremonially handed its independence by this or that minor branch of the royal family, I was usually there on the side-lines, applauding with academic but none-the-less vigorous enthusiasm the march of history. From time to time I was, I felt, markedly let down.

Over the years I formed a number of agreeable acquaintance-ships with political patriots dedicated to the removal of what they called my Imperial heel from their necks, an ambition that met with my strong approval. Indeed, much of my life seems in retrospect to have been spent in the company of putative national leaders passing through the process of being denounced and imprisoned for sedition, as part of the inevitable progression towards the Prime Ministership and the ritual tea-party at Windsor Castle. I find it difficult to catalogue the number of such anticolonial politicians with whom I have had troublesome and awkward rendezvous out of reach of the Special Branch, only to find myself a year or two later presenting my card with some humility at the Presidential Palace.

All this, as can be imagined, did not especially enhance my standing with what was then the Union, and is now the Republic, of South Africa. At one time I used to spend much time in that outstandingly lovely and melancholy country, and came to know it well. As year by year it retreated into the shadows, withdrew from an advancing world and sought its future in the dark neurotic corners of the past, I watched it with a mounting detestation that I tried to convey with what was, at least to begin with, a depressing lack of success. I was in South Africa in 1948 when the election of the Nationalists under the dour and sombre predikant Dr Malan finally confirmed the inevitable and ushered in the golden age of Afrikanerdom and *baaskap*, and the leaden years of apartheid, and in the following years as the darkness closed in. The story needs no telling now.

As time went on it became apparent that the fulsome welcome with which the Nationalist public-relations officers were wont to greet arriving journalists whom they deemed susceptible to hearty propaganda was waning in my case. No longer came the candid and matey endocrinations over the brandy-glass, the insistence that things were not what they were represented to be in the hostile foreign Press, and that in any case, man, we know our business best. It must have been manifest that by now I had seen enough of the back-alleys and barbed-wire aspect of their society to be invulnerable to any sort of soft sell manageable by an Afrikaner official. Very soon I was removed from the list of potential converts.

Relations that were never good became poor indeed, and the last time I visited, or shall visit, South Africa I was met at Cape Town airport by a plain-clothes officer of the Special Branch of an appearance so outstandingly conspicuous that I was surprised he was not surrounded by a brass band, who followed my cab to the hotel and who thereafter, with his colleagues, spent both day and night keeping watch in what I hope was some discomfort at the bottom of my stairway.

It is odd, and yet somehow characteristic, that the offence for which I was finally declared undesirable, and debarred from returning to the country, was not on the grounds of a false political attitude nor of untruthful journalism, but on those of pornography.

So rare an event is this for me that the occasion might have passed unnoticed had I not received through the post a copy of the Official Gazette of Pretoria, the government journal which puts on record the public developments of that grey legislature. This registered the fact that a book of mine had been examined by the Publications Control Board and adjudged Indecent, Obscene and Objectionable.

This was pretty high going for a simple man, unused to adjectives so stimulating. They looked if anything slightly more daunting in the Afrikaans version, in which this rather ordinary work was defined as *Onbetaamlik*, *Onwelvoeglik*, and, if you please, *Aanstootlik*. ('Not so much what it says, my dear Van Wyk, but there is a strong undercurrent of the *Aanstootlik*. I certainly wouldn't want to find my servants reading it.')

I had practically forgotten the book in question, in common with the greater part of the English-speaking world. It was several years old. It was in any case only a contemporary assessment of political developments over the whole continent, called, I suppose unfortunately, *The African Revolution*. As such books go I thought it was almost outstandingly inoffensive, not to say behind the times. It was, I believe, accepted as text material in one or two of the lesser universities of the Middle West – indeed years later I had an earnest letter from a student asking if I thought Mr Kenyatta stood any chance of acquiring office in a free Kenya. While this did not suggest any great perception on their part, at least it did not suggest any of the grosser indelicacies on mine. As a corrupting influence, the book had all the lewd excitement of a seed catalogue.

I expect it was the title alone that gave the book this particular quality of the *Aanstootlik*. One recalled that it was this same South African authority whose obsession with racial purity once caused it to ban a simple-hearted children's horse-book because it was called *Black Beauty*. Whatever the reason, these guardians of freedom finally proscribed a work that no one in his senses would have wanted to read, and was anyhow very difficult to find. It was odd to realize how long it took our white brothers of the *Raad van Beheer oor Publikasies* to catch on. It was also a little galling to be so long ignored, since even we pornographers have our pride.

Just as the honest citizen finding himself unexpectedly in the police-court waiting-room examines with a fascinated distaste the nature of his fellow-accused, I studied the company in which, under Sub-section (3) (a) of Section 113 of the Customs Act 1964, I was declared Indecent, Obscene and Objectionable. It was like finding oneself equiposed somewhere between King Street and the Charing Cross Road. There were *Beautiful Britons,* the *Magazine of Appeal*; *Dirty Book* by W. Rushton; *Jayne Mansfield's Wild, Wild World*; *A Nympho Named Sylvia* by Hank Janson; *De Spion die mij Beminde* by Ian Fleming; *J. W. Stalin, Werke* 5, 6, 7, 8, printed in Germany; *the Pyongyang Times of Korea*; and *The Theory and Practice of Photography*. This was like discovering oneself in a Black Maria that had wound up a general tour round the strip-clubs by collecting a few odd jobs for the Special Branch. We were in common bondage and contumely, Hank Janson and I; he with his Nympho and I with my norms. On the other bench the shade of Ian Fleming stared with sultry distaste at the spectre of the *Pyongyang Times*, united at last in the common front of gross indecency. But there were others.

In another list the publications were for some arcane reason described not as Indecent and Obscene, but merely as Undesirable (*Ongewens*). They included *An Absurd Affair* by Colin Spencer; *All Men are Mariners* by Calvin Kentfield; *Playboy's Females* by Jack Cole; *International Conference for Solidarity with the People of Vietnam against US Imperialist Aggression and for the Defence of Peace* (Hanoi 1964); the *Fundamentals of Political Economy* by P. Nikitin; and *Sex and the Divorcee* by Scott O'Neil.

This marvellous ragbag, this catholic catch-all of deviation, offered a great field for speculation. What was this enviably spacious attitude of mind that could equate the *Playboy* girls with Works 5–8 of the late J. W. Stalin? (And what was so okay about Works 1–4, for that matter?) In what strange human category did one simultaneously bracket the wild, wild world of Miss Mansfield and the presumably austerer conclusions of P. Nikitin? What *could* be the matter with *The Theory and Practice of Photography*?

And why, I wanted to know, was my little history book held to be as Indecent and Obscene as *The Nympho Called Sylvia*, when the *International Conference for Solidarity against US Imperialist Aggression* and so on and so on was only Undesirable?

I should like to have thought that some small marginal advantage might have accrued to me – that the South African bourgeoisie, inflamed with uncontrollable desire to possess my obscene book, would seek it after dusk in the byways of Johannesburg and Kimberley, paying great sums for it on the Black Market (or whatever it is called among decent Afrikaners), stealing home with suspicious packets in which, conceal them as they might inside copies of *Die Burger* and the works of Dr Balthazar Vorster, would really have been James Aleister Crowley Cameron's filthy statistics of Kenyan sisal-production in 1959, with several pages of lubricious maps.

It would have been agreeable to believe that the next time I went to South Africa I would have been met by coteries of panting frustrated Transvaal aesthetes who would bear me off to the pot-reeking cellars of Commissioner Street, and make me read out the really concupiscent bits from the section on the Devlin Report. Barring doors against the Vice Squad, they would hang on every word of the rarely-spoken quotations from the early Iain Macleod. Copies of page 114 would pass avidly from hand to hand, bearing the secret passages of erotica from the description of the Salisbury-Beira railway system. Orgiastic scenes would ensue at the unbearably sensual climax on the Gambian chicken-farms.

However, alas, these heady days among the sex-mad burghers of Bloemfontein were unlikely to come to pass. Soon afterwards I had a letter from the South African Secretary of the Interior, a man who could without flattery be described as not the most effusive of my pen-pals. He merely wanted to tell me that, while citizens of the UK visiting South Africa were exempted from visa requirements and the need for Aliens Permits, this exemption no longer applied to me, and he had Section 7 bis (3) and Section 24 (1) (c) of Act 22 1913 to prove it; and should I ever show up in South Africa without such documents I should be sorry, man, and he remained mine faithfully.

It surprised me at first, but in the light of this Indecency business the situation was, I argued, understandable. Clearly these people in Pretoria did not want all this lechery and obscenity let loose among the wholesome young womanhood of the Rand, who as was well known, were already obliged to protect their virtue with bra-holsters. They did not want this European salacity coming in to besmirch the straightforward solution of racial problems. No visa for Carnal Cameron, who would fill their papers with smut and their galleries with prurient rubbish and their radio with indecorous allusion, who wrote bawdy couplets on walls and who had not been seen with his trousers done up since the Bantu Education Act. Let the lustful lout stay in his own rotten UK stews and not come around South Africa seducing our innocent tanned blondes by whispering to them foul stories about East African light industry and suggestive production-figures from the Copperbelt. Let him be as *Aanstootlik* as he likes among his own decadent crowd, with Sylvia the Nympho and the *Pyongyang Times*. They did not want the likes of me, not even for 90 days.

Thus South Africa emancipated me. If I was taken seriously in the *Aanstootlik* belt, if only by a redneck Platteland peasant in Pretoria who moved his lips when he read, then cry havoc; old pussyfoot rides again.

Chapter Seventeen

OF the matter that in the end came to exercise and concern me most of all, which was the war in Viet Nam, there is little left to say that may still be relevant. For more than a year it sometimes seemed that I wrote and spoke of little else. My feelings were tremendously engaged in this uniquely brutal and muddled war, though they might have had no more value than anyone else's, but for the fact that I had seen both sides.

Through almost all of 1965 I had been trying – as I suppose had most Asia-leaning journalists in the Western world – somehow to enter the north of Viet Nam. It seemed impossible. In the south, Saigon seethed and hummed with hundreds of contending correspondents, most of them producing variants on the American theme, but the Northern Government of Hanoi consistently refused to entertain requests to observe the civil war from their side. Communication itself was difficult. The process of making contact alone was daunting, involving oblique and complicated channels. The chances of success seemed remote. I was by now much interested in film as a medium of expression. It seemed to me of some importance that the flow of repetitive and tendencious material from the south should be counterbalanced by something from the north that was other than the North's own crude and negative propaganda. I had the co-operation of two friends, accomplished cameramen, Malcolm Aird and Romano Cagnoni. For months we hung about, hoping with flagging optimism for permission to enter Hanoi. For twelve years no one from our part of the world had managed to break through; there seemed no particular reason why Hanoi should make any exception for us.

How this was finally and unexpectedly accomplished, and the results of the journey, have been pretty thoroughly described in a

film and in a book.[1] There is not much I can add to all that, and as
I write the war in Viet Nam grows more and more vile and crude
and senseless, assuming every day more and more aspects of
classic tragedy, driving more and more to a hopeless and despairing end. Nothing in my life – and I have been involved in my
share of political folly and seen rather too often the corruption of
the well-intentioned and the destruction of the innocent – had
been as lowering as this; I hated it then and I hate it now, but I
have said it all too often.

Late in 1965 the gears suddenly meshed, the permission suddenly arrived to go to North Viet Nam; the abrupt agreement
after months of frustration was a reproduction of what had
happened long ago with the Chinese: when you can go, you have
to go in a rush. It was an unprecedented occasion in all manner of
ways. We were sponsored by nobody; the expedition had to be
financed by private borrowing; it must have been one of the very
unusual occasions when three or four individuals had gambled so
heavily on the potential goodwill, or perhaps the curiosity, of the
big commercial communicators.

We travelled out in a laborious and circuitous way through
Pakistan and Ceylon to Canton, where we moved into the Chinese
economy and pipeline up to Peking, thus to Nanning and at last
Hanoi. For me, familiar with this miasmic mountainous mystery
from long ago, it was a searching experience, so changed and
changeless, full of vanished ghosts; full of uncertainty and regret,
and a simultaneous excitement that I know I will never lose at the
sight of those strange and somehow demanding Chinese hills
rising arbitrarily from the mists. It is like briefly living in the heart
of a sixteenth century water-colour: so many shifting dimensions;
all the grey of pearl and the sudden insistence of crimson; how I
love the landscape of southern China: even the solemn bureaucrats of the atrociously aseptic airports would pause in their
concrete questioning and say: wait, while the cloud comes thus it
is of an especial value; wait just a moment more. Or so they did
then; it is possible that things have changed today.

At this point, around the edges of Kwang-Si, is China and
South-East Asia indistinguishable, a blessed and accursed land;
how sweet it looks and sounds and smells. I find it hard not to be
tedious about this part of the world and its inhabitants, seemingly

[1] *Witness*: Gollancz 1966.

to me the one part of humanity that should not have been corrupted and abased by the west and involved to destruction by the imbecile ritual of the Cold War. But they were and they are; the vandals moved in too soon.

Anyhow, the results of this expedition to Hanoi and the north have been exposed and wrangled over enough. We reached Hanoi, as it were moving through the mirror into the looking-glass land, where all values were reversed. We were received initially with a marked if comprehensible coldness, which grew into a gradually developing cordiality that eventually permitted us unprecedented travel through the country, and culminated in an evening with the Prime Minister, Pham Van Dong, and the President, Ho Chi Minh, of such conviviality that I was heavily taken aback to have it rounded off an hour later by a summary order to leave the country by the following dawn. These, I have always found, are the forever-unexplained exigencies of Asian travel.

As it came to pass, however, that following dawn produced a prolonged air-raid alert over the Hanoi area, and the Chinese aircraft that was scheduled to leave for Canton most prudently did not take off. In consequence I and my friends lost every connection planned for the homeward journey, and were thus obliged to re-route ourselves through Peking and Siberia, and it was a mid-winter journey of no small acerbity for those compelled to travel through Irkutsk and Novosibirsk in a temperature a long way below zero, while equipped only with exiguous South-East Asian tropical clothes. Nevertheless we brought back with us our film, and not impossibly a little more information than had been current for some years.

To me personally this revisitation of Hanoi had been curiously poignant in a way that I suppose is meaningless to those who have been driven to consider the place in a context wholly political and symbolic, and not as a community of people, mostly very poor and mainly pre-occupied with the dreadful problems of survival. I had known this charming unlucky place well long ago; now its metamorphosis was terrible to see. Of all these things, and much else about Viet Nam, I have said so much that I am wearied and embarrassed to say more. My two companions and I spent many weeks in the north of Viet Nam, in conditions often of some difficulty and always of distress, and finally returned in a state of great uncertainty as to whether we should shortly be notorious or bankrupt.

At that time I had never in my life felt more in genuine need of a rest, and never did one seem more unlikely. I had hardly returned before I was whipped off to New York for a major confrontation on the television with an imposing and masterful cast of United States pundits, who were at some pains to imply that my observations and opinions on the Viet Nam war were not those of a sincerely objective journalist, as defined by strict American standards. *Time* magazine made its predictable assault on me, calling me a 'conduit'. To these and similar strictures I could only make the old response: that I had never in my life made any claim to being an 'objective' journalist, if 'objectivity' meant the uncritical presentation of wrong or foolish events and attitudes, and that since I had vigorous and bitter opinions about the war in Viet Nam there was neither honesty nor point in pretending otherwise.

Like almost everyone outside the US and not a few in it, I had always been greatly alarmed by the Americans. For many years they had been putting the wind up the world by actions of terrifying charity and menacing goodwill, but especially did they scare me, since the more I alienated myself from everything they did internationally the more I seemed to get mixed up with them personally.

The American nation is unprecedented in history: so rich, so strong, so vulnerable, so generous, so blind, so bountiful, so clumsy, so kind, so perilous, so unmanageable in their simple-minded craftiness, the brutal innocence of their lethal benevolence. Nobody but the Americans could have invented a President who posed as a peasant to conceal the expert ruthlessness that concealed the fact that he was a peasant all the time. Nobody ever knocked people about like the Americans to establish the warmth of their own hearts. (I recalled the genuinely tender consideration with which the army in Viet Nam provided artificial limbs for the children whose legs they had blown off.) The Americans were the people with whose good intentions the road to hell was so painstakingly paved.

It was after my return from Hanoi that I encountered what was for me perhaps the last wholly new experience in foreign travel, that of the huckster-propagandist, or the Billy Graham of the book section. It was my baptism of fire, enmeshed by day and by night in the whizzing machinery of the mass media, creature of a public-relations schedule of which I knew next to nothing. British publishers think books are things to be read, by those who can be bothered to find them; American publishers on the other hand argue that books are things to be *sold*, a point of view to which I imagine few writers will take violent exception. In this worthy cause, in the US, the author is supposed to play his part.

It happened that my small book on North Viet Nam had just been published in the United States, somewhat to my surprise, since it was hardly a paeon of praise for contemporary American policies. When asked over for a little 'promotional activity' I accepted gladly, anticipating a couple of quiet lunches with distinguished critics and perhaps one or two gentlemanly, unheard broadcasts at some relaxed time of day. To be sure I anticipated controversy, even hostility. It was, after all, only a short time before that I had been in New York and received, on the whole, with the tolerant hospitality that sacrificial victims were wont to find in the crocodile pools. To have been in North Viet Nam at all had been offence enough, to have talked to Ho Chi Minh compounded it, but to have argued the possibility that North Vietnamese were made of flesh and blood, and capable of both pain and anger, was heresy. If I could have been identified as a Commie bastard it would have been easier; that this could not be done was exasperating. However, I reckoned I could put up with it again.

My schedule of engagements was daunting. It involved programmes beginning at six in the morning, and others starting at midnight. It meant the Jerry This Show and the Johnny That Show and the Jane Show and the Marlene Show and University Forums and All-Night Call-Ins and several serious discussions on Viet Nam. It meant sometimes six shows a day, whirling from one alphabetical station-identification to another, edging in among the commercials, hopping in and out of trains and planes and taxis until I lost track of what State I was in, let alone what city. It was by far and away the most exhausting work I have ever done: fatiguing, repetitive, nervous and numbing. Nevertheless it was a realler America than I had known in the past, hitching on this or that bandwagon or presidential campaigns or freedom marches or other events particular and impersonal. Here I had to move round New York, Boston, Philadelphia, Washington, Chicago, at the total mercy of a changing, faceless cast of inter-locutors, spokesmen, inquisitors and masters-of-ceremony, with no purpose other than to say: I think your Viet Nam war is wrong and cruel and senseless, for them and for you and for me; I hold your values to be false and your ambitions unreal, and this is why I think so. One could have imagined easier jobs.

I embarked on this fantasy with a sinking heart. I remembered so well the routine challenges of five months before: 'But if you claim you aren't a red, how come they let you in?' 'What did your Chinese friends tell you to tell us?' and so on. It looked like being a fairly high price to pay for the flogging of one fairly unimportant book.

Yet what happened was unexpected. In most of the encounters the steam had gone out of the challenge and the chips from the shoulder; hostility was replaced with inquiry, suspicion with questioning, resentment with regret. Those who had demanded: 'Who the hell are you to tell us?' now said: 'What do you suppose can now be done?'

I came to realize later that I had drawn some very impulsive and optimistic conclusions from the company I had been keeping, which was clearly that of the more demanding and enlightened academics and communicators of the US, yet at the time I was so relieved not to be intellectually lynched that I felt that intelligent Americans everywhere had come to feel that many of their basic assumptions about Viet Nam had been shaken so seriously that a re-evaluation of the whole situation was becoming imperative.

It was visible in many factors: in the manifest re-orientation of the Press, the querulous uneasiness of the editorials that only the other day were unquestioning in support of the Administration's foreign policies; in the almost routine appearance in the most respected newspapers of immense and expensive advertisements of protest signed by people of eminence and reputation; in the overt mockery of the White House in the cartoons; in the almost tangible bitterness of almost all reference to President Johnson; in the new acceptance of Senator Fulbright's challenge, which had now evoked the most highly-publicized philosophical con-flict yet seen on the US political stage.

Those were the general terms; it narrowed down in my own experience to a kind of acceptance that was not easy at first to realize. The subject in hand was, after all, a book whose theme was by inference accusatory; suddenly I found it examined with understanding, or at least genuine inquiry; men and women long schooled in the conformity of US broadcasting would unexpectedly produce the book and recommend at least its examination.

A feature of US radio new to me was the listener-participation feature, or viewers' call-in, or whatever it is; after a long preliminary argument the air is thrown open to telephoned inquiries from anyone who happens to be interested. This would sometimes go on until the small hours of the morning. Who on earth were all these American insomniacs who spent the night watching the TV or listening to the radio I could not imagine; it was hardly possible that they could *all* be nightwatchmen.

Out of scores and scores of such interpolations I got practically nothing that was not of serious intent and courteous delivery – sometimes very sad, sometimes unimaginably ill-informed, sometimes plaintive, sometimes censorious, and sometimes intuitive or perceptive enough to make reply far from easy. I felt, for the first time in many years, that I had discovered an America that put *Time* in its place.

Once upon a time E. B. White, for so long my personal paragon of the journalistic word, had written: 'Anti-communism is strong drink. Already the lines are being drawn tighter; already fear produces symptoms of the very disease we fight – the tyrant fear, pricking us to fight tyranny.' It was hard to remember that had been eighteen years ago. He might, it seemed to me at that time, have been perhaps not as alone then as he was in his day.

So I returned home. It had for some time been clear to me that somewhere along the line of the Viet Nam journey, or any one of a hundred of its predecessors, I had acquired some sort of disturbance that was playing hell with my alimentary tract, that persecuted pipeline that had been subjected to so many years of assault and neglect, compounded by the stresses of my own intemperance. I had never given it much of a chance, and so long as it functioned in a minimally efficient way for the purposes of keeping me active and mobile I rarely gave its protests much heed. The time came now when I could forget about it no longer; eating had never been a strong point of mine but now it had become impossible, and I passed nothing but blood; my liver had become a pathological curiosity, a candidate for the Hunterian museum. Whatever

the illness that finally drove me into an English hospital for the
first time in my life was only partly brought about by infection
and fatigue; it was soon made clear to me that most of it was due
to the old mistaken belief that I could live forever sustained on
high hopes and alcohol. It was not shocking but it was saddening.
I became quite suddenly aware again of my old affinity with my
father; my life had been greatly influenced by his values and
attitudes; now it was reproducing his chemistry. This had never
occurred to me as a serious danger. I had vaguely, without much
conviction, held myself to be a man of a certain moderation; I had
indeed drunk too much too consistently but always, it had seemed
to me, for good reason and in good company and rarely, as far as
I knew, to the damage or discomfiture of anyone else. This
assessment had obviously to be modified intellectually; it remained to be seen if it could be corrected physiologically, for it
was already fairly late in the day. Many old friends and colleagues
had shared with me their responses to this situation; it was, after
all, said to be the occupational hazard of the trade. If so the less
excuse for me, who had long ago escaped the social exigencies of
the newspaper circus, who worked alone; it was not only somewhat suicidal that I should come to measure my night's work in
terms of so many thousand words to a bottle; it was absurd.

This information could hardly have come at a worse time. I was
deeply involved in the aftermath of the Viet Nam adventure,
hurrying around all over the place at the call, it seemed, of everyone of good will or bad who required to know about Hanoi.[1] The
process culminated in the numbingly taxing fantasy of the United
States tour. It seemed that for some two months I averaged some
three hours of sleep in every twenty-four. This, I felt, was no way
to behave for one who had newly become a grandfather, and who
moreover had for the first time in many years conceived a possible
reason for a little longer survival.

I went to hospital for some time and thereafter for a while was
very nearly well.

[1] From those seekers after news I must exclude officialdom; at no time after my
return from North Viet Nam was I ever required to see, consult, or inform anyone,
however minor or indirect, from the Foreign Office or the State Department. I do
not in the least complain about that, since it relieved me of yet one more obligation;
I was nevertheless mildly interested to note this total absence of diplomatic curiosity
in what was, after all, the most meaningful situation of all. My accounts of the thinking of the Hanoi hierarchy might doubtless have been suspect, but they might have
had secondary uses. Or perhaps, on reflection, they might not.

Chapter Eighteen

OUTSIDE the window now lies forty feet of rock and grass, and then the escarpment to the sea and the point where the sardonic seabirds sit like sentinels guarding the ocean, to the wild abrasive horizon of Roaringwater Bay and the Thousand Islands; the cottage hangs on the edge of Ireland with its fading white face lashed by the wind. From here only the Atlantic sighs and threatens between me and Manhattan – I was there a week ago, plodding unsteadily into the steaming loveless limbo of East 52nd Street; how near and how far; I am still momentarily there, breathing Third Avenue, in the howling empty solemnity of West Cork. I love this place; it will not last long; nothing lasts long.

For some twenty-five years I tried to combine the careers of a normal man and a professional nomad; it made for a vigorous and various life and it had its own transient rewards, but it fulfilled neither. The habit of loneliness over a long period engenders the wrong responses to love, and there is nothing, wherever it may be, to compensate for that.

It has been, when one comes to think of it – as I must do – a long time. I can hardly remember where it begun – in the forests of Burma, perhaps, or the paddyfields of Indo-China, with the echo of a lost Singapore behind and the shadow of Europe ahead; even then the shadow of the jailhouse was closing in, had one but known it. Still, it endured almost over a whole world – one was a camp-follower of the new age, trudging behind the witless caravan that finally reached Viet Nam.

We have all lived a long time since those early days; not many things seem as simple of definition, as easy of explanation.

I have spent thirty years of my life in this trade. Most of it was of necessity tangled in some way in the business of politics, and of politicians. I confess that I find their antics less amusing than I did.

Internationally they have, I think, become pretty nearly out of control, the human machinery sustained by various sets of myths and legends that may possibly be suitable for soldiers and statesmen and bishops and bureaucrats, but which in essence no longer make much sense to me. Two world wars within my lifetime, and a multiplicity of lesser ones, have anaesthetized our moral perceptions, and somehow produced the illusion that there can be a justification for killing millions of men, women and children in places like Dresden, Stalingrad, Hamburg and Hiroshima, and a hundred places more. I am obliged to say that I personally feel that *nothing* justifies it – neither Communism, Fascism, nationalism, tyranny nor freedom; the conquest of the earth or the preservation of *any* way of life: nothing. Nothing in the world, however base nor however good, nor however theoretically admirable, can justify murder as an act of policy. This is an argument hardly likely to be accepted in a society where even the professional priests bless the machinery of death in the name of Christ and anointed clergymen officiate at the launching of nuclear submarines. It will obviously be unpersuasive in a country that spends on its soldiers and their weapons in outmoded and improbable outposts more than a hundred times what it spends on the United Nations and its agencies. It is clearly, therefore, a point of view without political importance to anyone except myself.

I saw Adolf Eichmann tried and condemned in Jerusalem: a palliative thrown to the well-intentioned wolves in a world still liberally inhabited by Eichmanns; just as obedient, just as glib, just as simple, just as horrible, just as persuaded of the importance of their public function in the society that employs them, just as assimilated in our way of life – committed at the controls of Polaris vessels and V-Bombers, to obey the anonymous programmed command to deal more death in a second than the wretched and intolerable Eichmann did in four years. Mostly good family men, I understand.

At home they have left me far behind. It may well be that I was never the true material of a political observer: I have not the absorbed technical dedication to the detail of party conflict to sustain much curiosity in much love for a game that seems to me to have become so enmeshed in its piffling mechanics of personalities that it no longer invokes the issues of peace, social justice, and mutual comprehension, except as threadbare abstractions. As

I write this I see proof enough all around me that even good politicians, those at one time committed to renouncing a foreign policy based on threatened violence, are incapable of challenging the party machinery that sustains them, and who therefore accept – however reluctantly – everything that I oppose. They, even more than I, have acquired the emollient facility for self-deception.

I no longer argue the propriety of anyone's logic. All sides have now made so many errors so often that they are now wholly engaged in the occupation of trying to prove that at least one of their past misjudgments was sound. I should perhaps not complain too primly about that, belonging as I have for so long to an occupation whose own concentration of means over ends has been so obsessive, whose own values so accommodating, that its critical function is usually an impertinence. Today we journalists spend our time splashing in the shallows, reaching on occasions the rare heights of the applauded mediocre. It looks, perhaps, easier than it is.

To the individual in this machine it brings its own dilemma: the agonizing narrow line between sincerity and technique, between the imperative and the glib – so fine and delicate a boundary that one frequently misses it altogether, especially with a tight deadline, a ringing phone, a thirst, and an unquiet mind. Accept that, and the game is up.

Freedom of conscience must be an elusive thing; more often than not it requires not the adhesion to a script, but the departure from it. I have never had the responsibilities of a formal political attitude; I have been uncommonly lucky in avoiding the pressures of expediency. If I have been a gadfly at the heels of my friends I am sorry; they need not concern themselves for long.

The tale's told. I would not wish to contemplate a future in which I should not again see the surf-boats go out in Ghana, nor drink at the Cockpit in Singapore nor the Crillon in Paris, nor see the lotus-lakes in Kashmir or the Tung Tan Market in Peking or the Staten Island Ferry in New York, or the windmills of Mykonos or the Baie d'Along in Tonking. But if I do not see them again, then at least I have done so in my time, and more withal. I have comrades and competitors in them all; that is something in the way of riches, and God knows one has accumulated no other.

Most of us continue to survive, as we say, by the indulgence of our creditors and the generosity of our friends. I have had a multitude of both. May it continue – not necessarily long, but for a while. Hope subsides, but curiosity remains. Every day is, necessarily, and even now, a point of departure. We shall see.

INDEX